LIONS
of the
RED ROSE

The Percys *and*
the Wars
of the Roses

LIONS
of the
RED ROSE

The Percys *and*
the Wars
of the Roses

Ralph Percy
Duke of Northumberland

With a Foreword by John Sadler

Dedication

*For Jane, Katie, George, Melissa, Max,
and all their descendants.*

This edition © Northumberland Estates, 2024
Text and photography © Northumberland Estates, 2024

First published in 2024 by
Northumberland Estates
Estates Office
Alnwick Castle
Alnwick
Northumberland NE66 1NQ
www.alnwickcastle.com

ISBN 978-1-7385322-1-6 (Paperback)
ISBN 978-1-7385322-0-9 (Hardback)

Designed by Phillips Creative
Printed and bound in the United Kingdom

10 9 8 7 6 5 4 3 2 1

All rights reserved. No part of this book may be reproduced, stored in a retrieval system or transmitted in any form or by any means electronic, mechanical, photocopying, recording or otherwise, without the written permission of Northumberland Estates.

Every effort has been made to acknowledge correct copyright of images where applicable. Any errors or omissions are unintentional and should be notified to the Publisher, who will arrange for corrections to appear in any reprints.

Frontispiece: The Battle of Tewkesbury from an illuminated manuscript, 1471.

Contents

	Foreword by John Sadler	6
	The Percys in the Wars of the Roses, Battle Sites	7
	Introduction by Ralph Percy, Duke of Northumberland	8
1	Restoration – Back in Favour	12
2	Rivalries Old and New	18
3	Misrule and Anarchy	26
4	The Feud Develops	30
5	St Albans, 1455	38
6	The Seeds of Vengeance	44
7	Yorkists in Retreat	50
8	Blatant Betrayal	56
9	'The accursed blood of York'	60
10	'Upon ill Palm Sunday'	68
11	War in the North	78
12	The Last Brother	86
13	The Kingmaker Turns	94
14	The End of the Nevilles and Murder of a King	106
15	Power in the North	116
16	The Rise and Fall of Richard III	122
17	Restitution and Revolt	130
18	Epilogue	134

Appendix A	Map of Land Ownership in England & Wales during the Wars of The Roses	137
Appendix B	Timeline, 1377-1527	138
Appendix C	The Royal Houses of York and Lancaster	142
	The Percy Family Tree – Earls of Northumberland	144
	The Neville Family Tree 1 – Earls of Westmorland	146
	The Neville Family Tree 2 – Earls of Salisbury and Warwick	148
Appendix D	Maps showing the loss of English-held or Allied Territory in Continental Europe, c. 1429-1453	150

Index	152
Acknowledgements; Select Bibliography	158
Picture Credits	159

Foreword

John Sadler

For far too long, a detailed account of the role of the principal magnatial families in the North, the Percys and Nevilles, in the build up to what we now call the Wars of the Roses, has been lacking.

Just possibly, none of it need have happened if it wasn't for those two great houses. When Percy adherents tried to ambush a Neville wedding party on Heworth Moor in 1453, the affair may have appeared little more than a local, bloodless brawl. Nonetheless, it could be said to represent the first significant, armed clash between these two pre-eminent Northern affinities which were also active in the wider movement to reform and ultimately remove the Lancastrian administration.

Ralph Northumberland has helped to fill this gap with his insightful, impeccably researched history, examining the frequently pivotal part his 15th century ancestors played in this very bloody series of linked dynastic conflicts. Thanks to him, our understanding of events in the North and the participation of eminent Northerners, those *boreales bobinantes* who so offended Southern chroniclers, is fully contextualised and given the prominence it has long been denied.

Introduction

Ralph Percy, Duke of Northumberland

The English civil wars of the 15th century are fascinating but hard to follow. There were few contemporary accounts and later versions were often coloured by Tudor spin. There were many Richards and Henrys, Marys and Margarets, and titles changed hands as the winning side 'attainted' the losing magnates, confiscated their lands and titles and handed them out to others. Over the 30 years or so of conflict, sons followed fathers, generally bearing the same first names and titles, the Percys being a prime example. To add further confusion, titles were often acquired by marrying an heiress; the Earls of Salisbury and Warwick were two such beneficiaries. Some, like Sir John Neville, changed their titles through royal gift, on several occasions. It is easy to confuse people with places – Northumberland, Salisbury, Warwick, Gloucester, Bedford, Norfolk, Pembroke, Devon, Exeter, York and so on. In this book I have tried to make it reasonably easy to follow by adding titles to avoid confusion. Where this would be overly repetitive, I have just used the name – Warwick, for instance, rather than Earl of Warwick.

It appears that most of the 'great' men who fought during these civil wars did so for personal gain rather than public benefit: for more land, more wealth, more titles and more offices of state with accompanying wages and profits. They also wanted to settle old scores. 'Bastard feudalism' enabled them to raise significant private armies from retainers and tenants, and they settled disputes by force of arms rather than royal justice.

Until Sir Walter Scott popularised the name 'Wars of the Roses' in the 19th century, this conflict between different branches of the royal family was known as the Cousins' War, although Shakespeare and others created the more appealing concept of the red and white rose in the 16th century. The white rose was a principal emblem of the House of York, but there is little mention of the red rose of

The Tudor Rose from a mid-16th century illuminated charter in the Archives at Alnwick Castle.

LIONS OF THE RED ROSE

Lancaster until Henry Tudor adopted it before the Battle of Bosworth, enabling the creation of the Tudor rose, the union of white and red symbolising the unification of the two houses through Henry's marriage to Elizabeth of York.

It is inaccurate to think of these periods of warfare as a single conflict for they were a series of linked wars interspersed with relative peace and prosperity. There weren't long-lasting campaigns and battles barely lasted a single, blood-soaked day, Towton being the bloodiest with over 20,000 killed. The population of England at this time was about two and a half million, drastically reduced from around four million at the start of the 14th century due to the ravages of the Black Death that flowed along trade routes throughout Europe, wiping out more than a third of the population. Under those circumstances, it was extraordinary that such large armies could be mustered and how many died during these battles.

I embarked on this book because of my family's involvement in the wars and a desire to learn more about their lives and deaths, particularly those of a father, the 2nd Earl of Northumberland, and four of his sons, Henry Percy (3rd Earl of Northumberland), Sir Thomas Percy (Lord Egremont), Sir Richard Percy and Sir Ralph Percy. These sons sought revenge for their father who was hunted down and butchered, on the orders of Yorkist leaders, in the first Battle of St Albans in 1455. By 1464 all the brothers had been killed in different battles supporting the Lancastrian cause, although the last to die, Sir Ralph, spent some time on the Yorkist side before reverting to Lancaster and dying heroically in a last stand on Hedgeley Moor in Northumberland. These brothers bear some responsibility for the conflict because of a bitter feud they conducted with their Northern rivals, the Nevilles, which forced each side to seek important noble allies for their cause, polarising the aristocracy into two powerful and ambitious forces, which weak kingship could not control, and corrupt government exacerbated. The tragedy continued into the next generation with the murder of the 4th Earl of Northumberland four years after Bosworth and two years after Stoke Field, the final battle of the Wars of the Roses.

For the Percys, these wars weren't the only conflicts that stained their swords with blood in the 15th century; Scotland was ever knocking at the door, testing English resolve. The Percys' traditional

Portrait of Henry VI (1421-1471), English School, 16th/17th century.

role involved keeping the Scots at bay and dealing with constant lawlessness on both sides of the Border while, in France, the Hundred Years War saw most English magnates, including the 2nd Earl of Northumberland, fighting for territory on the Continent. The ever-present threat of the 'Auld Alliance' between both of these prickly neighbours added spice to the complex politics of the era, and the Percys were right in the thick of it. Since they purchased Alnwick Castle and its estates, benefits and responsibilities in 1309, the Percy Lords (Earls of Northumberland from 1377) were responsible, when in royal favour, for maintaining order on the east side of the Scottish Border, as Wardens of the Eastern March. Financially, this came with a significant royal grant to cover military and other costs whilst perks normally included ransom fees for the return of captured Scottish prisoners. This position involved regular communication and cooperation with opposite numbers on the Scottish side as well as with Wardens of the Middle and Western Marches on the English side, but rivalries along and over the Border sometimes made this task extremely difficult.

King Henry VI is the central figure in this saga but only in an ethereal way, almost as a bystander to the momentous events that surrounded him, yet tragically responsible for the disasters that destroyed his dynasty. Compared to his father and grandfather, contemporaries saw him as a big disappointment throughout a reign that lasted for nearly 40 years. As he succeeded to the crown at the age of nine months he cannot be blamed for the initial problems of his reign but he could never truly rule, leaving it to others to act in his name. His weakness made it impossible for the Crown to control the power of aristocratic factions and royal contenders, and thereby helped to create the conditions for civil war. He was mentally unstable, probably schizophrenic, and his catatonic coma in 1453, lasting 18 months, was the start of a downward spiral which manifested itself in similar, shorter episodes of mental stupor. Abbot Wheathampstead of St Albans knew Henry from a child, and maintained that he was easily led and influenced by those with ulterior motives. A few years later his views were even more damning, describing Henry as 'his mother's stupid offspring, not his father's, a son greatly degenerated from the father, who did not cultivate the art of war... A mild-spoken, pious king, but half-witted in affairs of state.' In effect, Henry was completely unsuited to the task he was born to perform. He was brought along to four battles during the wars, as an emblem of sovereignty that gave legitimacy to his aristocratic commanders rather than as a true royal commander himself. He was undoubtedly a hopeless king but he was a good and deeply devout person who left lasting legacies, like the founding of King's College Cambridge and Eton College. He did not deserve to be murdered by his usurpers.

We denizens of the British Isles are often ridiculed for our obsession with the weather but, in our defence, the ensuing account of military and occasional naval escapades clearly demonstrate our climate's dramatic effect on the course of history. Wind, rain, and snow were powerful forces that wrecked ships, bogged down cavalry, rendered artillery useless, altered the flight of arrows and left heavily armoured and exhausted soldiers floundering in the mud, weakened by hypothermia and drowning in flooded streams.

The land and landscape was very different in the Middle Ages. Without the modern concept of land drainage, rivers were generally less well defined, meandered more, held large volumes of water for much longer than now, and their valleys were full of treacherous marshland. Throughout history, wet land played a pivotal role in success or failure. French knights, for instance, floundered in the boggy ground while charging Henry V's army at Agincourt; the Earl of Surrey destroyed the Scottish army by forcing them to charge through cloying mud at Flodden Field; Napoleon's cannon were rendered useless by the soggy ground at Waterloo. Defeated armies, trying to flee the battlefield, were often bogged down and slaughtered by the pursuing victors, as at Homildon Hill where huge numbers of Scottish soldiers were killed by the forces of Harry Hotspur, the 1st Earl of Northumberland's eldest son, or drowned in the swollen Rivers Till and Glen as they tried to flee home.

The Wars of the Roses could have ended the Percy dynasty; it very nearly did. They 'backed the wrong horse' in their adherence to the House of Lancaster and yet, against all the odds, by 1485, the year of the Battle of Bosworth, virtually all their titles, estates and political influence had been restored to them by the House of York. That they continued to thrive after Bosworth, and into the Tudor period, shows remarkable dexterity combined with a large slice of good fortune.

It might be helpful to the reader to put this period of British history into the context of a few events further afield. During the 15th century, the Middle Ages gradually gave way to a more cultured, modern (though no less violent) era in Europe and beyond. Johannes Gutenberg invented the printing press around 1440, initiating a revolution in the circulation of global information, news and ideas. The Renaissance was establishing itself throughout Europe, bringing advancement in the arts, sciences, banking, accountancy, humanism and diplomacy. Constantinople fell to the Ottomans in 1453, heralding the fall of the Byzantine Empire and accelerating the development of the Renaissance through the migration of displaced Byzantine artists and scholars.

By the end of the century, lands and opportunities had been discovered in the Americas by the Italian, Christopher Columbus, while Vasco da Gama, the Portuguese explorer, reached India by sea, opening Asia to European colonialism. In Spain, seven centuries of Islamic rule came to an end and the country became united through the marriage of Ferdinand II of Aragon and Isabella I of Castile. The Islamic faith spread through Africa. In China, the Ming dynasty completed the construction of the Forbidden City in modern day Beijing. Moctezuma I's reign turned the Aztec Empire into the preeminent power in Mesoamerica and Machu Picchu was constructed by the Incas in Peru.

1   Restoration – Back in Favour

For months the 1st Earl of Northumberland's leonine head, pickled in a mixture of cloves, cumin and anise, still bearing some of its once silver mane, stared sightlessly southwards from the London Bridge Gatehouse, reminding passers-by of the perils of treason. On the 19th February 1408 it had been hacked from his corpse on a snowy, bloodstained battlefield in Yorkshire by the 'turn-coat' victor, Sir Thomas Rokeby, who had lured the Earl to his death with promises of support against the King. This doomed battle brought an end to the Percy rebellion which had intermittently faced King Henry IV for the previous five years. The Earl's son, Sir Harry Hotspur had been killed at Shrewsbury on 21st July 1403, felled in the midst of battle by an arrow through his raised visor. His dismembered body parts were displayed in various major cities and his head was placed on Micklegate Bar in York. Northumberland's brother Thomas, Earl of Worcester, was executed a few days after that battle, and his pickled head preceded his brother's on London Bridge; an ignominious end for a man who had served under the Black Prince and John of Gaunt, rose to the rank of Admiral to the North and West, had loyally served under Kings Richard II and Henry IV, and had acted as tutor to the Prince of Wales, the future King Henry V.

The Earl of Northumberland and his army had failed to reach Shrewsbury before hearing the disastrous news of defeat and the loss of his son and brother. He turned around and fled north, pursued by a royal army under Ralph Neville, Earl of Westmorland, his Northern rival and Warden of the Western March. Throwing himself on the King's mercy, Northumberland received a royal pardon but his overwhelming thirst for vengeance led him to join the Archbishop of York's doomed rebellion in summer 1405. The King then pounded the Percys' castles

Seal of the 1st Earl of Northumberland, 1400.

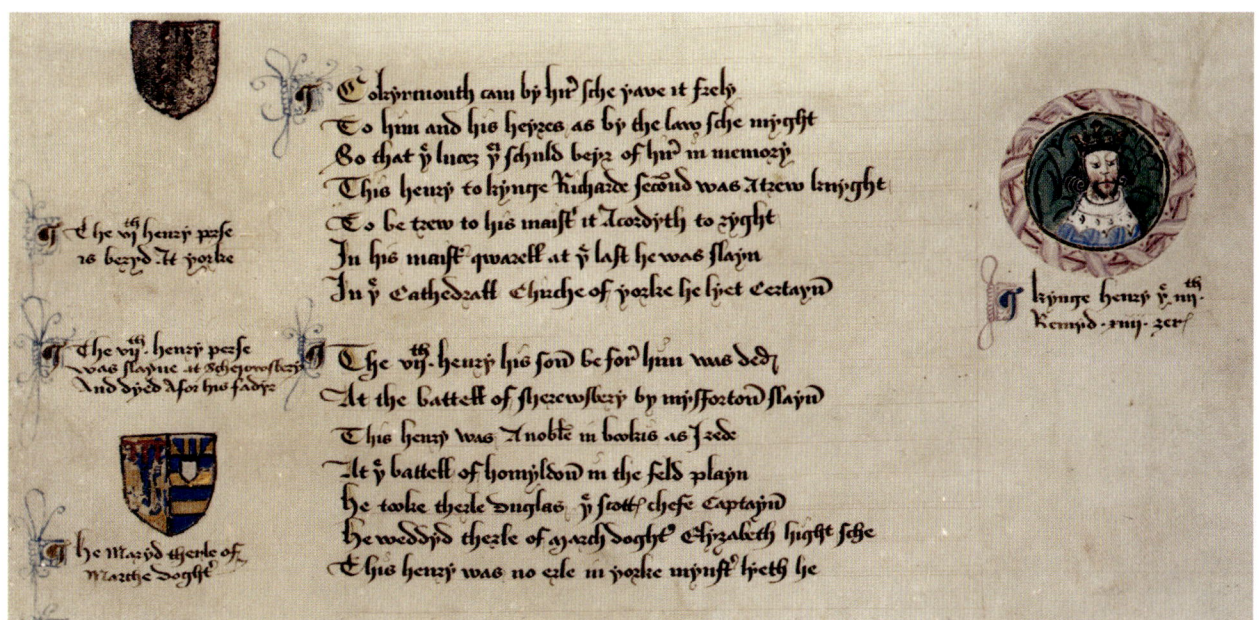

with powerful new artillery which brought them under royal control. Northumberland fled to Scotland, then travelled to France, avoiding royalist traps and seeking allies before returning to Scotland. His subsequent ill-fated and poorly executed 'invasion' attracted little support and ended in bitter defeat and death on Bramham Moor. In 1408 the Percys were utterly destroyed, their estates forfeit and titles lost.

Hearing of the defeat at Shrewsbury in 1403 and the death of her husband, Elizabeth, Hotspur's widow, had fled with their ten year old son, Henry, to Scotland where they remained under the protection of King Robert III. Henry became a friend and companion to the King's eldest surviving son, James. These boys were educated under the same tutor in St Andrews, but in 1406 the ailing King feared for James' life under the regency of the boy's ruthless and ambitious uncle, Robert Stewart, Duke of Albany, so he sent his heir to further his education at the royal court in France, accompanied by Henry Percy. En route, however, their ship was captured by privateers near Flamborough Head and the boys were sent to the English King who held them captive, albeit in comfort at court.

While Prince James remained an extremely well treated prisoner, Henry Percy appears to have escaped and returned to Edinburgh, resuming his studies in St Andrews. With the death of King Robert III, in April 1406, the Duke of Albany

Excerpt on the 1st Earl and Hotspur from a pedigree roll of the Percy family in rhyming verse by William Peeris, Chaplain to the 5th Earl of Northumberland, c. 1510.

"This henry to kynge Richarde second was A trew knyght,
To be trew to his maister it Acordyth to ryght,
In his maister qwarell at the last he was slayn,
In the Cathedrall Chirche of Yorke he lyet Certayn.

"The vijth Henry his son before him was ded,
At the battell of Sherewsbery by myssfortone slayn,
This Henry was A noble in bookis as I rede,
At the battell of Homyldon in the feld playn,
He tooke therle Duglas the Scottes chefe Captayn,
He weddyd therle of March doghter Elyzabeth hight sche,
This henry was no erle in yorke mynster lyeth he."

Left: Memorial brass to the widow of Hotspur and her second husband, Lord Camoys, in Trotton Church, Petersfield.

ruled Scotland in the absence of his nephew, and acted as Henry Percy's guardian. Percy had some military action under Albany, taking part in 'civil feuds' in Scotland and, although there is no proof, popular Northumbrian folklore tells of secret, personal missions across the Border to Northumberland, narrow escapes and a clandestine marriage to Eleanor Neville at the Warkworth Hermitage several years before their actual marriage. Perhaps they made a pledge to marry at this time although she was engaged and perhaps even married to Lord Spenser. He died in 1414, thereby removing any obstacle to this Percy Neville marriage.

> "Ah! seldom had their host, I ween,
> Beheld so sweet a pair:
>
> The youth was tall with manly bloom
> She slender, soft, and fair."

The two lovers were the heroes in a lengthy Northumbrian ballad, written in 1771, called 'the Hermit of Warkworth' by Bishop Thomas Percy, of which this is a verse.

In no hurry to provide ransom money and obtain the release of the uncrowned Scottish king, the Duke of Albany was nonetheless keen for the return of his own son, Murdoch Stewart. He had been captured by Hotspur in 1402 at the Battle of Homildon Hill, and remained Henry IV's prisoner. Fruitless negotiations proceeded until 1413 when the English King died, ravaged by a flesh wasting disease, probably leprosy. Henry Percy, now Albany's prisoner due to his value as a hostage, had become well acquainted with the former Prince of Wales, now Henry V, whilst a prisoner at Henry IV's court, and saw his future in England. Permitted by the courts to lobby for the return of his

The Hermitage at Warkworth, engraving by Thomas Bewick.

titles and estates, he acquiesced in 1415 to an Anglo-Scottish treaty to trade him for Murdoch Stewart. Enactment of this treaty was delayed until Percy had cleared his name from implication in the Earl of Cambridge's 'Southampton' plot to assassinate the King; he was absolved in 1416 and became free to return to England on payment of the ransom for Murdoch's release.

In 1416, the 23 year old Henry Percy was restored to the Earldom of Northumberland. Henry V, who, as Prince of Wales, had fought with courage and skill against Percy's father, Hotspur, at Shrewsbury, knighted the young Henry Percy and made him Earl of Northumberland on 16th March that year, after considerable petitioning by Percy's future mother-in-law, Joan Neville, Countess of Westmorland, the King's aunt. We know this Henry Percy as the 2nd Earl to avoid confusion but the King intended the title as a new 'creation' since his grandfather's treachery and resulting attainder had extinguished his own title. At about this time, Percy married Eleanor, one of the Earl of Westmorland's 23 children, in a love match which helped, temporarily, to bring the two rival families together. Percy's sister Elizabeth, Hotspur's only daughter, married John, Lord Clifford at around this time, helping to forge a bond between two families that would fight and die together for the Lancastrian cause over the coming years.

King Henry V desired strong leadership in the North to protect the Border from Albany's increasing belligerence, and so the new Earl of Northumberland was made Warden of the Eastern March, the position held by many of his forebears. The restoration of the family estates was more complicated since most had been given to the King's brother, the Duke of Bedford. These were eventually restored to the Earl by an act of parliament in 1439, four years after Bedford's death, but the question of ownership relating to other Percy estates created sparks that ignited the flames of war.

In 1416 Northumberland had brought his family back from the brink of destruction and, for the faith shown in him, he repaid his charismatic King with fervent loyalty. Still in exile in Scotland when Henry V won his stunning victory at Agincourt in 1415, Northumberland hastened to France the following year with 40 men-at-arms, including four knights, and 80 archers. Little is known of his involvement in this part of the Hundred Years War but he accompanied King Henry on his triumphant entry into Rouen in 1419, with nine other earls, and took part in the siege of Melun in 1420. Henry V rounded off his victories with the Treaty of Troyes, on 21st May 1420 which made him and his heirs the lawful successors to King Charles VI of France. As part of

Charter, 1417, by the reinstated 2nd Earl of Northumberland, confirming grants made by his ancestors to the Chaplains of Alnwick Castle, such as milling rights and the right to gather honey and wax from the bees in the Earl's parks. The brown areas are 19th century repairs where leather patches have been used to infill rodent damage.

Catherine of Valois, from a 15th century drawing of her wedding to King Henry V.

the arrangement which followed this victory, he married the French King's youngest daughter, Catherine of Valois. The Earl of Northumberland took part in these negotiations and officiated as Lord High Steward at the Queen's coronation.

Despite Henry V's success in France against the unhinged French King (who managed to kill several of his men with a sword during one psychotic episode), Charles, the Dauphin (his father's eleventh child) and his mother, Queen Isabeau, set up an alternative court in Bourges and continued to threaten English territories. Henry V returned to France in 1421, leaving his pregnant queen behind, and she gave birth to the future Henry VI while her husband was besieging Meaux. Six months later she left the infant in the care of his uncle, Humphrey, Duke of Gloucester, and sailed for France to attend to her husband who was gravely ill with fever and dysentery. Henry V died on 31st August 1422 having brought England to a pre-eminent position in Europe, united his people and greatly enhanced the House of Lancaster.

The Earl of Northumberland became a member of the Council of Regency after Henry V's death and, in 1422, Ambassador to the Court of France and Ambassador to Scotland 1423-1424 and 1429-1430.

Henry V's widowed queen, Catherine, secretly married Owen Tudor, a Welsh nobleman. Their grandson, Henry Tudor, was to become King after defeating Richard III at the Battle of Bosworth in 1485.

Portrait of King Henry V, oil painting, English School, 16th/17th century.

1 / RESTORATION – BACK IN FAVOUR   17

2   Rivalries Old and New

Scotland had proved troublesome, as the Regent, Robert Stewart, 1st Duke of Albany, took advantage of Henry V's absence in France. In 1417, Albany besieged Berwick while the Earl of Douglas simultaneously bombarded Roxburgh Castle, an English stronghold on the north bank of the River Tweed, with artillery, in an attack known as the 'Foul Raid'. Both attacks were repulsed and, after reinforcing the walls of Berwick and Roxburgh, the Earl of Northumberland sought retribution and unleashed his ruthless lieutenant, Sir Robert Umfraville, who created mayhem in south-east Scotland for the next two years. In 1419, Sir William Halliburton, a Scottish leader, attacked Wark Castle on the south bank of the River Tweed, and slaughtered the garrison, whereupon the Earl of Northumberland's other loyal henchman, Sir Robert Ogle, entered through the castle's sewer, and captured Halliburton and 23 other Scotsmen who had survived the engagement. Ogle then beheaded them all.

The 1st Duke of Albany died in 1420 and his successor, Murdoch Stewart, proved to be a poor regent, incapable of keeping order. Meanwhile Prince James, the rightful but uncrowned King of Scotland, had remained a prisoner at the English court where he had been treated well, received a good education and gained extensive

> ### Wark Castle, Northumberland
>
> This stronghold was built with the permission of King Henry I of England in 1136 on the south side of the River Tweed, a few miles downstream of Roxburgh Castle. It overlooked an important ford over the river between England and Scotland. Constantly attacked and besieged by the Scots, it was rebuilt by Henry II in 1157, was destroyed by the Scots in 1216 and rebuilt again thereafter. Legend has it that Edward III established the Order of the Garter there after rebuking his sniggering courtiers as he gallantly retrieved Lady Salisbury's garter from the floor during a ball. The King gave the castle to Edmund of Langley, his fifth son, and it continued to be subjected to Scottish raids. Although destroyed by James IV of Scotland prior to the Battle of Flodden Field in 1513, it was rebuilt, then regularly attacked and eventually abandoned in the 1600s.

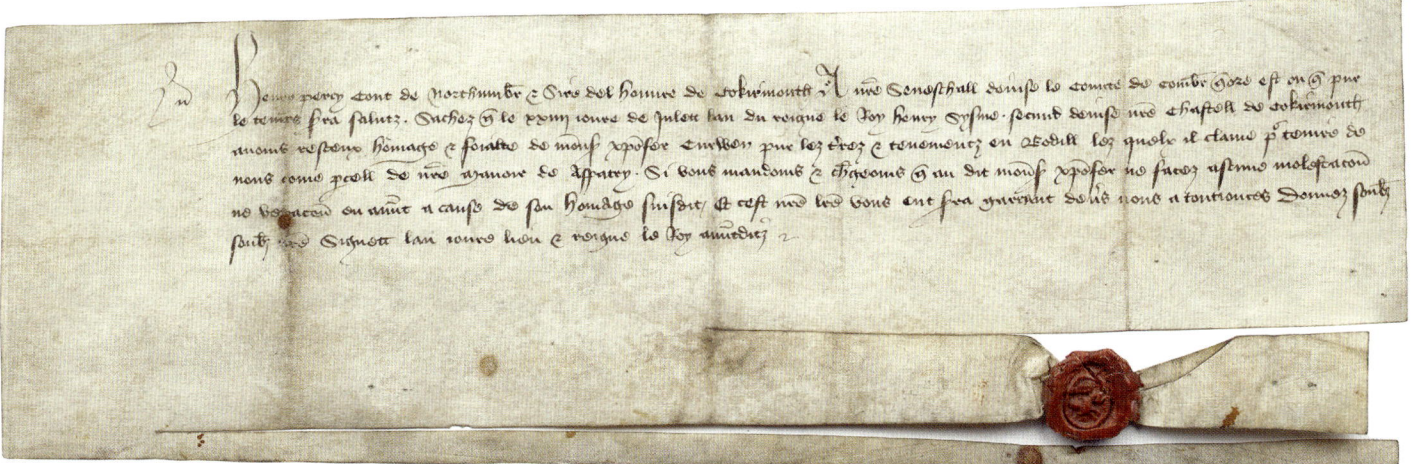

military experience in France. In 1421 Henry V made James a Knight of the Garter and, in 1424, the Treaty of London was concluded, allowing his return to Scotland as its king on the payment, in instalments, of a £40,000 ransom. The unenviable and difficult task of retrieving this ransom fell on the Earl of Northumberland, who needed these monies to pay for the maintenance of order on the Border. Under the terms of the treaty, the Scots promised not to send more troops to France, although no mention was made of troops already there, and they also agreed to a seven year truce. To seal his relationship with the English royal family, the new King James I of Scotland married Joan Beaufort, daughter of John, Earl of Somerset, and niece of the powerful Henry Beaufort, bishop of Winchester, two key figures of the period. Her grandfather, John of Gaunt, a younger son of Edward III, had acted as England's regent during Richard II's minority.

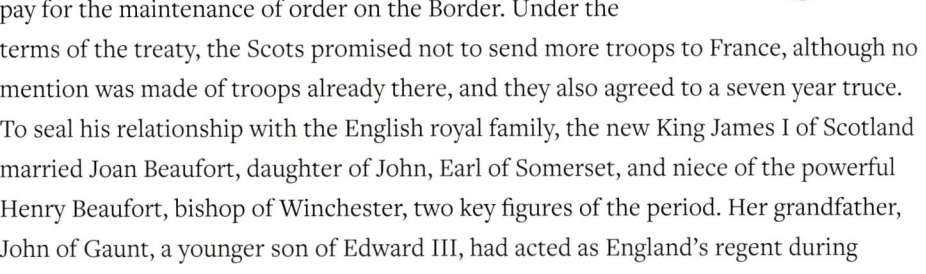

Letter under the 2nd Earl's signet seal, 1424, informing his Steward that he had received the homage and fealty of Christopher Curwen at Cockermouth Castle for Curwen's lands in Aspatria, Cumberland.

The Earl of Northumberland was instrumental in the Treaty of London and was one of the nobles who escorted King James from Durham to the Border. Almost as soon as he arrived at Melrose the Scottish King focused on revenge against the Duke of Albany and his treacherous faction, although two of his main foes, the Earls of Buchan and Douglas, were out of range of retribution, fighting against the English in France.

Meanwhile, the Earl of Northumberland had become one of the Duke of Bedford's assistants in the initial Protectorate, taking an active part in maintaining the rule of law in the North, as Warden of the Eastern March and Governor of Berwick. In 1424 he joined the Duke of Bedford in a French campaign which culminated in an overwhelming victory over the Comte de Narbonne and his Franco-Scots army at Verneuil where, much to King James' delight, the Earls of Douglas and Buchan, along with most of their

Signet ring found near the battlefield of Towton, which has in the past been attributed to the 3rd Earl of Northumberland, though the motto is not a known Percy motto. A ring like this would have been used to form an impression in soft wax to authorise a deed. The lion and motto are in mirror image, so that the seal impression appears the correct way round.

2 / RIVALRIES OLD AND NEW

followers, were killed. This carnage changed the balance of power in Scotland and allowed King James to dominate the political arena north of the Border. Further vengeance on remaining enemies came swiftly and, within a year, the Duke of Albany and his two sons, Walter and Alexander, had been tried and executed, securing the King's complete control over the Scottish nobility.

The mid to late 1420s were a relatively quiet period for the Earl of Northumberland, perhaps dominated by domesticity. By his wife, Eleanor, numerous children were born between 1418 and 1430, nine of whom survived childhood (six boys and three girls) including Henry, his heir, born in 1421.

In France, however, there was a terrible reversal of fortunes. In 1428, while besieging Orleans, Thomas Montagu, 4th Earl of Salisbury, England's finest commander, was killed by an iron shard from an exploding cannon ball. The Earl of Suffolk, his utterly inadequate replacement, was forced to lift the siege by a small French force commanded by a pious farm girl known as Joan of Arc, the Maid of Orleans. Later, Joan was at the head of French troops when they overwhelmed the town of Jargeau by the River Loire and captured Suffolk who was clearly taken by surprise in this engagement for he had just managed to seduce a French nun. A week later the English suffered a major defeat at Patay and, a few weeks after that, Joan encouraged the Dauphin to be crowned Charles VII in Reims Cathedral. In September however, believing in her divine invincibility, Joan joined the Duc de Alençon's

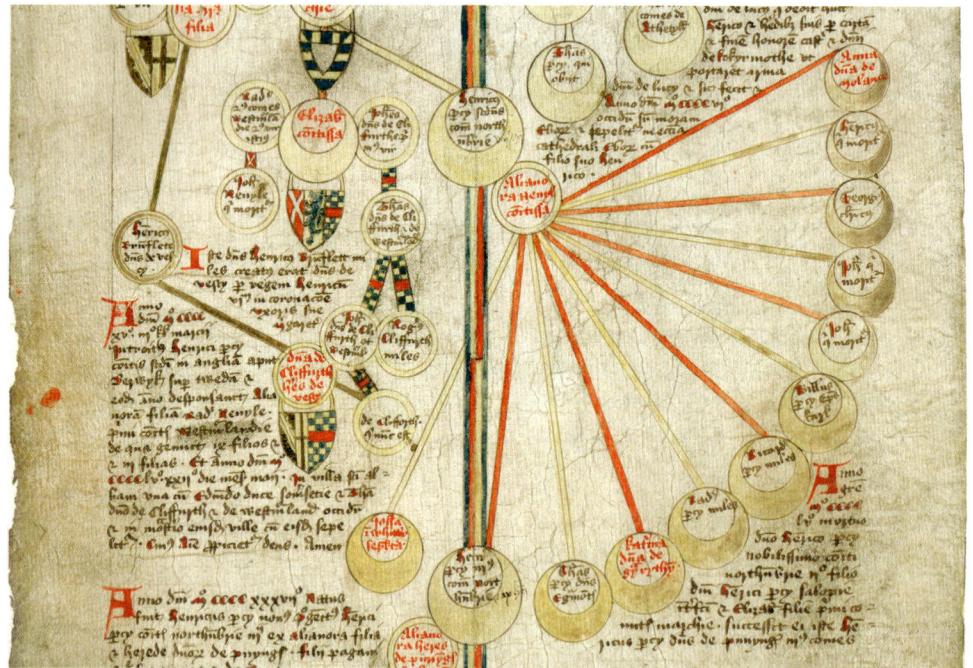

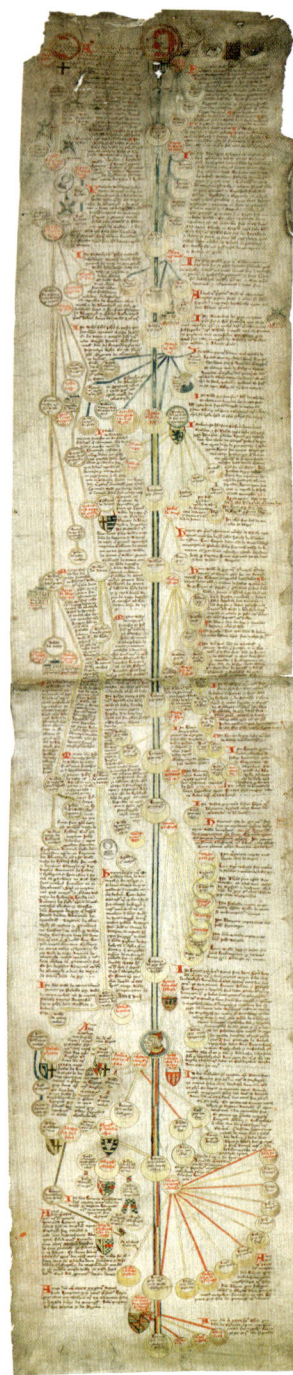

Above: 15th century pedigree roll illustrating the descent of the Percys since the Norman Conquest.

Left: Detail from the roll showing the children of the 2nd Earl of Northumberland.

20   LIONS OF THE RED ROSE

ambitious plan to take Paris itself though they were easily repulsed and her reputation was mortally damaged. In May 1430 she led a force of mercenaries out of Compiegne but was captured by a Burgundian knight, handed over to the English and burnt as a heretic in Rouen a year later, on 30th May 1431. Cardinal Henry Beaufort, second son of John of Gaunt by his third wife, lord chancellor to Henry IV and Henry V, and de facto prime minister, ruled on her fate. On 2nd December that year, the child King of England, Henry VI, entered Paris and on 16th December was anointed and crowned by Cardinal Beaufort in Notre Dame Cathedral. In early January the new King and his entourage left for England; Henry VI never set foot in France again.

Joan of Arc, illuminated portrait from a 15th century manuscript.

In 1431 an Anglo-Scottish Truce was due to expire. The King of Scotland was fully aware that friendly communication with King Charles VII of France, at this extremely sensitive time, had the double benefit of encouraging the English to avoid pressing for the outstanding part of King James's ransom, and to offer favourable terms in negotiations for the renewal of the truce. King James prevaricated until the Duke of Bedford changed the balance of war in France in England's favour, and then he signed for another five years of peace. As the years passed, however, the Scottish King renewed his negotiations with France, and the Border slowly reverted to regular threats of violence. In 1434 the Earl of Northumberland was granted a royal licence to enclose and fortify the town of Alnwick against a threatened invasion from the north.

Two years later he and George Dunbar, 11th Earl of March, led a force of around 5000 men from Alnwick into Scotland in an effort to restore March to Dunbar Castle, his family stronghold overlooking the harbour in Dunbar, which had been confiscated the previous year by William Douglas, 2nd Earl of Angus. Despite years of service, negotiating with England on behalf of the Scottish Crown, the Earl of March was accused, at a parliament in Perth, of holding his earldom and estates illegally since they had been forfeited after his father's treason. He pleaded that his father had been pardoned by the regent Duke of Albany, but it was ruled that a regent had no right to issue such a pardon. The Earl of March's father (also called George Dunbar) earned his attainder by defecting to the English and providing his considerable military skills, defeating a Scottish army at Nesbit Moor and supporting Hotspur in his devastating victory against the Scots under Sir Archibald Douglas at Homildon Hill. March changed allegiance, fought for Henry IV and greatly contributed to Hotspur's defeat and death at the Battle of Shrewsbury. Despite this, Hotspur's son

Bondgate Tower from Bondgate Without, Alnwick. Part of the 15th century town walls.

2 / RIVALRIES OLD AND NEW

was sympathetic to the Earl of March's cause, perhaps due to the confiscation of his own family estates after his father's rebellion, and supported his claim. The Earl of Angus, wanting to avoid a lengthy siege, ambushed this force in or near the Cheviot Hills, at Piperdean (there is confusion as to the exact location), and routed them, killing a good number of English troops and knights, including Sir Richard Percy, a kinsman of the Earl of Northumberland, while the Scots were relatively unscathed and lost few men. The English force retreated to Alnwick, and the Scots, buoyed by this success, were soon on the rampage again, this time with their king at the helm.

In 1436, King James' young daughter, Margaret, was sent to France to be married to the new young Dauphin, sealing an alliance with King Charles VII who supplied the Scots with the latest artillery, as well as German gunners, for their Border campaign. With a force of up to 30,000 men, they laid siege to Roxburgh Castle but Sir Ralph Grey defended it with a small force and great fortitude. When the Earl of Northumberland's army arrived to relieve the castle, the Scots 'were driven back with great slaughter', according to De Fonblanque, a somewhat biased Percy historian. Other accounts maintain that the Scots fled as soon as they saw Northumberland's army, leaving all their artillery and baggage behind. Whatever happened in reality, a peace treaty was concluded soon after.

King James I's iron grip on the Scottish nobles unsurprisingly created many enemies and, in February 1437, the Earl of Atholl sent a group of assassins to break into Blackfriars Monastery in Perth, where the Scottish King had been staying with his family since Christmas. The King heard suspicious sounds and hid in a vault or sewer while the gang threatened his servants and nearly cut the Queen's throat. Eventually King James was discovered and, after a brief fight, was stabbed to death by Sir Robert Graham, a staunch enemy. The plotters unwisely allowed the Queen to escape and within weeks she had her young son crowned. The plotters, Sir Robert Graham and Sir Robert Stewart, were tortured and executed, and the Earl of Atholl beheaded.

With the six year old James II now on the Scottish throne and the 16 year old Henry VI on the English one, the Scottish Border became relatively calm, allowing the English government to avoid renewing the Earl of Northumberland's wardenship of the Eastern March, despite his recent victory at Roxburgh Castle. His involvement with the Earl of March had irritated Cardinal Beaufort who advised the King to appoint Northumberland's worthy lieutenants, Sir Ralph Grey and Sir Robert Ogle, to protect the Border instead.

Roxburgh Castle, Scotland

Built on a bluff between the Rivers Tweed and Teviot, near Kelso, by King David I of Scotland, the castle surrendered to the English in 1174. It remained an important strategic fortress until its ruination by King James II (1460) who was killed by an exploding cannon called 'The Lion' during the bombardment. His queen, Mary of Guelders, continued the campaign and completed the castle's destruction. A timber and earthwork fort was built on the site in 1547.

LIONS OF THE RED ROSE

Left: Seal of the 2nd Earl, 1435.

In 1435 the Earl of Northumberland arranged for the marriage of his heir, Henry, to Eleanor Poynings, a wealthy heiress from Sussex. Her father had predeceased her and when her grandfather died in 1446, she was left substantial lands in the south; Henry Percy thus inherited the title of Lord Poynings. Taking possession of Eleanor's estates in Sussex and Kent proved acrimonious and involved the forceful eviction of her cousin, Robert Poynings. According to contemporaries, Lord Poynings became a fine, upstanding man like his father. He had five surviving brothers: Thomas, William, Richard, Ralph and George. George became a rector in Rothbury and William became Bishop of Carlisle at the age of 24, but the other three were warriors. Unfortunately they had an outlet for their warlike tendencies in their growing feud with the junior but wealthier branch of the Neville family, headed by Richard Neville, Earl of Salisbury who was based at Middleham Castle in North Yorkshire. The Earl of Westmorland's branch were at Raby Castle in present day County Durham. Westmorland, who was Northumberland's brother-in-law, had himself fallen out with Salisbury but the two Neville branches buried their differences in 1442-3 as the feud between the Earls of Northumberland and Salisbury intensified. Northumberland made things worse by claiming, in a fit of pique, that his enemy had married his title, sidelined the Earl of Westmorland and cheated the Percys to try and take control of the Border Marches. The Earl of Salisbury, then Warden of the Western March, countered with barbed references to Percy treachery and rebellion, still a raw subject 40 years after the death of Hotspur.

The Earl of Salisbury had the upper hand; he was closer to court and had more powerful allies than the Earl of Northumberland.

Tomb of the Reverend George Percy in Beverley Minster (he now lies inside the Minster shop).

2 / RIVALRIES OLD AND NEW 23

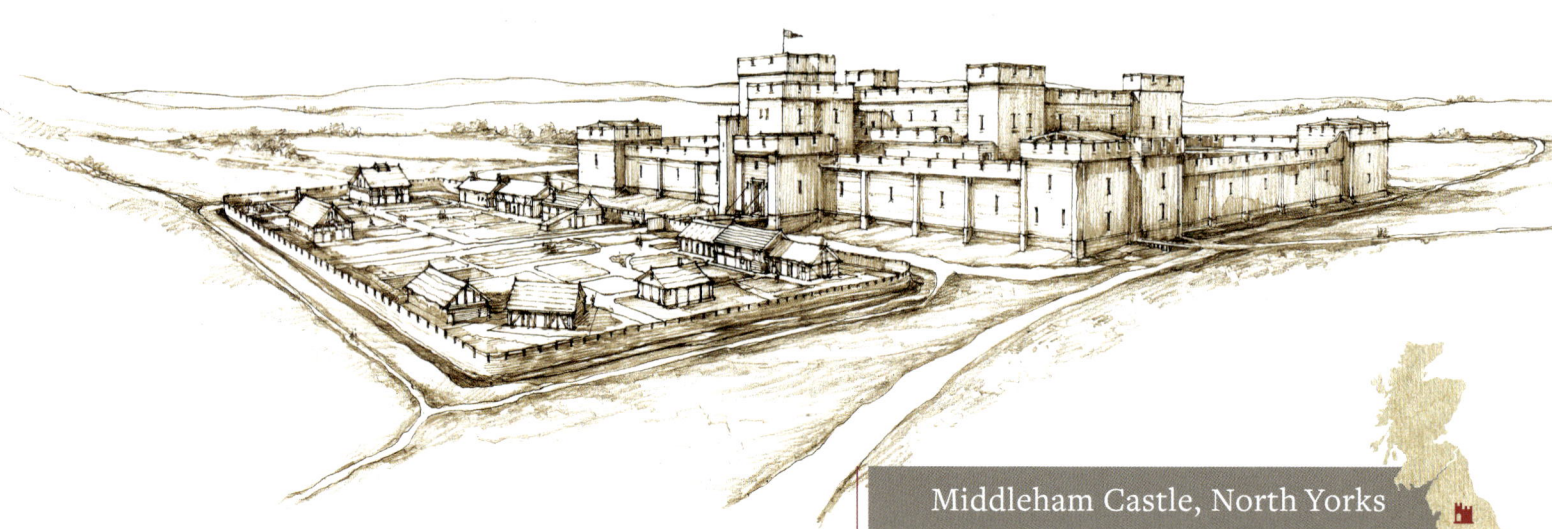

The latter recently held the support of Henry V's brothers, the Dukes of Bedford and Gloucester but Bedford was now dead and Gloucester was being accused of treason by his powerful rivals, the Earl of Suffolk, Cardinal Beaufort and his nephew Edmund, Earl of Somerset. With little more than circumstantial evidence, they accused Duchess Eleanor, Gloucester's wife, of witchcraft through her attempts to discover, with the help of priestly astrologers, whether she would one day become Queen. The evidence was twisted by the Duke of Gloucester's foes and presented in a way that was sufficient to condemn the Duchess for encouraging the King's death rather than seeking to foresee it. She was forced to perform humiliating public penance while her astrological associates were tortured and executed. Her condemnation implicated her husband beyond repair and Gloucester was forced to divorce her and suffer imprisonment in Bury St Edmunds, where he died, in suspicious circumstances, in 1447. John Holland, Duke of Exeter, another powerful ally, also died that year, and his immature son, Henry, was little help to the beleaguered Earl of Northumberland at this time. The Earl of Westmorland was too weak, and Lord Clifford, Northumberland's brother-in-law, friend and ally, had little power or influence beyond the North.

The Earl of Salisbury also held a major trump card in the form of Richard, Duke of York, grandson of Edmund, Duke of York, Edward III's fifth son. Richard's father, the

Middleham Castle, North Yorks

Built in the late 12th and early 13th centuries in Wensleydale, North Yorkshire, it became a principal Neville property in 1270. It was enlarged by Ralph Neville around 1300 and further expanded in the 15th century when a new gatehouse was built, probably by Richard Neville, Earl of Warwick. After the Duke of York was killed at the Battle of Wakefield in 1460, the Earl of Warwick looked after York's children at Middleham, including Edward (later Edward IV), George (Duke of Clarence) and Richard (Duke of Gloucester and later Richard III). Middleham became the home of the Duke of Gloucester in 1471 when he married Warwick's daughter, Anne Neville. Their son Edward was born there but died in 1484. Middleham Castle reverted to the Crown after Richard III's death in 1485 and was eventually 'slighted' by Parliament during the Civil War and condemned to decay.

Earl of Cambridge, had been executed for his involvement in the plot to kill Henry V in 1415, the same year his uncle, the previous Duke of York, was killed at Agincourt. Inheriting his childless uncle's title and lands, young Richard was brought up in the Earl of Salisbury's household until he came of age in 1432. His mother, Anne, was the elder sister of Edmund Mortimer, 5th Earl of March, whom Hotspur had intended to place on the throne if he had defeated Henry IV at Shrewsbury. Edmund died childless, and so Richard inherited the Earldom of March from his maternal uncle and the Duchy of York from his paternal uncle, giving him a strong claim to the throne derived from two of Edward III's sons. He married the beautiful Cecily Neville, 'the Rose of Raby', the Earl of Salisbury's youngest sister, firmly placing this powerful and extremely wealthy man in Salisbury's camp. Henry VI's incompetent and corrupt council made the enormous error of largely ignoring the Duke of York's pedigree and capabilities, denying him senior office whenever possible and thereby forcing him into the open arms of the Nevilles.

Cecily Neville, 'the Rose of Raby', wearing a green and yellow patterned dress, from a 15th century illuminated book of hours owned by the Neville family.

2 / RIVALRIES OLD AND NEW

3 Misrule and Anarchy

William de la Pole, Earl of Suffolk, was elevated to a dukedom and became the King's principal adviser, using his position to further his own and his friend's interests and wealth. In the 1444 Treaty of Tours, he incurred national disapproval by arranging the King's marriage to Margaret of Anjou in return for a truce which included the transfer of the province of Maine to King Charles VII of France. To further endear himself to the French King, he also discussed the potential renouncement of Henry VI's claim to the French Crown, thereby causing outrage amongst the majority of Englishmen, including many who had made their homes and livelihoods in England's French territory, and saw France as the enemy. In the King's absence, it was the Duke of Suffolk who stood in for Henry VI at the initial marriage ceremony in France, placing the ring on the 14 year old Margaret's finger and reciting the marriage vows on Henry's behalf. Suffolk and the young Queen became devoted friends and, despite a significant age difference, there were unfounded rumours of a physical relationship.

For the general population, Suffolk's misjudgements and failures at home and abroad were significant enough but, five years later, King Charles VII of France launched a massive campaign against the underfunded and woefully protected English territories and, by 1450, all that remained of England's ancestral French lands, and Henry V's more recent conquests, was Aquitaine and the Channel Islands (see appendix D). The Duke of Suffolk was chiefly responsible for this disaster and became the most hated man in England. In April 1450, fearing retribution, he fled for France only to be intercepted in the Straits of Dover, probably on the Duke of York's orders, by a gang of men on a ship called the *Nicholas of the Tower*. A few days later

Top: Frontispiece of an illuminated manuscript of 1445 depicting its presentation to King Henry VI and Queen Margaret of Anjou by John Talbot, 1st Earl of Shrewsbury.

Above: Detail from the manuscript showing Queen Margaret of Anjou.

he was 'tried' by the gang, found guilty, taken onto a rowing boat and beheaded with a rusty sword in the hands of an inebriated Irishman who took six strokes to sever his head. His body was left on the sands of Dover where it lay rotting for a month, with the head on a pole beside it, a macabre allusion to his family name – de la Pole.

In the spring of 1450, Suffolk's failures, mismanagement and corruption ignited a rebellion in Kent under a veteran called Jack Cade, supported by many embittered Anglo-Norman refugees landing in Dover, and inflamed by Richard, Duke of York's propaganda machine. The rebels poured into London, breached the Tower of London, murdered the Treasurer, Lord Saye and Sele, and threatened to plunge the country into bloody civil war. It took until July to bring the rebellion to a halt and, thanks mainly to the Queen's intervention, most of the rebels were pardoned, although the main ringleaders, like Cade himself, were hunted down and killed over the following year. Thanks to weak kingship and corrupt government the country was descending into anarchy, fuelled by deep dissatisfaction with state and church. One unscrupulous prelate, the Bishop of Salisbury, was murdered by his congregation, and other priests were threatened. Cade's most strident demand was for the King to dismiss his grasping favourites because 'his lords are lost, his merchandise is lost, his commons destroyed, the sea is lost and France is lost', a succinct description of the degenerate realm in 1450. If Cade himself had maintained the moral code he demanded of others the rebellion might have been even more serious but he sought to enrich himself with plunder and thereby lost the support of many of his allies, nobles and commoners alike.

Richard of York as depicted in the 'Talbot Shrewsbury Book', 1445.

Edmund Beaufort, now Duke of Somerset, replaced Suffolk as the King's principal adviser, much to the chagrin of the Duke of York who loathed Somerset and saw himself, as did many others, as the best hope for stable government. York had proved himself an able commander and administrator in France and Ireland, spending vast sums of his own money defending the interests of the Crown, for little thanks or reward. However, the self-centred clique around the King saw the Duke of York as an existential threat and the Queen held him responsible for the death of the Duke of Suffolk, her friend and mentor. The Duke of Somerset, on the other hand, was little improvement on Suffolk. He had suffered spectacular failures and defeats in France, provided inadequate control over royal spending, persuaded the King to give him an outrageously high salary, accumulated wealth through the grant of royal offices and the fees and rents that came with them, and yet managed to persuade the King to exclude the vastly more capable Duke of York from positions of power. His incompetence led to further disasters in France and, on 17th July 1453, King Charles VII utterly defeated the English army at Castillon, the final battle of the Hundred Years War. All English territories in France were lost except Calais. A month later, on hearing this catastrophic news, Henry VI's mind shut down and he fell into a catatonic coma. The Duke of Somerset was helpless without the Crown's support and, in November 1453, the Duke of York and his allies took full advantage of the situation, accusing Somerset of treason and, with Parliament's approval, sending him to the Tower of London.

While all this was playing out in the south of England and in France, the Scottish Border was rumbling with discontent. The Earl of Salisbury was in charge of the Western March while the Earl of Northumberland's heir, Henry Percy, Lord Poynings, was responsible, since 1440, for the Eastern March. In 1447 the nine year truce with Scotland expired and by the following year Poynings, desperate for action, decided to attack and burn the town of Dunbar. His Scottish counterpart, William, 8th Earl of Douglas, retaliated by burning the towns of Alnwick and Warkworth so Poynings' father marched a force of 6000 Northumbrians through the Earl of Salisbury's Western March, a breach of etiquette that infuriated his fellow warden, then crossed the Border at Gretna and encamped by the River Sark in Annandale. He

Commission, 1446, from Lord Poynings as Warden instructing Christopher Spencer to capture and detain a large number of Scots who had invaded the Marches. Seal of the Crescent and Fetterlock type, used by Lord Poynings as Warden.

was attacked by the Earl of Ormond with a force of about 4000 Scots. After furious fighting, the Northumbrians seemed to be prevailing when Lord Maxwell appeared with Lanarkshire reinforcements, turning the battle in favour of the Scots as the Solway's tide rose to cut off the Earl of Northumberland's retreat. Many of his men drowned in the sea and mud, and Northumberland only managed to escape with the aid of his son who helped him onto his horse as the enemy bore down on them. Lord Poynings was captured along with Sir John Peynington, one of the commanders, but both were ransomed soon after.

Casualty figures at that time were notoriously unreliable but as many as 2000 Englishmen may have perished in the battle, whereas the Scots lost about 600. To avenge this overwhelming Scottish victory, the Earl of Salisbury was ordered to attack the Scots as soon as possible but, as he marched towards the enemy in atrocious weather, thieves stole most of his horses and provisions, and fighting became impossible. He returned, humbled, to Carlisle only to find the Scots ravaging the area around the city.

The King's council raged at these failures, both Wardens' fees were cut and peace negotiations with the Scottish King initiated without the involvement of either the Earl of Salisbury or Earl of Northumberland. Fortunately for the latter, his reputation was restored the following year when James II led an army across the Border which was repulsed by the Earl and his son Ralph. They received formal thanks from Henry VI for their 'diligence in protecting the Marches and rebuking and resisting the malice of our enemyes the Scottes.'

Portrait of Henry, 2nd Earl of Northumberland. English School, mid-18th century.

3 / MISRULE AND ANARCHY

4 The Feud Develops

As far as the Percys were concerned, malice was not only held by 'the Scottes'. The feud with the Nevilles escalated, mainly due to the ferocious nature of the sons of the Earls of Northumberland and Salisbury. Apart from the traditional rivalry between Northern magnates, the feud was inflamed by the diminution of Percy wealth, lands and influence in the aftermath of Hotspur's disastrous rebellion against King Henry IV at the start of the century, and the corresponding rise in the Nevilles' power and wealth in the vacuum created. They had risen in political importance with the two marriages of Ralph Neville who was created Earl of Westmorland by King Richard II, much to the irritation of the Percys despite their own recent elevation under the same king. The Earl of Westmorland first married Margaret Stafford and, after her death, Joan Beaufort, daughter of John of Gaunt and Katherine Swynford. In total, he fathered 23 children. Several sons married heiresses: Richard married Alice, heiress to the Earl of Salisbury, and her husband acquired that title from her; William, George and Edward gained the important baronies of Fauconberg, Latimer and Bergavenny. Some of Westmorland's daughters also married well, to the Dukes of York and Norfolk and the Earls of Stafford and, of course, Northumberland.

Sheriff Hutton Castle, North Yorks

It was built in the late 14th century on the site of a former motte and bailey castle in North Yorkshire, by John, Lord Neville. His son, the 1st Earl of Westmorland, left his Yorkshire estates, including Sheriff Hutton, to his eldest son by his second marriage, Richard Neville, Earl of Salisbury. After the death of Salisbury's son – Warwick 'the Kingmaker' – at the Battle of Barnet in 1471, Richard, Duke of Gloucester, used the castle as a Northern base. After his death at the Battle of Bosworth, it fell into the hands of Henry VII and was occupied by Thomas Howard (later 2nd Duke of Norfolk), the King's lieutenant in the North.

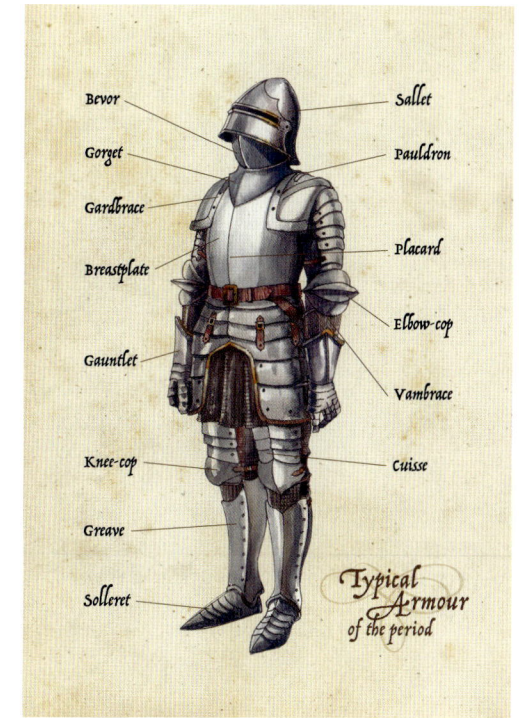

This canny and clearly virile Neville left the Earldom of Westmorland to his eldest son but, realising the political importance of Joan Beaufort's issue, he left the bulk of his lands to Joan's son, Richard, Earl of Salisbury, including the castles and lordships of Middleham and Sheriff Hutton in Yorkshire, and other estates in Westmorland and Essex. Salisbury's son, another Richard, married Anne de Beauchamp who inherited the vast Beauchamp estate and Earldom of Warwick thereby giving the future 'Kingmaker' his title as well as great riches and power. The Percys' recovery under King Henry V brought back their titles and some of their property but they still lacked much of their former holdings, some of which had ended up in Neville hands. They were also now considerably less wealthy than the Nevilles, and found it harder to receive their dues from the Crown for protecting the Eastern March, creating more debt and greater resentment. An agrarian crisis in the 1430s continued to reduce the income of both families but the Earl of Salisbury's greater influence at court enabled him to recoup losses from his wardenship and other high offices.

Thomas Percy, Northumberland's second son, born at Leconfield in 1422 and bearing his grandfather Hotspur's fiery temper and love of combat, is described by contemporaries as 'quarrelsome, violent and contemptuous of all authority'. He had the charisma to draw men to his banner, particularly men of a similar nature and equal disdain for the Nevilles. In 1446, a complaint was made by the former Sheriff of Cumberland relating to an incident in which Percy's men had beaten and wounded his under sheriff and bailiffs, and that Percy had said in front of witnesses that he would have the Sheriff's head! The Sheriff put this complaint to the Earl of Salisbury, that he might put the matter to the King. In the hope of improving his temper and maturity, Thomas Percy was created Lord Egremont by Henry VI in 1449 and granted the full barony of Egremont in Cumberland, former Percy territory, despite Neville

4 / THE FEUD DEVELOPS 31

claims that their family had been granted the barony after Hotspur's rebellion. As Warden of the Western March, Salisbury saw northwest England as his sphere of influence but Lord Egremont became a malevolent force in the area and, in 1452, he was joined by his 24 year old brother, William, the newly appointed Bishop of Carlisle. These brothers stirred up anti-Neville dissent and initiated riots on the Western March before moving to Yorkshire and inciting trouble in the traditional heartland of both families, where the rivalry was at its most toxic. Percys and Nevilles had large property holdings in the area, employing vast numbers of retainers, and receiving rent and military service from a multitude of tenants. The Earl of Salisbury eventually alerted the King to Lord Egremont's troublemaking, and the errant Percy was commanded to take himself and his violent followers to Gascony where they could be more use and less trouble. Egremont, however, ignored the royal summons three times in the summer of 1453 while Gascony burned. A vicious, personal vendetta grew between Lord Egremont and Salisbury's third son, Sir John Neville, who spent June and July stalking his Percy enemy throughout Yorkshire. The protagonists' retainers were unleashed on each other's properties, breaking into houses, smashing windows and creating mayhem, Egremont's equally violent brother, Richard, personally involving himself in the robbery and looting. According to King's Bench papers, Richard and his followers, 'the sons of the devil and heretics' burst into Gargrave church in Craven, and attacked Lawrence Catterall, the Bailiff of Staincliff Wapentake, then jumped onto the altar, almost on top of the vicar who was saying mass. He begged them to cease their hooliganism but they kidnapped Caterall and locked him in Cockermouth Castle until he ceased to be bailiff. The situation became so bad that the King commanded Salisbury and Northumberland to rein in their sons and disband

The family of the 2nd Earl of Northumberland as depicted in a stained glass window (no longer surviving) of St Denys Church, York. Illustration from Drake's 'History of York', 1736.

32 LIONS OF THE RED ROSE

their forces but Egremont and John Neville ignored all orders to keep the peace.

In August 1453, as the King fell into a mental abyss, the Percy-Neville feud took an even more dangerous turn. 50 years earlier, after the Battle of Shrewsbury and Hotspur's death, the 1st Earl of Northumberland's brother, Thomas, Earl of Worcester, was executed and attainted by Henry IV. His Yorkshire castle and manor of Wressle and the manor of Burwell were later acquired by Ralph, Lord Cromwell, a Lincolnshire baron with Beaufort connections. The Earl of Northumberland hoped that this important part of the Percy empire would one day revert to his family and he may even have promised it to his second son, Lord Egremont. However, the marriage of Cromwell's heiress, Maud Stanhope, to Sir Thomas Neville, John Neville's older brother, meant that Wressle would, on Cromwell's death, pass into Neville hands and be lost to the Percys for evermore. This was utterly unacceptable as far as Egremont and his brother Richard Percy were concerned. Accompanied by John Clifford, heir to Lord Clifford, they recruited 700 men and, with murder on their minds, ambushed the wedding party on Heworth Moor to the east of York, as it made its way from Tattershall Castle to Sand Hutton, the Neville stronghold. Faced with a larger force than they expected, the Percys refrained from a full-on attack and there was little more than a scuffle and some name-calling but continuing pressure for violent redress was growing.

The King's mental

Wressle Castle, East Riding

It was built in the East Riding of Yorkshire in the 1390s, probably designed by John Lewin, who was also responsible for parts of Warkworth and several other castles of that period. It was created for Thomas Percy, Earl of Worcester, younger brother of the 1st Earl of Northumberland. Worcester was executed after the failed Percy rebellion against Henry IV in 1403, and Wressle Castle was confiscated by the King. In 1471 Edward IV returned many of the Percy properties, including Wressle, to Henry Percy, 4th Earl of Northumberland. It remained in Percy ownership until the 18th century but was badly damaged during the Civil War.

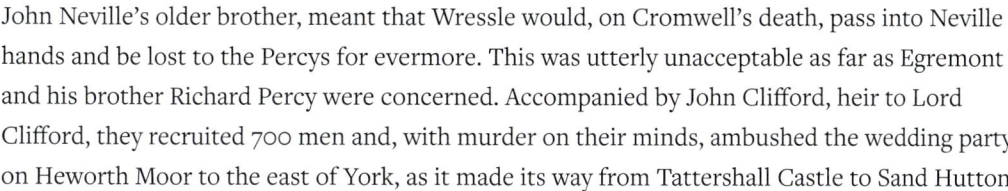

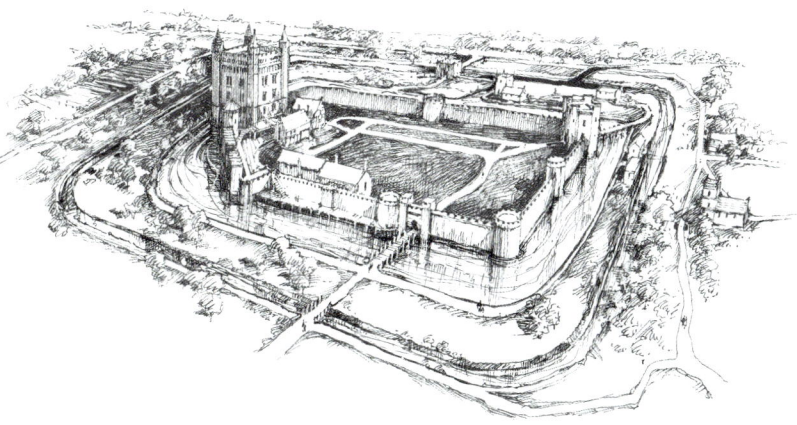

Left: Tattershall Castle

4 / THE FEUD DEVELOPS

incapacity made royal intervention unlikely and each side sought strong allies for a final reckoning. The Earl of Salisbury needed the Duke of York's political strength and military might to defeat the Percys, and York needed Salisbury's support in his ambition to become Lord Protector during the King's illness which, for all anyone knew, could have been permanent. The Percys had a strong ally in the Queen, Margaret of Anjou, who hated the Duke of York as much as she adored the Duke of Somerset. They also gained the support of Henry Holland, the young Duke of Exeter, who believed that his descent from John of Gaunt and his first wife, Blanche of Lancaster, gave him a greater right than York to be Lord Protector. The Percys could also rely on the support of the loyal Northern barons, Lord Clifford and his son John.

On 13th October 1453, the Queen gave birth to Prince Edward, Duke of Cornwall, which should have dashed any belief by the Dukes of York, Somerset or Exeter, that they might one day claim the crown. However, the council could not acknowledge the child's right to succession until he had been acknowledged by the King who, at this stage, was incapable of acknowledging anything. Rumours spread that the child was another man's offspring, perhaps the Duke of Suffolk's or Somerset's. After all, Henry's piety and views in support of celibacy were well known and the Queen had failed to conceive in the first seven years of her marriage. The Earl of Warwick then incurred the everlasting loathing of Queen Margaret by referring to her son as a fraud and bastard in front of a packed assembly of magnates in the Palace of Westminster, where the child was born.

South West View of Egremont Castle, 1739.

As tensions increased, Lord Egremont and Sir John Neville continued to create havoc in Yorkshire, becoming increasingly brazen and lawless. Egremont even beat up Cumberland's Deputy Sheriff and bailiffs when they were collecting taxes, incurring the wrath of the government who threatened to downgrade the ranks of the Earls of Salisbury and Northumberland, and remove the titles of Lord Egremont and Sir John Neville if the rancour continued. This warning and the mediation of the Archbishop of York probably came just in time to avoid a bloody showdown, for both sides were

gathering large forces at their bases in Yorkshire, the Percys at Topcliffe, and the Nevilles, including the Earl of Warwick, at Sand Hutton.

In his bid for power, the Duke of York's wealth, ability and experience proved decisive and he was made Protector in 1454, supported by the Earls of Salisbury and Warwick. Salisbury saw York as a valuable ally against the Percys while Warwick's dispute with the Duke of Somerset over land in Glamorgan also drew him closer to York's side. The land in question was an old Beauchamp family property, including the Lordship of Glamorgan. Warwick had held this land, albeit with a questionable legal right, since 1450 but, early in 1453, the King granted it to the Duke of Somerset, thereby further antagonising the Nevilles. With the Duke of York now Regent and the Duke of Somerset imprisoned by his enemies in the Tower, the Earl of Northumberland had lost a vital ally at a crucial time, and Salisbury's influence on the Duke of York ensured that there was little respite for the Percys. In May 1454 the Earl of Northumberland, Lord Poynings, Lord Egremont and their brother, Sir Ralph, were summoned by the council to London to explain their recent, anarchic activities in Yorkshire – they all ignored this. Instead, Lord Egremont, his younger brothers and the Duke of Exeter, who was also in dispute with Lord Cromwell, raised a rather amateur army, kidnapped the mayor of the City of York and tried to instigate rebellion in the North. They had some success in Lancashire but since most people longed for stable government and saw the Duke of York as the best man to provide it, the rebellion dissolved at the arrival of a relatively small but more professional army led by the Duke of York, accompanied by the Earl of Salisbury, now Chancellor of England. The Duke of Exeter fled to seek sanctuary in Westminster Abbey but was dragged out and imprisoned in Pontefract Castle, fortunate to avoid execution.

Lord Egremont hid in Cockermouth, his Cumbrian property, before heading south-east to Yorkshire, to join his brother Richard in ravaging Neville property once more. At Stamford Bridge they finally clashed with a Neville force led by Sir Thomas and Sir John Neville, and were roundly defeated mainly thanks to the treacherous desertion of Peter Lound, the Bailiff for the (Percy) Manor of Pocklington, and his followers. According to a Latin chronicle at Trinity College, Dublin, hundreds were killed and many wounded in the fighting. Lord Egremont surrendered to the Nevilles and was taken to Middleham Castle, fined a huge amount of money

Left: Portrait of Thomas Percy, Lord Egremont, English School, mid-18th century.

(£11,200) by the Earl of Salisbury for all the damage the Percys had inflicted on him in recent years, and sent to the debtors' prison of Newgate with his recently captured brother, Richard, to be held there until this debt was paid. The Earl of Northumberland and Lord Poynings had sensibly stayed clear of the Stamford Bridge debacle, and the Duke of York, attempting to mollify the Percys, magnanimously accepted their innocence, rewarding Poynings with a significant sum for his role as Warden of the Eastern March.

Richard Plantagenet, Duke of York brought stability and good governance to England during his protectorate and much of the population fervently hoped that this would continue indefinitely. For all they knew the King might have been permanently incapacitated while Prince Edward was just a baby who had not yet been recognised by his father as his son and heir, and would almost certainly fail to be recognised as such by the barons or general populace. However, on Christmas Day 1454, York's worst fears were realised when Henry VI suddenly came out of his mental stupor. As he regained most of his faculties and recognised the child as his heir, Queen Margaret's influence blossomed and, a month later, the Duke of York was removed from his position as Lord Protector. The Duke of Somerset was released from prison, cleared of any charges, reinstated at court, made Captain of Calais, replacing the Duke of York there, and became Henry's principal royal councillor once more.

The Duke of Exeter, though still a prisoner, was moved from Pontefract Castle to the more comfortable Wallingford Castle, away from the Earl of Salisbury's

Cockermouth Castle, Cumbria

At the junction of the Rivers Cocker and Derwent in Cumbria, this castle was built around 1134 using stone from an old Roman fort at nearby Papcastle. Towers were added in the 13th and 14th centuries and Robert the Bruce destroyed part of the castle in 1315. It was owned by the Percys from the 14th century and then inherited by the Wyndham family in the mid-18th century. It played an important role in the Wars of the Roses, as a base for Thomas Percy, 1st Lord Egremont. As a Royalist stronghold in the Civil War, it was 'slighted' by the Parliamentarians and fell into disrepair. It was partly repaired in the 19th century but much of it is now in ruins.

North West view of Cockermouth Castle, 1739.

malign influence. Salisbury refused to release him and was threatened with a large fine for disobedience, then dismissed as Chancellor and replaced by the Archbishop of Canterbury. Lord Cromwell, who was despised by the Lancastrians, stepped down as Chamberlain of the King's household, whilst the Earl of Worcester, Salisbury's son-in-law, was dismissed from his post as Lord High Treasurer. For the Earl of Northumberland and the faction now centred on the Duke of Somerset, revenge was sweet. They now held all the cards, or so they thought.

In mid-April 1455 a great council was summoned at Leicester, scheduled for 21st May, to which the Duke of York and Earl of Salisbury were summoned but, believing that this council, brimming with their enemies, had malicious intent, they withdrew to their Yorkshire castles, Sandal and Middleham, and started to recruit an army. It is possible that the intention of this council, perhaps with the King's active involvement, was to reconcile the opposing factions, but the Duke of York and the Nevilles were not going to risk it. York now planned to seize the initiative and regain the power so recently lost. He marched south with his allies, the Earl of Salisbury, Lord Clinton, Lord Grey of Powys and Sir Robert Ogle who had raised a substantial force of men from the Welsh Marches. The Earl of Warwick and his 1000-strong army linked up with the Duke of York on Ermine Street, the old Roman road, and together they converged on St Albans.

When the council belatedly became aware of this threat, the Duke of Somerset quickly amassed forces to protect London from the Yorkists, enlisting the support of the Duke of Buckingham, the Earl of Northumberland and Lord Clifford, together with three other earls and five other barons who were present in London at the time. They left the city on 21st May accompanied by one cleric, the Earl of Northumberland's son, William Percy, Bishop of Carlisle. They marched towards Leicester, spending the night at Watford on the way, whilst the Duke of York marched from Ware to St Albans, mid-way between the two armies, and called for negotiation, making it clear that this rebellion was against the Duke of Somerset not the King. Two other appeals had been sent by York during the march south but both were intercepted by Somerset and never reached the King. At this point Henry VI, who had replaced Somerset with the more neutral Duke of Buckingham as commander of his army, agreed to negotiate with York, believing that the latter would submit to the royal command.

Richard, 5th Earl of Salisbury, from a Roll of Arms, c. 1463.

5 St Albans, 1455

Early next morning, the royal army arrived at St Albans from the west but they found the Yorkists already blocking the road running north out of the town from St Peter's Street. They halted, strung out down the main street, into the market place and back into Holywell Street where the King and his entourage waited. The Duke of York was based on Shropshire Lane while the Earl of Salisbury covered Sopwell. The Earl of Warwick, commanding the reserves, was placed between them, opposite the King's position, but hidden by a row of houses. The Lancastrians reinforced the barricades to prevent the Yorkists from entering the main part of the town, the Earl of Northumberland and Lord Clifford taking charge of the Shropshire barricade and Sopwell Lane defences respectively. They had several hours to undertake this work as the Duke of Buckingham, who was respected by both sides, was deep in negotiation with the Duke of York, trying to find a peaceful solution. York's terms, however, were emphatic; the Duke of Somerset must be turned over to him or there would be no truce. The King was said to be furious, exclaiming 'By the faith that I owe to St Edward and the crown of England, I shall destroy every mother's son and they shall be hanged and drawn and quartered'. This pronouncement sounds unlike anything Henry might have uttered so it is more likely to have been the words of Somerset, Northumberland or Clifford.

Since there were around 6000 Yorkist troops, with longbows, crossbows and cannon, to 3000

38 LIONS OF THE RED ROSE

The First Battle of St Albans
22nd May 1455

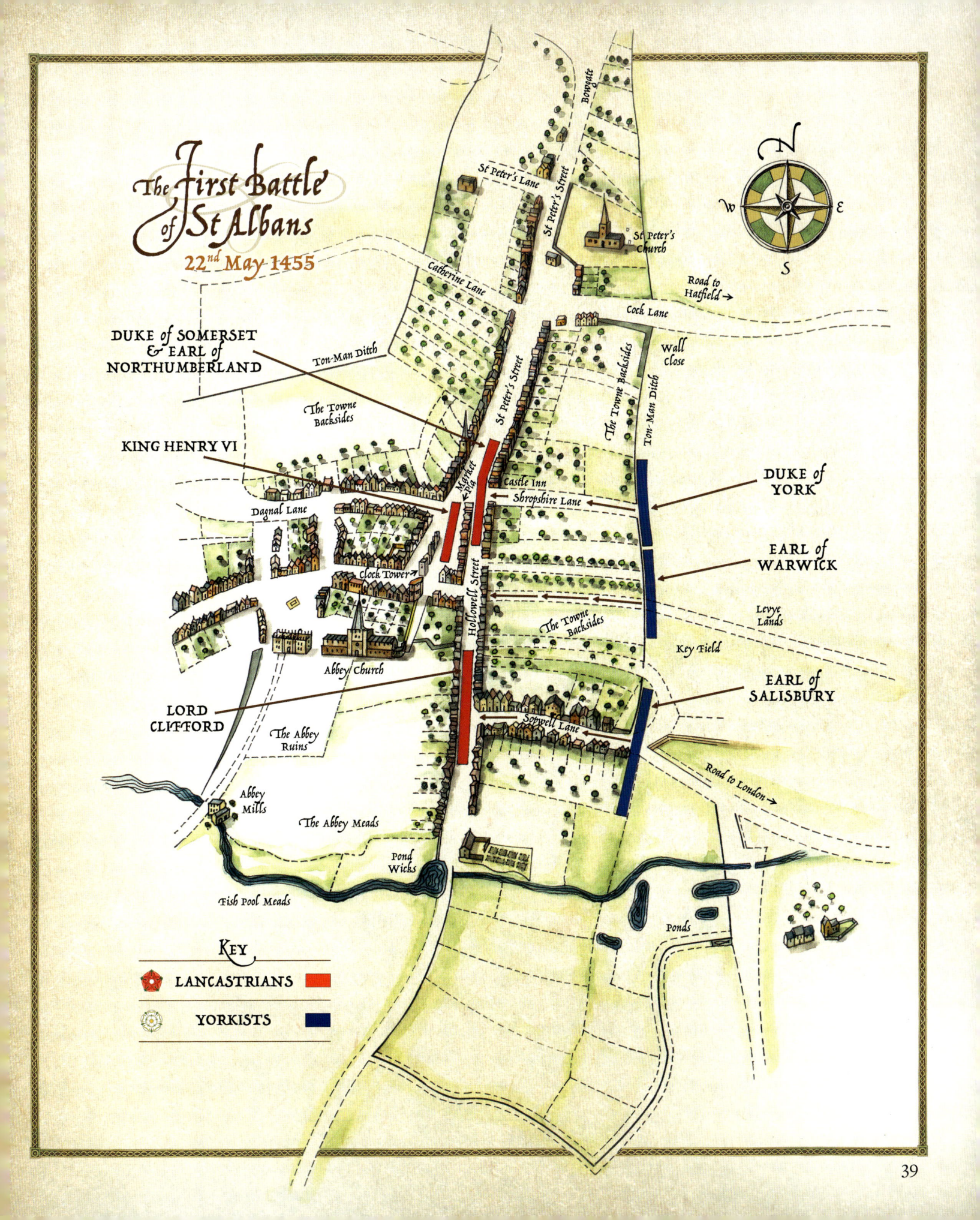

DUKE OF SOMERSET & EARL OF NORTHUMBERLAND

KING HENRY VI

LORD CLIFFORD

DUKE OF YORK

EARL OF WARWICK

EARL OF SALISBURY

Key
- 🌹 LANCASTRIANS
- 🌼 YORKISTS

Labels on map: Bowgate, St Peter's Lane, St Peter's Street, St Peter's Church, Catherine Lane, Road to Hatfield, Cock Lane, Ton-Man Ditch, Wall close, The Towne Backsides, Ton-Man Ditch, Market Pla, Castle Inn, Shropshire Lane, Dagnal Lane, Clock Tower, Hollowell Street, The Towne Backsides, Levye Lands, Key Field, Abbey Church, Sopwell Lane, The Abbey Ruins, Road to London, Abbey Mills, The Abbey Meads, Pond Wicks, Fish Pool Meads, Ponds

39

inadequately equipped Lancastrians, this absurdly arrogant end to negotiations was a tactical disaster. While the talks continued, the Nevilles had moved their forces round to the west of the town and when York and Salisbury sounded the charge, Sir Robert Ogle broke through to the market place while Warwick broke through the gardens and houses onto Holywell Street, his men screaming 'A Warwick! A Warwick!' He had split the enemy line and panicked the Lancastrians defending the barricades who, fearing a devastating rear attack, rushed into the market square to protect the King, leaving the Earl of Northumberland and Lord Clifford overwhelmed and unable to stop the enemy from scaling the barricades. They attempted to hold back the Yorkists while retreating slowly to the market square where Warwick's troops were shooting longbows and crossbows at close range at the disorganised Lancastrians protecting the King, who was slightly wounded in the neck. The Duke of Buckingham was injured by an arrow in the face while many others received wounds to the arms and hands. Lord Clifford reached the main street but was killed while trying to relieve those who were trapped, while the Earl

Crossbowman, or arbalist, with typical crossbow bolts of the period.

South West View of St Albans Abbey.

LIONS OF THE RED ROSE

of Northumberland tried to regroup with his remaining guards at the Castle Inn, on the corner of Shropshire and St Peters. He was trapped against a wall and hacked to death by an overwhelming force of Yorkists. The Duke of Somerset made it to the Castle Inn and held it for a while but, assuming that the Duke of York would not allow him to live if he surrendered, he rushed out of the inn and cut down four Yorkist soldiers before being felled by an axe. His son, the Earl of Dorset, was badly wounded in the fracas, but survived. William Percy, Bishop of Carlisle, managed to flee for the North.

The battle had taken the lives of barely 200 men, mostly Lancastrians, but it set the scene for far greater loss of life in the future. It also marked a troubling change in strategy, from following the chivalric code of former engagements, which would have protected enemy nobles from the carnage, to the purposeful, brutal assassination of Somerset, Northumberland and Clifford. Ironically, the Earl of Northumberland was a strict observer of the code of chivalry for which his father, Hotspur, was celebrated and, from the time of his restoration, he had presided as judge in courts of chivalry. Traditionally, the vanquished would be ransomed for considerable sums of money but the ruthless and ambitious Earl of Warwick had little need of more money and was certainly not squeamish about breaking with tradition to rid himself of his principal enemies. The older, wiser Duke of York and Earl of Salisbury might have had qualms, and with good reason, for it set a dreadful precedent by which all three Yorkist leaders would ultimately suffer.

The battered corpses of the three Lancastrian nobles, stripped of their armour and any valuables, lay in the streets until John Wheathampstead, the Abbot of St Albans, arranged for their bodies to be gathered and their burials to be conducted in the Lady-Chapel of St Albans Abbey, close to that of Humphrey, Duke of Gloucester, Henry V's famous younger brother. De Fonblanque states that the 2nd Earl of Northumberland's body was later taken

Above: the great St Albans town bell, called Gabriel, which hangs in the Mediaeval Clock Tower in the Market Place, rang out the alarm in 1455 at the First Battle of St Albans.

to York Minster to lie with his father and grandfather, but this is disputed and weight of evidence suggests that his body remains in St Albans Abbey, the location unknown due to later alterations to the building.

History tends to focus on the martial side of the 2nd Earl of Northumberland's life but there were long periods of peace and prosperity within it. We know, for instance, that he was well educated and was one of the benefactors of University College, Oxford, where he founded three fellowships for those born in the dioceses of Durham, Carlisle and York. He was also a pious man who funded various Christian institutions including Alnwick Abbey, Tynemouth Priory (to establish a chantry on Coquet Island) and Durham Cathedral Priory.

The Oxford Almanac, 1735, featuring a view of University College, Oxford, with the main historical benefactors of the College in the foreground. The 2nd Earl is depicted third from the right, in full armour and carrying an earl's coronet.

Excerpt from the 1443 Account roll of Robert Cotes, Receiver for the County of Northumberland to Henry Percy, 2nd Earl of Northumberland. Payments are listed to the Friars of Hulne Priory, the Chaplains of Alnwick and Warkworth Castles, Alnwick Abbey (for 3 stones of wax), the Sacrist of Durham Cathedral for lights around the tomb of St Cuthbert, and a new annual rent to Tynemouth Priory for the augmentation of the living of two monks on Coquet Island, who will pray for the souls of the Lord, Eleanor his consort, and their ancestors.

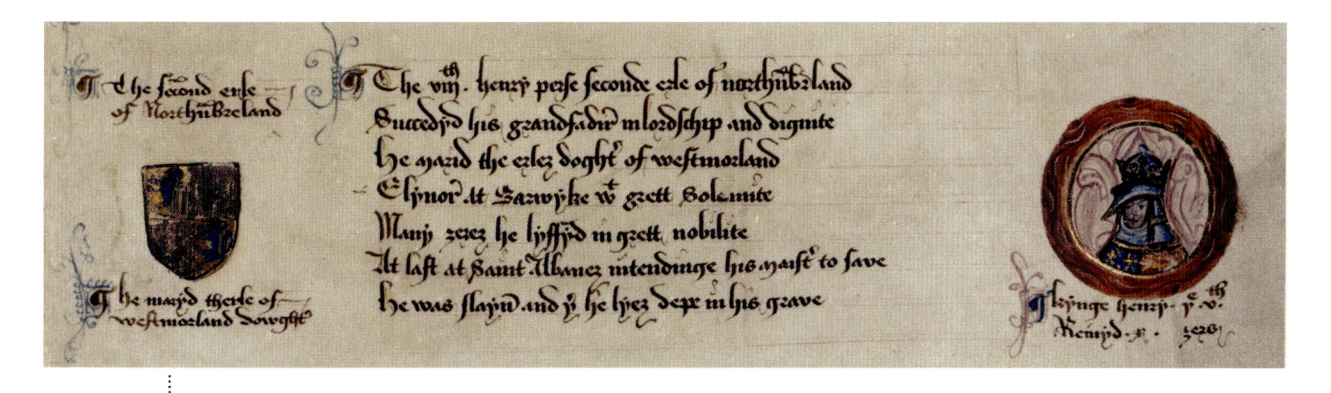

Excerpt on the 2nd Earl from William Peeris' pedigree roll.

"The viijth Henry perse seconde erle of northumberland,
Succedyd his grandfadir in lordschip and dignite,
He marid the erles doghter of westmorland,
Elynore At Barwyke with grett Solemite,
Many yeres he lyffyd in grett nobilite,
At last at Saint Albanes intendinge his maister to save,
He was slayn and ther he lyes depe in his grave."

5 / ST ALBANS, 1455

6 The Seeds of Vengeance

As the battle in St Albans reached its chaotic climax, the King had withdrawn into the stinking confines of a tanner's house to escape the arrows and, from there, the Duke of York took him into the Abbey for protection. York, Salisbury and Warwick then declared themselves to be the King's true liegemen who had rid the kingdom of traitors. The following day they escorted Henry VI back to London where, in a ceremony in St Paul's Cathedral on Whit Sunday, 25th May, his monarchy was reaffirmed. The Duke of York re-established the Earls of Salisbury and Warwick as joint Wardens of the Western March until 1475, at a greatly increased salary. He put Warwick in charge of Calais and, as the King lapsed into insanity once more, formed a new protectorate with the support of Parliament and, for what it was worth, the vague approval of the occasionally lucid King. The Duke of York tried to calm the troubled country with generosity in victory, pardoning 'rebels', including Lord Egremont and Sir Richard Percy, both of whom remained in debtors' prison, and allowing Lord Poynings, who took no part in the battle, to become the 3rd Earl of Northumberland and retain his full inheritance. Similar generosity was shown to Henry Beaufort who had fought at St Albans yet inherited the Somerset dukedom, and John Clifford who became Lord Clifford. But this generosity came with a sting, particularly for the Earl of Northumberland. He was owed £6000 by the Exchequer for his work on the Border but this was wiped out by a fine of £6050 for Percy transgressions prior to the engagement at St Albans. Since his father had left significant debts, mainly from having to pay the costs of a private army, the 3rd Earl was financially hamstrung.

The Duke of York may have thought that order was now

Sir Richard Percy, locked in a Newgate Prison debtors' cell.

restored but he would have been wiser to further purge the court and dissolve remaining Lancastrian influence. Instead, he had kicked a hornets' nest, releasing a group of disaffected young nobles, outraged by the assassination of their fathers, united in their loathing for him and his Neville sidekicks, and drawn to a furious queen who would do anything to protect her weak husband and young child. When the King recovered, in late February 1456, the Duke of York was released from his protectorship although he was retained as the King's 'chief and principal councillor' while his Yorkist appointees also kept their positions. The Duke of Buckingham and Earls of Wiltshire, Shrewsbury and Pembroke, and various other lords, made peace with York and tried to reconcile the two sides while the Queen began to develop an alternative plan; she moved her family to Kenilworth Castle where a battery of 26 new cannon had been placed on the walls.

Newgate Prison

Nearby Coventry, in the heart of Lancastrian country, became her seat of government. She created a 'shadow cabinet' to replace the Duke of York's administration, appointing Bishop Waynflete as her Chancellor, and Laurence Booth as Keeper of the Privy Seal, thereby giving her complete power of the administrative machinery of government. She recruited the Earl of Shrewsbury as Treasurer, and the Duke of Exeter, the Duke of Somerset, his brother Edmund Beaufort, Owen Tudor and his sons (the Earls of Richmond and Pembroke), the Earl of Northumberland, Lord Egremont, Sir Richard Percy, Sir Ralph Percy, Lord Clifford and Lord Grey as members of her Council.

In November Lord Egremont and Sir Richard Percy made themselves available for the Queen's Council having made a daring escape from Newgate Prison. They released other prisoners who diverted the guards while they scaled the walls and

6 / THE SEEDS OF VENGEANCE

jumped onto horses left at a pre-arranged site. Their brother, the Earl of Northumberland, on the other hand, was late owing, inevitably, to trouble on the Border.

From the time of his coronation, King James II of Scotland had struggled to shake free from the political domination of the Douglases and, in 1452, he confronted William, 8th Earl of Douglas, at Stirling Castle, accusing him of forging an alliance with the Earls of Ross and Crawford to threaten royal authority. When Douglas refused to break this alliance, the infuriated King stabbed him 26 times and threw his body from the window whereupon the battered and bloody corpse was further savaged by court officials on the ground. Civil war inevitably ensued but, on 1st May 1455, King James finally defeated the 'Black' Douglases at Arkinholm, consolidated his power and turned his attention to England. Taking advantage of the chaotic aftermath of the St Albans skirmish, with the 2nd Earl of Northumberland dead and the 3rd Earl in the South, he marched on Berwick where, to his great embarrassment, he was easily rebuffed.

The following year, James renounced the Anglo-Scottish Truce, marched to the Border and set up camp beside the Kale Water, a tributary of the River Teviot, believing that the Duke of York was going to claim the English throne, thereby giving him the opportunity to proffer his support and potentially make territorial gains as a result. This misunderstanding may have been encouraged by the Earl of Salisbury, trying to make trouble for the Earl of Northumberland, but it provoked a crass letter from Queen Margaret's court to the Scottish King which reminded him of his subservience to the English Crown and described him as a rebel. The furious King immediately marched into the county of Northumberland, destroyed various military targets, including 17 towers, and created mayhem for a few days before marching home with minimal casualties. The Earl of Northumberland was sent to negotiate with King James but, despite the Earl's diplomatic skills, he came away with a truce of a mere six months, at the end of which King James immediately assaulted Berwick again, only to be rebuffed once more. In February 1457 the Queen awarded the Earl of Northumberland a ten year wardenship of the Eastern March, made him Keeper of Berwick and gave him sufficient resources to force the slightly humbled Scottish King into a five year truce, which was later extended for a further five years.

Portrait of Henry, 3rd Earl of Northumberland. English School, mid-18th century.

The rift between the two English factions was escalating into more violence during 1456-7. Threats and assassination attempts were made on the Duke of York and Earl of Warwick, mainly by the more bloody-minded young Lancastrians, particularly the Dukes of Somerset and Exeter, and Lords Clifford and Egremont. On one occasion the severed heads of five dogs were left on poles outside York's London home, with lurid rhymes stuck in their jaws. In September 1456 Somerset attacked York in the street and would have killed him but for the intervention of a local official. With the King under the Queen's control, and power shifting into Lancastrian hands, Yorkist influence was steadily eroding as Queen Margaret's increased. But the Queen's power was not used to govern properly for the health of the nation, as the Duke of York had done, but to consolidate her own position, feather the nests of her supporters and focus on the destruction of her enemies, particularly York and Warwick. Corruption was rampant and 16 sheriffs were on the royal payroll, expected to favour the Queen's supporters and hinder the Duke of York's. Some of the magnates that supported her were in league with pirates, sharing in the plunder from foreign shipping, increasing their wealth to the detriment of English merchants who found that foreign traders now avoided England where possible.

Queen Margaret knew that the Duke of York would not stand idly by so she prepared for war, ordering a vast stock of arms and ammunition to be delivered to Kenilworth. However, in the name of the King, the Duke of Buckingham, the only magnate respected by both sides, instigated a final attempt at mediation. A great council was called in London in January 1458. Virtually all the protagonists turned up, attended by heavily armed retinues who needed to be fed and provided with sleeping quarters. To Londoners, people from the North were considered barbarians and the Earl of Northumberland is said to have turned up with so many rough Northerners that he was turned away at the city gates. This was probably Yorkist propaganda, but he and Lords Egremont and Clifford did bring 1500 Northern retainers and housed them between Temple Bar and Westminster, while the Dukes of Somerset and Exeter added another 800 men. The Duke of York had 140 cavalrymen and 260 foot soldiers while the Earl of Salisbury brought 80 knights and 420 foot soldiers. York had persuaded the King to

6 / THE SEEDS OF VENGEANCE

appoint the Earl of Warwick as Captain of Calais in April 1456, and Warwick managed to retain this appointment during the ensuing troubles despite the huge strategic advantage this gave the Yorkists. Its fortress, garrison and location gave Warwick a springboard for invasion, and a base for dealing with piracy, at which he had considerable success before later resorting to piracy himself. Warwick brought 600 guards from Calais to London for the council, all dressed in scarlet tunics with his heraldic badge, the ragged staff, embroidered on the front and back.

This peace congress lasted for two months but acrimony pervaded the city and little was achieved. The protagonists could hardly be in the same room together without fighting and they relied on messengers and negotiators to scuttle from one side to the other. The two factions were ordered to remain separated but, even so, the usual trouble-makers, Exeter, Somerset and Egremont, could not resist trying to ambush the Earl of Salisbury and Duke of York as they rode through their designated area at Westminster. In February, Lord Clifford, the Earl of Northumberland and the Duke of Somerset arrived at Temple Bar with a large force, angrily demanding compensation for the deaths of their fathers at St Albans. The King was so intimidated that he had no choice but to agree, forcing the Duke of York, and the Earls of Salisbury and Warwick to join together to found and endow a chantry in St Albans, in which masses for the souls of those killed in the battle could be sung forever. The Yorkist lords were also ordered to pay Clifford, Northumberland and Somerset a considerable amount of money. The Duke of Somerset's widowed mother received 5000 marks from the Duke of York, while the Earl of Warwick paid Lord Clifford 1000

Richard Neville, 16th Earl of Warwick as depicted in the armorial roll chronicle known as the 'Rous Roll', c. 1483.

marks. As part of the agreement, Lord Egremont's debt to the Earl of Salisbury was cancelled as long as he kept the peace for ten years, an impossible task for such a hot-head, and, much to the Nevilles' fury, he was given life ownership of the castle and manor of Wressle. On 24th March, a public 'reconciliation' between the opposing parties was staged, later known as the 'Loveday'. The leaders of both factions went in procession together through the streets of London to St Paul's Cathedral, where a service was held. The attendees were not plainly recorded and there is some suggestion that some or all of the Percys were absent. This reconciliation was a farce but the King believed he had achieved a great peace between the opposing nobles, and gave thanks to God. In fact, as his mind shied away from the realities of kingship, he became increasingly immersed in worship and absorbed in his foundations, particularly Eton College and King's College Cambridge, and he retreated further from political life, leaving his embittered queen to run the country.

St Paul's Cathedral, London

St Paul's has existed in several incarnations since pre-Norman times. It was destroyed by fire in 1087, after which the Normans started to rebuild it. Another fire in 1135 interrupted the rebuilding and a new Cathedral was not consecrated until 1240.

St Paul's was rebuilt by Sir Christopher Wren after the Great Fire of London destroyed it in 1666.

St Paul's Cathedral in the 15th century.

6 / THE SEEDS OF VENGEANCE

7 Yorkists in Retreat

The 'Loveday' may have calmed the troubled waters for a time, temporarily satisfying malcontents like Lord Egremont and the Duke of Somerset, but the Queen remained resolute in her destructive determination and focused her bile on the Earl of Warwick who had treated her with such profound disrespect, spreading lies about her and the legitimacy of her son. On Warwick's return to Calais after the 'Loveday', subsidies for the fortress's defences were slashed, forcing the Earl to dig deep into his own pockets to fund the garrison. With several ships under his control, the temptation to augment his finances through piracy became too strong. Gamekeeper became poacher and Warwick further stung the English government by attacking merchant ships belonging to non-enemy nations, thereby undermining English foreign policy. With sharp political instinct, he attacked French but not Burgundian ships, believing that a Yorkist England, allied to Burgundy, might resume war with France and attempt to regain its lost lands.

Warwick was eventually summoned to answer for his actions, arriving in London at the head of 600 armed retainers. The Queen demanded that he stand trial and on 31st July 1458 the Council instituted an inquiry. The Queen and court completely underestimated the considerable popularity that Warwick's exploits had engendered and, the following day, Warwick felt powerful enough to publicly denounce the Queen for trying to undermine him despite his achievements on the high seas on behalf of England. Riots broke out in the streets of London, supporting him and demonstrating against the Queen and authorities, during which the Attorney General was killed. The Council's inquiry was inconclusive and the Earl of Warwick returned triumphant to Calais. That autumn, however, he returned to Westminster and became involved in an unseemly scuffle. As he passed the kitchens, accidentally one of the King's scullions nearly impaled him on a spit. A fracas broke out between the royal servants and Warwick's men who managed to grab the unfortunate scullion and haul him before the Queen. She knew that if she defended him, she would be accused of attempting to assassinate Warwick, so she ordered the man's execution and then secretly allowed him to escape. The furious Margaret then persuaded the Council to draw up an order for Warwick's arrest and committal to the Tower, but the Earl managed to flee back to Calais. In November the Queen and Council demanded that Warwick surrender his post to the Duke of Somerset but, on returning to London, Warwick defiantly refused to resign unless Parliament revoked his appointment, since it was Parliament that had appointed him in the first place. As he left the chamber, he was attacked by retainers of the Duke of Somerset and the Earl of Wiltshire, and only narrowly escaped, fleeing back once more to his sanctuary of Calais.

For Warwick, the lucrative harvest from piracy became a vital alternative source of revenue to government funding. By targeting merchant ships from countries that competed with the Calais 'Staple' and their allies, the merchants of London, particularly the Italians and the Germans of the Hanseatic League, Warwick's popularity increased in the capital and south of England, and helped to merge the interests of the Yorkists with those of the commercial classes. This in turn helped to finance Yorkist military activity and pave the way for mass recruitment in the south of England.

Above, typical weapons of the period, clockwise from top left: 1. Pikes 2. Swords and dagger 3. Axes and mace

7 / YORKISTS IN RETREAT

Warwick's behaviour was tantamount to rebellion and even the moderate Duke of Buckingham was disgusted by it. He declared his full support for the King and the two factions made ready for war, 3000 bows and sheaves of arrows being ordered for the royal armoury. In June, fearing a Yorkist attack on Kenilworth to kidnap the King, a great council was called at Coventry to which the Duke of York and Earls of Salisbury and Warwick were summoned. They and others of their faction failed to attend but York and Salisbury desperately called for Warwick's support as they feared an immediate attack by the Queen. Warwick quickly raised a force of 200 men-at-arms and 400 archers, mostly seasoned veterans, all dressed in his red livery, and sailed from Calais, landing at Sandwich in Kent. On 21st September he marched into London unopposed, recruited a large force and marched north to rendezvous with York and Salisbury at Ludlow. En route, he realised that the Duke of Somerset was shadowing him with a large West Country army, but he managed to avoid it and continue on his way. The Earl of Salisbury, meanwhile, led his army from Middleham towards Ludlow but the Queen was aware of his plan and sent an army of Cheshiremen to intercept him before he met up with the Duke of York. This force was nominally under the command of a young boy, the Prince of Wales, but in reality it was led by Lords Audley and Dudley.

Salisbury had about 3-4000 men and some cannon, compared to Lord Audley's 6-12,000, including a number of crack archers, but he was a considerably more experienced general. On Sunday 23rd September, he was blocked by Audley's army on his approach to Market Drayton. He drew up his forces on nearby Blore Heath, formed extensive defences on the boggy ground, using ditches and sharpened stakes, and waited for Audley to attack. When Audley arrived, Salisbury requested free passage, which was denied, then feigned preparations for either a retreat or advance which lured Audley into ordering a charge. 500 of the Lancastrian cavalry galloped into a hail of arrows which so unnerved them that they defected to the enemy, creating chaos on the battlefield. Audley's line broke, he was killed, many

Eccleshall Castle

Left: Ludlow Castle

of his men deserted and Dudley was captured. About 2000 Lancastrians were killed to about 1000 Yorkists and the remnants of Audley's army fled to join the King and Queen at Eccleshall Castle. Deeply shocked by the defeat, the Queen immediately sent troops to find and attack the Earl of Salisbury's army. They were confounded by a cunning ploy: Salisbury left his cannon on Blore Heath where they were fired at intervals during the night by an Augustinian Friar, thereby luring the royal army to the vacant battlefield, while the Yorkist army headed for Market Drayton. There, Salisbury discovered that two of his sons, Sir Thomas and Sir John, had been captured by Lancastrians at Acton Bridge in Cheshire.

Salisbury joined the Duke of York in Ludlow, followed soon after by Warwick, and their forces converged. However, a much greater Lancastrian force of over 30,000 men, including hardened Yorkshiremen and Northumbrians, was now heading for Ludlow with the Earl of Northumberland, his brothers Lord Egremont and Sir Richard Percy, and Ralph Neville, Earl of Westmorland. The Percys had persuaded the latter to join the struggle against his hated kinsmen, particularly the Earl of Salisbury with whom he was involved in an acrimonious feud over the inheritance of estates from his grandfather's second wife, Lady Joan Beaufort. In the early evening of 12th October, the Yorkist forces encamped at Ludford Bridge saw the King appear in full armour at the head of a huge army flanked by the Earl of Northumberland and his brothers, plus the Dukes of Somerset, Buckingham and Exeter, the Earls of Westmorland, Arundel, Devon and Shrewsbury, and at least ten lords. To the Yorkist troops, cold and soaked by heavy rain, this display of royal might only served to emphasise the treason they were committing. Moreover, attempts to recruit more forces had born limited fruit and they were badly outnumbered. Apart from the duplicitous Lord Stanley, the Yorkists had only managed to attract two minor barons, Lord Clinton and Lord Grey of Powys. That morning, the leaders sent a manifesto to the King, declaring their loyalty to him but determination to remove those degrading the realm's 'common weal', in an attempt to counter accusations of treason. In return, the King offered to pardon those who laid down their arms but to charge as traitors those who continued to face his royal banners. York tried to spread a rumour that Henry VI was dead, but as the King was clearly in view of the Yorkist army, the Duke lost credibility with many of his men who gradually started

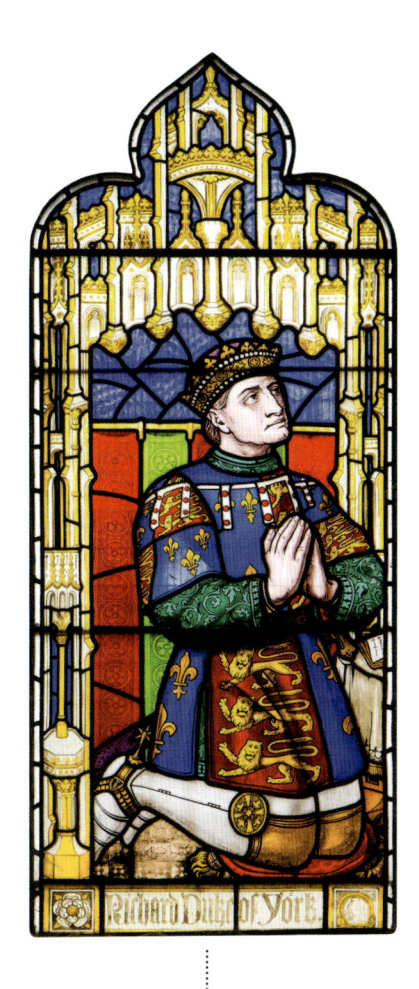

Richard, Duke of York, depicted in a stained glass window.

7 / YORKISTS IN RETREAT

to desert. The Duke of Buckingham persuaded the King to repeat his offer of a pardon which effectively increased the flow of deserters. Just as the pardon was being proclaimed at the town gates, the Yorkist cannon opened fire, but instead of stirring the troops into battle, panic broke out and there were mass desertions in the Yorkist ranks. Even the Earl of Warwick's professional army from Calais, led by the normally reliable Andrew Trollope, followed suit and defected to the other side. For once Henry VI acted like a true king rather than a puppet, and rallied his army with a rousing speech.

At midnight, the Duke of York and Earls of Salisbury and Warwick, seeing no hope of victory, left their forces to 'refresh' themselves in the river but, as soon as they were out of sight, fled with a few followers, leaving their army drawn up in battle order with banners displayed. Next morning, the remnants of the Yorkist army knelt before the King and begged for mercy, which he willingly granted. York's apparent cowardice was compounded by the discovery that he had abandoned his duchess, Cecily, and their two younger sons, George (aged

Petition of the 3rd Earl to King Henry VI for full reinstatement of his inheritance from his father, grandfather and great grandfather. It begins: 'Mekely besecheth youre highnes youre true liegeman Henry Percy, Erle of Northumbrie, Sonne and heire to Henry late Erle of Northumbrie, benyngly to considre that Where as the moost Cristen Prynce, the kyng your fader... graunted ordeyned and accepted the said late Erle to the name and habilite to be Sonne and heire to Sir Herry Percy his fader [Hotspur] ... And hym restored to the name and habilite to be Erle of Northumbrie the rebellions and forfaitures of [his father and grandfather] ageyns the moost noble Prynce, kyng Herry the fourth, your graundfadre... notwithstonding ...'

11) and Richard (7), as well as their daughter Margaret (13), all of whom stood in the market place at Ludlow as Lancastrian soldiers laid waste to the town. The Duchess and her children were captured and placed under the care of her sister, the Duchess of Buckingham. Meanwhile, as his properties were ransacked by Lancastrians, the Duke of York fled to Ireland with his son, Edmund, while his eldest son, the 17 year old Edward, joined Salisbury and Warwick as they fled to relative safety in Calais. Once ensconced there, Warwick returned once more to piracy and Calais became the seat of Yorkist rebellion, from which a stream of propaganda flooded through Southern England, denouncing the King's 'evil' counsellors.

By the end of the year York, Warwick, Salisbury and 20 other associates had been legally attainted for high treason by 'the Parliament of Devils', as the Yorkists named this totally biased Lancastrian assembly. Their lands were distributed among loyal followers like Lord Egremont, who gained Conisbrough Castle in south Yorkshire, and the Earl of Northumberland who became even more dominant in the North, being appointed chief justice north of the River Trent and Constable of Scarborough Castle. Government of the North was now entirely the responsibility of the Earl of Northumberland and his friend and ally, Lord Clifford. The Duke of Somerset was made Captain of Calais, although he was unable to take up his position while Warwick controlled the town. Similarly, the Earl of Wiltshire became Lieutenant of Ireland in place of the Duke of York, although the Irish parliament resolved to ignore the appointment and protect York. Wiltshire's unfortunate messenger, who carried a writ for York's arrest, was hanged, drawn and quartered for his efforts. The Lancastrians once again appeared strong and victorious, but this was an illusion, for their dangerous enemies were still at large and more determined than ever to reverse the situation.

Henry VI triumphant at the Battle of Ludford Bridge, while Edward of York, Salisbury and Warwick set sail for Calais. From an illuminated manuscript of the 1460s.

8   Blatant Betrayal

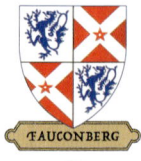

With the compliance of Burgundy, the Earl of Warwick's attacks on French territories and shipping helped to replenish his coffers, and in June 1460 his men established a bridgehead at Sandwich, where the Earl's heroism on the high seas became a powerful recruitment tool. Yorkist propaganda in the form of thousands of leaflets reaffirming their loyalty to the King and detailing once more their case against his 'evil counsellours' was spread throughout England and when Warwick and Salisbury stepped ashore on the 26th June, they were joined by an army of Kentishmen. After worshipping at the tomb of Thomas Becket, another victim of royal injustice, and receiving the Archbishop of Canterbury's blessing, they marched on London and were welcomed by a populace fed up with Lancastrian misrule. To the utter dismay of the confused royal court in Coventry, the Yorkists were in London and had raised a popular army of about 40,000 men, outnumbering any force that the Queen could quickly muster, particularly as there were hardly any peers at court that summer.

This wasn't the Queen's only predicament, for the Scots were threatening to invade from the North, potentially joining a Neville rebellion in Yorkshire, and the Duke of York was threatening to attack from Ireland. Moreover, a Burgundian invasion by sea from the South was quite possible. In early July, the Earl of Northumberland was guarding the Scottish Border while the Duke of Buckingham, Earl of Shrewsbury, Lord Egremont and his brother-in-law, Lord Grey of Ruthin, remained with the King. Having reinforced the army, they moved to Northampton and camped in a meadow between the village of Hardingstone and Delapré Abbey where they made substantial defences, digging deep ditches and a palisade of stakes around the whole camp before blocking the road from London with cannon. The Duke of Buckingham, who led the royal army, wanted to get this battle over with quickly so that he could march on London, but he completely underestimated the military skills of the Earl of Warwick and the young Earl of March, who were rushing towards Northampton. On 10th July their army arrived there and Warwick sent the Bishop of Salisbury and Cardinal Coppini, the Yorkist supporting papal representative, to ask the

LIONS OF THE RED ROSE

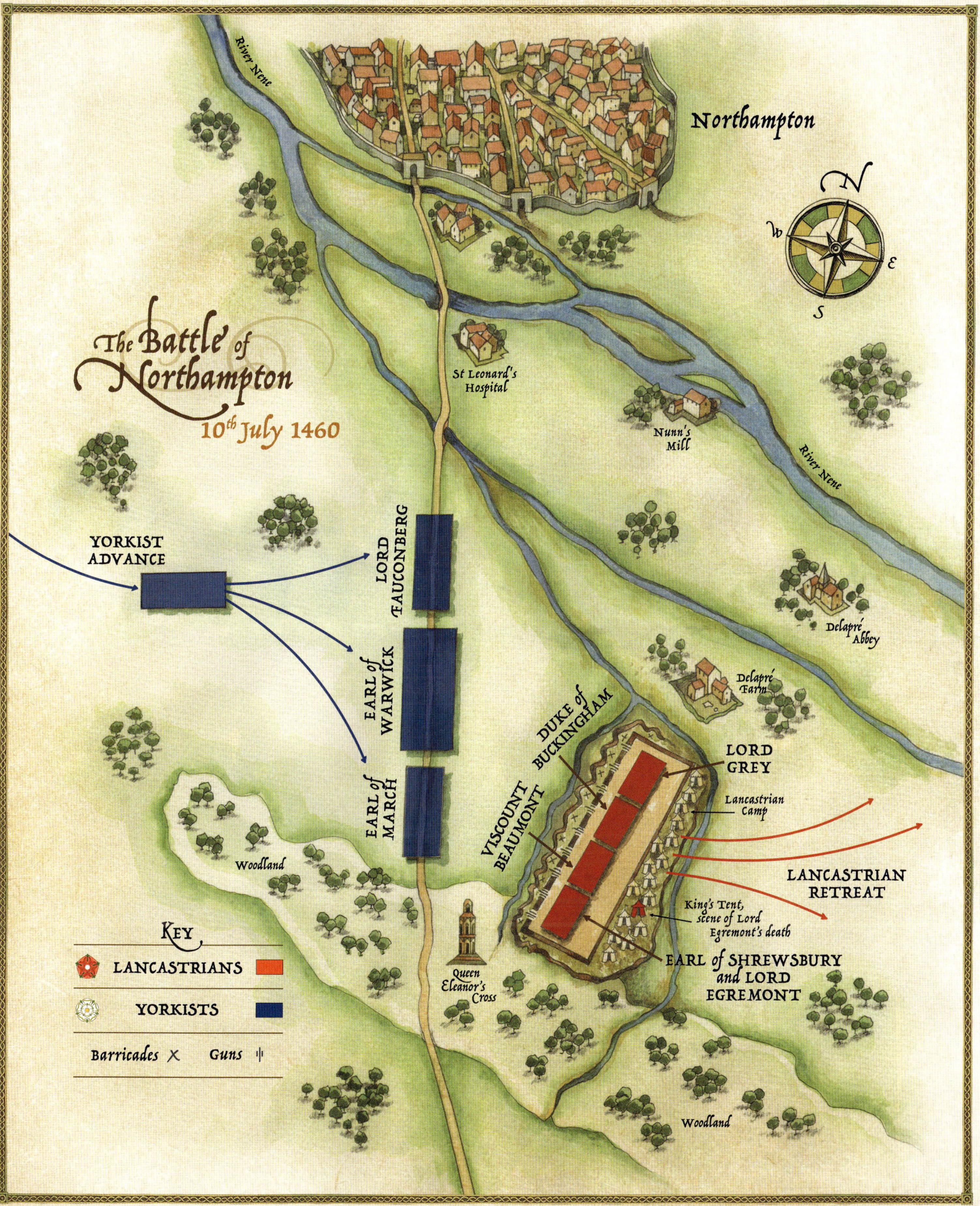

The Battle of Northampton
10th July 1460
Northampton
River Nene
St Leonard's Hospital
Nunn's Mill
River Nene
Delapré Abbey
Delapré Farm
YORKIST ADVANCE
LORD FAUCONBERG
EARL of WARWICK
EARL of MARCH
DUKE of BUCKINGHAM
VISCOUNT BEAUMONT
LORD GREY
Lancastrian Camp
LANCASTRIAN RETREAT
King's Tent, scene of Lord Egremont's death
EARL of SHREWSBURY and LORD EGREMONT
Woodland
Queen Eleanor's Cross
Woodland
KEY
LANCASTRIANS
YORKISTS
Barricades
Guns
N
W
E
S

King to hear the grievances of the Yorkist lords. The Duke of Buckingham, believing the Lancastrian position was unassailable, advised the King to dismiss the plea and prepare for battle.

In reality, the royal army was not in a strong position. Lancastrian reinforcements failed to arrive in time, rain had turned their camp into a quagmire and their army was half the size of Warwick's. This unfortunate state of affairs was compounded by the treachery of one of the commanders, Lord Grey of Ruthin, husband to Katherine, the sister of the Earl of Northumberland and Lord Egremont. He sent the Earl of March a secret message offering to change sides and fight for the Yorkists if they would back him in a land dispute with Lord Cromwell and the Duke of Exeter over the manor of Ampthill in Bedfordshire. Naturally the Earls of March and Warwick agreed to this and may also have offered high office to Grey as further inducement – he did become Treasurer of England in 1463. Before the attack, Warwick ordered his men not to lay hands on the King or any soldiers wearing Grey of Ruthin's 'black ragged staff' motif, to spare ordinary men where possible, but to kill rather than capture any magnates.

The young Earl of March's advance across the marshes next to the River Nene was met with a storm of arrows from the Lancastrian centre but the Yorkist forces ploughed on towards the Lancastrian defences led by Lord Egremont and the Earl of Shrewsbury on the left flank, the Duke of Buckingham in the centre, and Lord Grey of Ruthin on the right. Torrential rain flooded the entrenchments and rendered the Duke of Buckingham's cannon useless whilst many of the royal cavalrymen were forced to dismount and fight on foot in the deep, sticky mud. As the Yorkist army reached the defences, Lord Grey signalled to his men, who breached the barricades to allow the Yorkists to surge through the gaps, while his troops turned to fight their erstwhile allies. Within half an hour the battle was over and many Lancastrians fled and drowned in the swollen River Nene. Buckingham lay dead

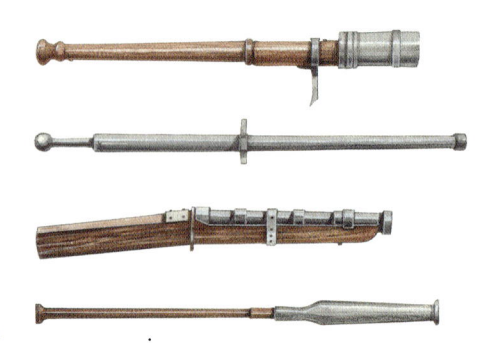

Left: Artillerymen in action. Above: Typical field artillery of the period.

The Earl of March kneeling before King Henry VI outside his tent, with the dismembered remains of Lord Egremont alongside. From an illuminated manuscript of the 1460s.

LIONS OF THE RED ROSE

on the battlefield along with about 400 others. Lord Egremont, Viscount Beaumont (Constable of England) and the Earl of Shrewsbury bravely defended the King who was cowering in his tent, but they were overpowered by the Earl of Warwick's Kentishmen and killed outside the royal tent or executed after the battle. Henry VI was confined until the battle was over and when the Earls of Warwick and March and Lord Fauconberg entered the tent, they knelt before him, craving his forgiveness and assuring him of their loyalty once more.

Percy history gives a more heroic, if less accurate, view of Lord Egremont's death at the battle of Northampton. Claiming that it was by Warwick's sword that the 2nd Earl had been slain at St Albans, the four Percy brothers supposedly focused their hatred on him and determined to kill or capture him. Another historian of the Percy family, Gerald Brenan, notes 'the impetuosity of the Lancastrian attack upon the future 'king-maker's' forces is traceable to this unfortunate resolve.' Seeing that the day was lost, Northumberland is said to have sent Egremont to protect the King while he retreated with the Queen and Prince Edward to ensure their safety. Egremont hastened to the royal tent only to meet a furious charge led by Warwick himself. Drawing his sword he placed himself directly between the trembling Henry and the whole host of York, killing two of Warwick's knights before falling, 'pierced by many wounds at the very feet of the King.' In fact, the Earl of Northumberland was marching south and had not crossed the River Trent when the battle was fought. The Queen and her son had been sent to Staffordshire as news broke of the imminent arrival of the Yorkist force.

The Earl of Warwick now controlled the King, but the Queen and her son were still at large. On hearing the news from Northampton, they fled from Eccleshall Castle, were robbed and nearly killed by one of their servants, then rode hard for Wales. At Harlech Castle, Jasper Tudor, the Earl of Pembroke, welcomed them with open arms and set them up at Denbigh, one of the Duke of York's castles, now controlled by Pembroke. Queen Margaret was joined by the Duke of Exeter and other Lancastrian nobles and, on their advice, she sent messages to the Duke of Somerset, Earl of Devon and other allies, asking them to raise forces and meet her at Hull.

Lord Egremont's fingerprint, a tangible link with the past, captured in the wax of a seal impression on a title deed of 1458.

8 / BLATANT BETRAYAL

9 'The accursed blood of York'

At more or less the same time that the Earl of Northumberland heard the news of his brother's death, his brother-in-law's treachery and the King's capture at the Battle of Northampton, James II of Scotland, now supporting the Lancastrian side, launched an attack on the Yorkist garrison in Roxburgh Castle. Excited by the prospect of pulverising the walls with his new, powerful, siege cannon, recently imported from Flanders, he invited his queen, Mary of Guelders, to come and watch the spectacle and bolster morale among his men. On 3rd August 1460, James ordered an artillery salute in her honour but the inquisitive King stood too close to one of the guns, known as 'the Lion,' which exploded on recoil, smashing his thigh. He was 'stricken to the ground and died hastily' but his queen continued the bombardment and Roxburgh fell a few days later. Although this helped the Lancastrian cause, it drastically limited English control over the Scottish Border as Roxburgh was a strategic outpost that had stood as a mighty symbol of English rule in southern Scotland. Percys had been responsible for it, on and off, for a hundred years or so, and Queen Mary reduced it to rubble.

With the Duke of York in Ireland and the King under his control, the Earl of Warwick ruled England, except in the North where the Earl of Northumberland and other Lancastrian magnates held sway. Until now, the Yorkist leaders ostensibly sought to oust Henry's 'evil counsellours' and set up good government under

Below: Named after the Belgian town where she was made, the Mons Meg cannon was given to King James II in 1457. Bottom: Typical field cannon of the period.

60 LIONS OF THE RED ROSE

their anointed king. By October, however, the Duke of York saw no value in continuing with this objective. Subservience to a weak king, a loathsome queen and their Lancastrian child heir was, to the Duke of York, no longer tenable. Believing that he would have widespread support, he arrived at Westminster seeking approval to claim the throne of England. He touched its cushion and turned to the stunned assembly, expecting encouraging murmurs and nodding heads to demonstrate approval for his regal ambition, but there was none, even from his closest allies. The Earls of Warwick and Salisbury were staggered at his arrogance. The Archbishop of Canterbury suggested that he seek an audience with the King to discuss his claim, stirring York to anger; 'I know of no one in the realm who would not more fitly come to me than I to him,' he retorted. York had misread the public mood and it was clear that, despite his weaknesses, the crown would remain on Henry's head as long as he lived. However, the Lords accepted the Duke of York's clear position as de facto ruler of England as well as his hereditary claim to the throne through the Mortimer connection so, by the Act of Accord on 24th October 1460, they sought to satisfy York, his allies and the general populace, by promising the throne to the Duke and his heirs after Henry's death. This clumsy 'solution' raised serious questions over the future inheritance rights of noble families while the disinheritance of Prince Edward added greater resolve to Queen Margaret's cause. Under the Duke of York's control, Henry VI sent a message to his queen, commanding her to bring Prince Edward to London and denouncing her as a rebel if she refused, which, of course, she did.

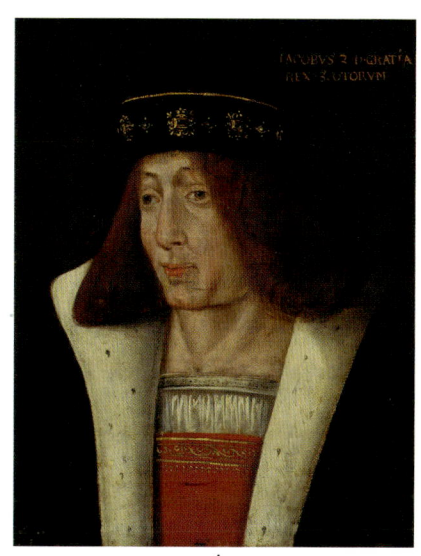

In August, Queen Margaret and Prince Edward left Denbigh and sailed from Wales around the coast to Berwick, hoping to find refuge in Scotland where James II, whose mother was a Beaufort, would surely offer sanctuary. The timing was unfortunate

Portrait of King James II of Scotland, contemporary oil painting.

as King James had just been killed during the siege of Roxburgh Castle, and Scotland was in mourning: his widow Queen Mary was in Edinburgh for the King's burial and then Kelso for the coronation of James III, her nine year old son. Mary, however, sent an envoy, Duncan Dundas, to escort Margaret and her son to Dumfries and thence to Lincluden Abbey where they were looked after as Mary's guests. Although Mary of Guelders was raised at the Burgundian Court, she had no desire to support the Yorkist cause and the two queens bonded from the start, even discussing a potential marriage between Prince Edward and the new Scottish King's sister, Mary. In due course, the Scottish Queen agreed to lend money and provide men for a campaign against the Yorkists on condition that Queen Margaret surrender Berwick to Scotland, to which she readily agreed. She was unaware of the stunned disapproval this plan would receive from many of her husband's subjects, including the Earl of Northumberland, particularly after the fall of Roxburgh which left Berwick as the only remaining English stronghold north of the River Tweed.

Spurred on by tales of the plunder they might expect in the rich south of England, provided they avoided pillaging the area north of the Trent where the Earl of Northumberland ruled in the King's name, the Earl of Angus escorted Queen Margaret back into England. Despite this, Northumberland could be forgiven for having serious reservations about an Anglo-Scottish Alliance since he and his forebears had fought the Scots for generations. Now, however, Scottish support was essential because, since the Duke of York had grasped power over most of England in October, the Earl of Northumberland's territory north of the Trent had become, more or less, an independent Lancastrian state. Instructions from London were ignored and Neville lands from Yorkshire to Cumberland were laid waste under his authority. In Parliament the Percys were damned as 'ravagers and misdoers' but, in his domain, the Earl of Northumberland held ultimate power and assumed martial authority, according to Alexander Rose, ordering all men over the age of 16 to arm themselves in readiness for war.

In late November, the Duke of Somerset, who had been unsuccessfully trying to oust the Earl of Warwick from Calais, joined the Earl of Devon at the City of York where they met the Percys and then rode on to Hull to join the Queen and

Silver groat depicting King James III of Scotland, issued 1484-1488.

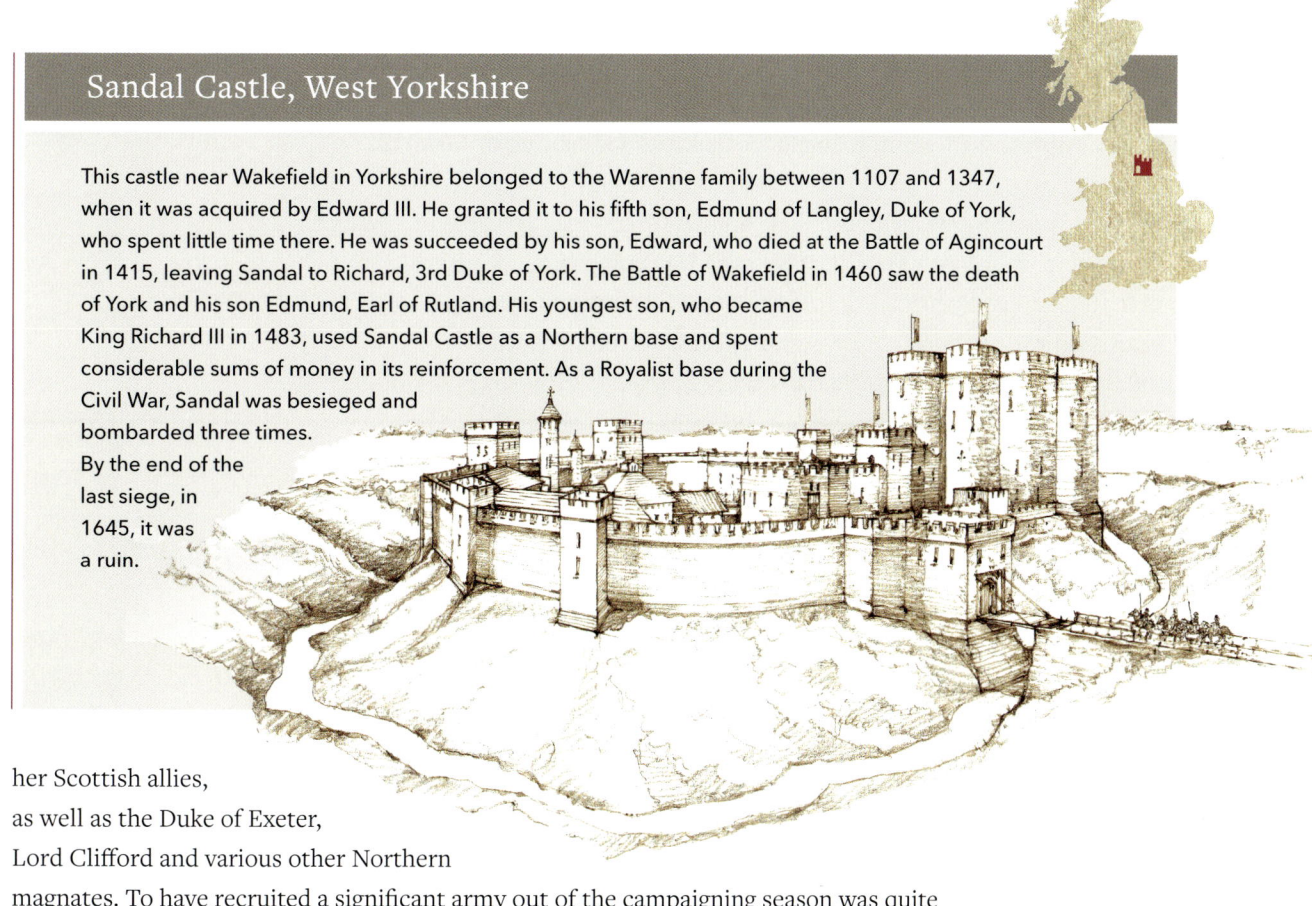

Sandal Castle, West Yorkshire

This castle near Wakefield in Yorkshire belonged to the Warenne family between 1107 and 1347, when it was acquired by Edward III. He granted it to his fifth son, Edmund of Langley, Duke of York, who spent little time there. He was succeeded by his son, Edward, who died at the Battle of Agincourt in 1415, leaving Sandal to Richard, 3rd Duke of York. The Battle of Wakefield in 1460 saw the death of York and his son Edmund, Earl of Rutland. His youngest son, who became King Richard III in 1483, used Sandal Castle as a Northern base and spent considerable sums of money in its reinforcement. As a Royalist base during the Civil War, Sandal was besieged and bombarded three times. By the end of the last siege, in 1645, it was a ruin.

her Scottish allies, as well as the Duke of Exeter, Lord Clifford and various other Northern magnates. To have recruited a significant army out of the campaigning season was quite a feat for which the Earl of Northumberland was mainly responsible. It also reflected the disgust that many nobles felt at the Act of Accord and its ultimate transfer of power to the Duke of York. On 8th November, York was proclaimed heir apparent to the throne and Protector of England, and all the Lords spiritual and temporal swore allegiance to him as he swore allegiance to the King and the Lords. He now ruled England in the name of the King.

In Hull, the Queen learned of the disinheritance of her son, which hardened her resolve and determination to destroy her enemies, release her husband and restore her son to his rightful inheritance. By the time her army, now under the command of the Earl of Northumberland and Duke of Somerset, reached the City of York, it numbered about 20,000. At York, Queen Margaret made a public protest against the Act of Accord and challenged the Duke of York to settle the issue in battle. In late November, the Lancastrian army marched south, and as they did so, they ravaged the estates of the Duke of York and Earl of Salisbury, particularly around Sandal Castle, York's mighty fortress close to Wakefield. The Duke of York, meanwhile, began preparations to march north. He acquired a loan of 500 marks from the Common Council of the City of London who, incidentally, had received a similar request from the Queen which they turned down. On 9th December, he and the Earl of Salisbury marched north with around 5-6000 men and several cannon commandeered from the Tower of London, while the Earl of Warwick stayed behind to maintain order in London. They marched via Nottingham, recruiting more men on the way, and made their way to Sandal Castle, where they had heard of Lancastrian activity in the area. On arrival there, the Duke of York enhanced his defences, dug trenches around the castle and strategically placed guns on the walls before settling down for Christmas, waiting for the Earl of March to arrive with reinforcements. The Earl of Northumberland and Duke of Somerset didn't have enough resources for a siege, so they planned to lure York out of the castle and make him fight before the Earl of March arrived. Their army of 20,000, including the forces of the Duke of Exeter, Earl of Devon and Lord Clifford, greatly outnumbered the Duke of York's force of around 12,000 men, which lacked any peer apart from the Earl of Salisbury. Lord Neville responded to the Duke of York's summons, bringing 8000 men, but he defected to the Lancastrians on arrival at Sandal.

By the end of December, supplies in the castle were dwindling and new supplies were blocked by the Lancastrian forces. An agreement was made between the Dukes of Somerset and York that a truce would prevail until after the feast of Epiphany on 6th January, but the Queen's commanders had no intention of honouring the agreement. A herald was sent to provoke the Duke of York into action, sneering at his 'want of courage in suffering himself to be tamely braved by a woman'. On 30th December the Duke of York rode out of Sandal, probably with a foraging party, and was attacked and sent back inside the castle. The Duke of Somerset then advanced with the centre of the Lancastrian army to a position near the castle and waited for York to attack while the Lancastrian right and left flanks, commanded by the Earl of Wiltshire and Lord Roos, lay in wait, hidden in woods on either side of the entrance to Sandal. The ruse worked and the Duke of York, Earl of Salisbury and York's 17 year old son, the Earl of Rutland, rode out of Sandal at the head of their army, across the drawbridge and downhill to open land south of the River Calder, an area known as Wakefield Green. The Lancastrian centre charged to meet them and there was a furious clash. Meanwhile, under the direction of Sir Andrew Trollope, who had deserted the Earl of Warwick and defected to the Lancastrians, the Duke of Somerset and Lord Clifford ordered the Earl of Wiltshire to take the castle and commanded Lord Roos to block the Duke of

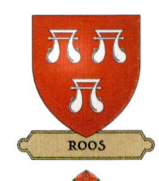

The Battle of Wakefield
30th December 1460

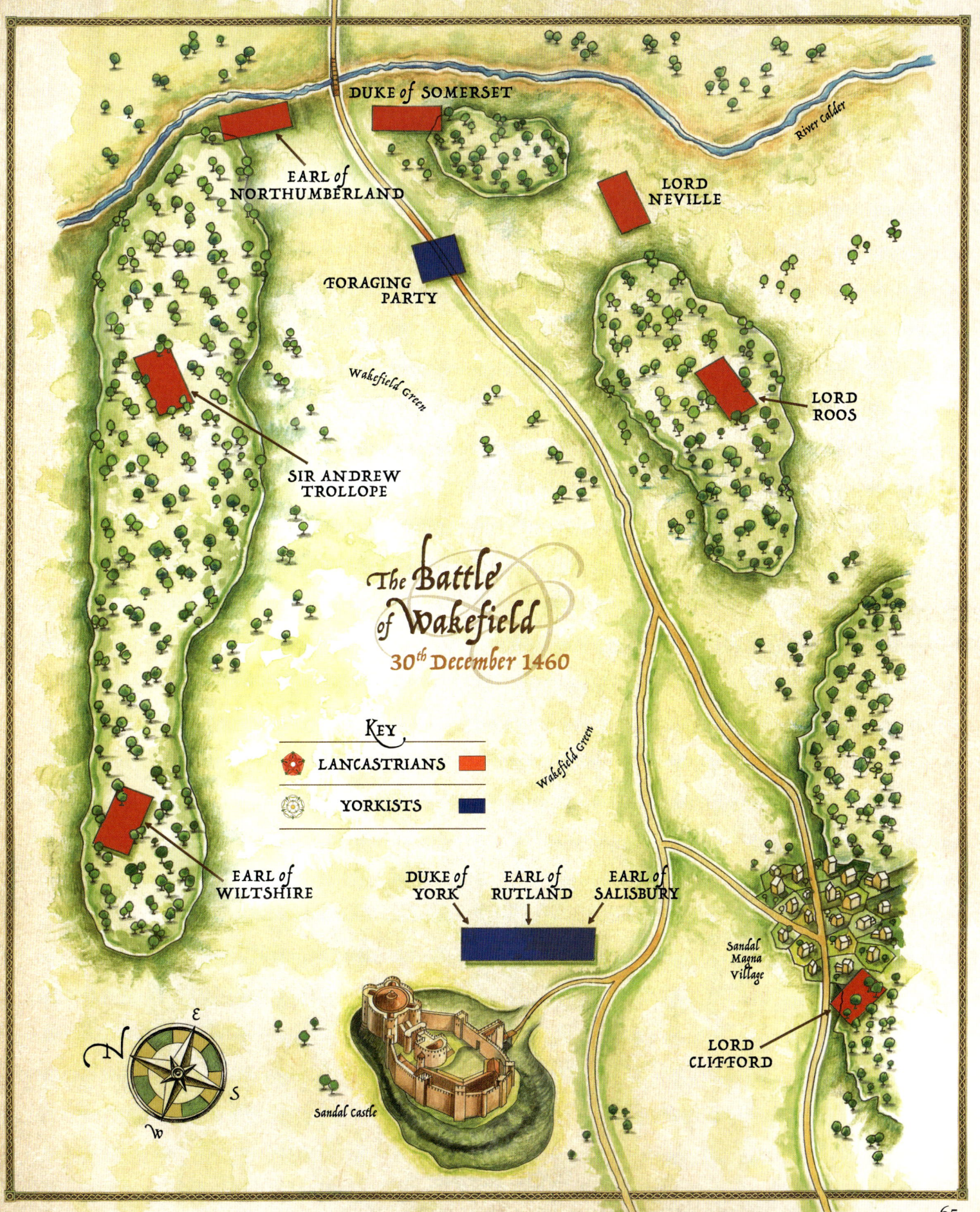

KEY
- Lancastrians (red)
- Yorkists (blue)

Duke of Somerset
Earl of Northumberland
Lord Neville
Foraging Party
Lord Roos
Sir Andrew Trollope
Earl of Wiltshire
Duke of York
Earl of Rutland
Earl of Salisbury
Lord Clifford

River Calder
Wakefield Green
Sandal Magna Village
Sandal Castle

York's retreat. As the two flanks surged out of the woods and enveloped York's army, the Yorkists were trapped.

Many were slaughtered and many surrendered, but not before the Duke of York was pulled from his horse and killed in the midst of battle. Then Lord 'Butcher' Clifford earned his nickname. Seeing the young Earl of Rutland leaving the field with his tutor, Sir Robert Aspsall, Clifford rode up and asked who the boy was, to which Aspsall stupidly replied 'Spare him, for he is a king's son, and good may come to you!' Clifford stabbed the boy through the heart with his dagger, shouting 'By God's blood, thy father slew mine! So will I slay the accursed blood of York!' According to Shakespeare, 'Northumberland, then present, wept to see it.' On the whole, the great bard was generous to the Percys and since there is no contemporary evidence of the Earl of Northumberland's tears of sorrow at Rutland's murder, one can only surmise that Shakespeare sought to present the Earl in a kindly light. After all, the Percy family retained significant status during Shakespeare's writing career – the 9th Earl of Northumberland was a neighbour of Shakespeare at Blackfriars – and he would, perhaps, wish to maintain a good relationship with this influential family.

About 1000 men were killed at the Battle of Wakefield, including the Earl of Salisbury's son, Sir Thomas Neville, whose wedding had provoked Lord Egremont's murderous attack some years before. The Earl of Salisbury was captured by one of Trollope's men the night after the battle and taken to Pontefract Castle, where he was imprisoned. He bribed his gaoler to let him escape but was caught in the act and 'the common people of the country, which loved him not, took him out of the castle by violence, and smote off his head'. Lord Clifford took the heads of the Duke of York, and Earls of Rutland and Salisbury, to the City of York and placed them on pikes above the Micklegate Bar, the main entrance to the city, leaving two empty pikes to await the heads of the Earl of Warwick and Edward of York. Richard Duke

Left: Richard, Duke of York as depicted in a mid-15th century stained glass window at Trinity College Cambridge.

Portrait of Lord John 'Butcher' or 'Blackfaced' Clifford.

Left: Micklegate Bar, York

of York's head bore a paper crown, a mocking reference to the end of his regal ambitions. His death, however, did not end the Yorkist campaign.

Queen Margaret had returned to Edinburgh before the battle, staying there as a guest of the Scottish Queen, but she rushed south to the City of York on hearing news of the great victory against her hated foes. In the New Year she marched south from Edinburgh, with a large Scottish army that drooled at the prospect of English plunder and, since Margaret lacked the funds to pay them properly, she encouraged their appetite for booty.

The severed heads of the Earl of Rutland, the Duke of York and the Earl of Salisbury.

9 / 'THE ACCURSED BLOOD OF YORK'

10 'Upon ill Palm Sunday'

The Earl of Salisbury's death left the Earl of Warwick the richest magnate in England, with additional lands in the North, the castles of Middleham and Sheriff Hutton and the Earldom of Salisbury, but Queen Margaret and the Lancastrian lords intended to capitalise on their recent victory at Wakefield, crush Warwick and rescue the King from his clutches. On the 20th January, she and her army met the main Lancastrian force at the City of York, where her nobles confirmed the agreement between Margaret and the Scottish Queen to surrender Berwick to the Scots and allow the Prince of Wales to marry the Scottish Princess Mary. Charles VII of France, Scotland's ally, also promised to allow Queen Margaret to use harbours in Normandy if she needed them. On the same day, the Lancastrian army set forth under the command of the Earl of Northumberland and Duke of Somerset, marching via Grantham, Stamford, Peterborough, Huntingdon, Royston and St Albans. Once past the River Trent, the Northern soldiers began looting, raping and laying waste to abbeys, priories, towns and villages that stood in their way. Thieves and robbers boosted the Queen's army hoping for booty, and terrified people fled south with tales of horror, filling the Southern population with alarm. The terror caused by this rapacious Northern army confirmed the Earl of Warwick's propaganda and encouraged the Council to grant him a loan of 2000 marks for the defence of the realm.

Warwick was slow to react to the threat though, and waited until the Lancastrian army reached Hertfordshire before he began recruiting his army. He awaited the enemy near St Albans, forming his lines on Barnet Heath, a large, flat field north-east of the town. When the Lancastrian army reached Luton, a former Yorkist, Sir Henry Lovelace, realised that Warwick had laid an ambush south of the town, with nets concealing spikes and caltrops covering the road to cripple horses and impede cavalry. He alerted the Queen who swung her army west towards Dunstable rather than St Albans. In Dunstable she destroyed a small Yorkist force, then headed down Watling Street towards St Albans. Warwick was still expecting the enemy to appear from Luton which would bring them right to his assembled army, in front of which he had laid more traps for enemy cavalry. He also had a contingent of Burgundian mercenaries with the latest weapons, small firearms called ribaudkins. Although his main force faced towards Luton, Warwick had allowed for the fact that the Lancastrians might come from the direction of Dunstable so he placed archers to defend that flank. When the attack did indeed come from this direction, on 17th February, the Lancastrian force was pushed back by a storm of arrows. However, Warwick lacked the time to wheel his main ranks around to face the enemy. Some Northerners, led by Trollope, found a way to circumvent the town centre, via Catherine Lane into St Peter's Street, and attack Warwick's vulnerable flank and rear. They burst through, surprising the Yorkist left, which soon broke and caused a collapse of the entire force. When he realised the battle was lost, Warwick marched west through the night with a force of about 4000 men, aiming to link up with Edward of York. He left behind a battlefield strewn with corpses and a bemused King sitting in his tent once more, this time surrounded by frightened Yorkist nobles, Lord Bonville and Sir Thomas Kyriell. King Henry insisted that they be spared but was overruled by his vengeful wife. She asked the seven year old Prince Edward, recently knighted by his father, how the two knights should die. The child replied, 'Let them have their heads taken off'.

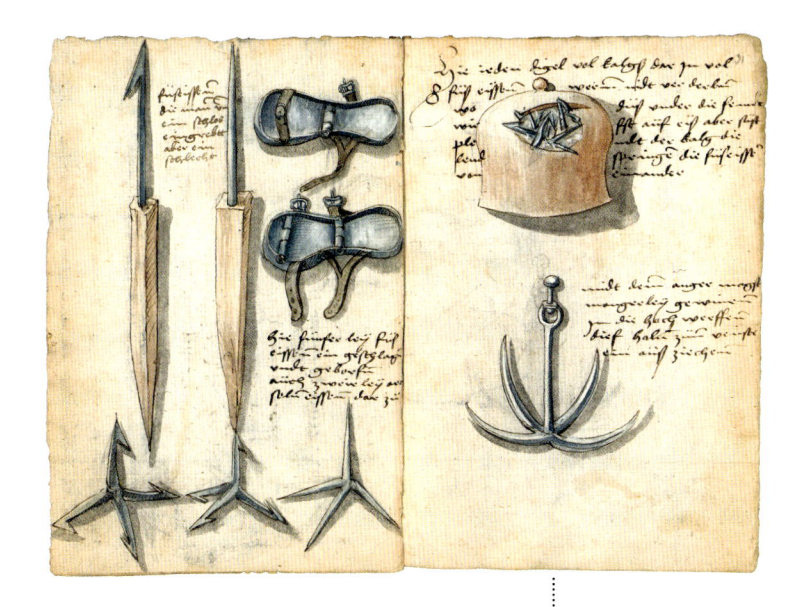

On 2nd February, Edward of York had won a stunning victory against an army of Welsh soldiers,

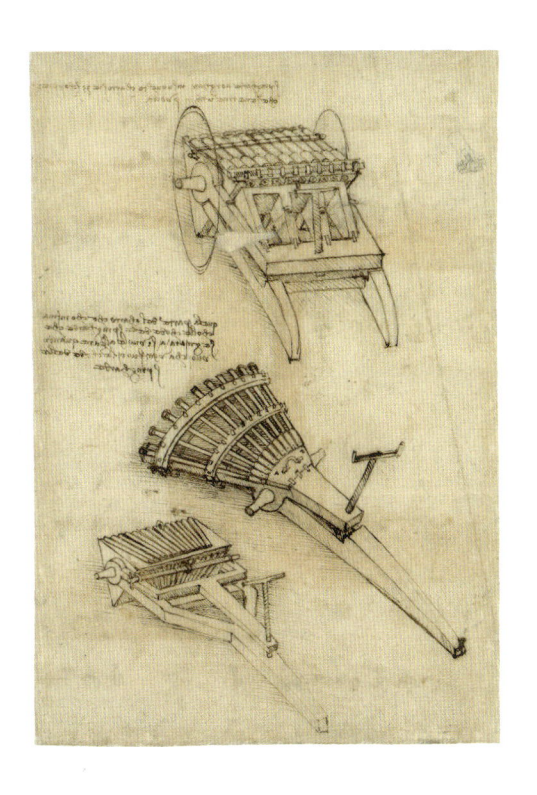

An illustration of caltrops, lower left, from a Codex dated 1505.

Left: Leonardo Da Vinci's designs for ribaudkins.

and French, Breton and Irish mercenaries under Owen Tudor and the Earls of Pembroke and Wiltshire. They had been marching east to join the Queen's army as it marched south to attack the Earl of Warwick, but Edward, having recruited an army in south-west England and the Welsh Marches, intercepted them at Mortimer's Cross, a hamlet on a crossroads between Ludlow and Leominster. Edward was encouraged by an unusual natural phenomenon known as 'parhelion,' whereby three suns appeared to rise at dawn, and he took this event to represent divine support from the Holy Trinity. He led about 5000 men, including seasoned archers, to the Lancastrians' 4000 troops. Mortimer's Cross was a particularly bloody battle, with about 4000 dead, most of them Lancastrians. On seeing the day was lost, the Earl of Pembroke fled, leaving his men and his father, Owen Tudor, to the mercy of the victorious Edward. On 3rd February, Owen Tudor was executed in the market square at Hereford, on Edward of York's orders, perhaps in revenge for his own father's death at Wakefield. Pembroke tried in vain to rally Welsh allies to avenge his father but was forced to flee abroad, leaving his nephew Henry Tudor, for whom he had been responsible since his brother Edmund's death, hiding in Pembroke Castle. There the future Henry VII was discovered by Yorkists and put under house arrest at Raglan Castle, under the watchful eye of William Herbert.

Edward of York sees the Parhelion event at the Battle of Mortimer's Cross, from an illuminated manuscript of the 1460s.

Edward of York's army met up with the Earl of Warwick in the Cotswolds and together they marched to London in just four days. The citizens, who had refused to allow Queen Margaret's army of 'Northern devils' to enter the city, opened their gates with delight at the arrival of the Yorkist force which, to them, represented salvation. In this supportive atmosphere, the 18 year old Edward of York, with the Earl of Warwick's backing and the support of Lords and Commons, claimed the crown of England. He forcefully maintained that the Lancastrian kings from Henry IV to Henry VI were usurpers whose rule led to 'unrest, inward war and trouble' among the nobles. Edward's claim 'by God's law, man's law and the law of nature' apparently trumped all others. He was descended from two sons of Edward III, Edmund Duke of York, the fifth son, and Lionel Duke of Clarence, the third son, whose great-grandson was Edmund Mortimer, Earl of March. The latter's claim had been championed by Hotspur and his father, the 1st Earl of Northumberland, in their rebellion against Henry IV. Above all, Edward held London and now had a strong military advantage over Henry VI. On 4th March 1461, Edward was acclaimed by the people and heard the Te Deum in St Paul's Cathedral before entering the Great Hall at Westminster where, clad in royal robes and invested with the cap of Estate, he swore the oath and sat on the marble seat known as the King's Bench. The coronation was postponed by Edward, who vowed that he would not be crowned until Henry VI and Margaret of Anjou, his queen, had been executed or exiled. Edward of York was young, affable, intelligent and even-tempered, well over 6 feet tall, handsome (if vain) with a fondness for fighting, hunting, feasting, drinking and womanising. He was a king that shone brightly in contrast to the shrivelled, ageing, weak-minded Henry VI.

With few friends in the south, King Henry and Queen Margaret retreated north leaving a ravaged country and a population that despised them. Nonetheless, they camped outside the walls of the City of York and called for reinforcements. The Scottish Queen, Mary of Guelders, responded with a small force of men and, gradually, the Lancastrian army swelled to a total of roughly 30,000 under the command of the Duke of Somerset, Earl of Northumberland and Lord Clifford, the vengeful sons of the leaders slaughtered at St Albans six years earlier. They persuaded the King and Queen to remain in York while they marched south to meet their enemy.

Portrait of Edward IV. English School, 16th/17th century.

Edward IV victorious in battle, from an illuminated manuscript of the 1460s.

10 / 'UPON ILL PALM SUNDAY' 71

On 5th March, Edward IV sent the Duke of Norfolk to recruit forces in East Anglia, and the Earl of Warwick to do likewise in the Midlands. On the 11th, his mainly Kentish and Welsh troops marched out of London and headed north, followed by King Edward himself on the 13th. As he rode north, his ranks swelled with new recruits that flocked to the cause, determined to rid the country of malignant Lancastrian rule. By the 22nd, Edward had arrived at the City of Nottingham where he received intelligence that the Duke of Somerset, Lord Rivers and a large force were positioned to defend the river crossing at Ferrybridge, in Yorkshire. By the 27th he had reached Pontefract, gathering increasing numbers of recruits to his banner. He led up to 25,000 men and was expecting to be joined imminently by the Duke of Norfolk's and Earl of Warwick's armies. Eight Yorkist peers were present; the Duke of Norfolk, the Earl of Warwick and Lords Bourchier, Grey de Wilton, Clinton, Fauconberg, Scrope and Dacre.

The Lancastrian army blocked the road to the City of York. At least 19 Lancastrian peers were present, led by the Dukes of Somerset and Exeter, the Earls of Northumberland and Devon, the Lords Fitzhugh, Hungerford, Beaumont, Dacre of Gilsland, Roos and Grey of Codnor, and Sir Andrew Trollope. Somerset, the Lancastrian commander-in-chief was only 24 years old while his enemy, King Edward IV, was still 18. Somerset and Exeter commanded the Lancastrian reserve, stationed in the village of Towton. The Yorkist vanguard was commanded by Lord Fauconberg.

On 27th March King Edward sent Baron Fitzwalter and the Earl of Warwick to secure the bridge over the River Aire, south of Ferrybridge, but they were ambushed and massacred by a large force of Lancastrian cavalry under Lord Clifford who was killed in the melee, along with the Earl of Westmorland's brother, Lord Neville. On the Yorkist side, Fitzwalter was killed and Warwick was wounded in the leg by an arrow. Morale plummeted when the Yorkists heard this news, so, in full view of the army, Warwick grabbed his sword and killed his horse, vowing that he would rather fight on foot and die with his men than concede another inch.

The pious King Henry VI sent a message to the new King Edward IV, seeking a truce as the following day, 29th March 1461, was Palm Sunday and King Henry would normally spend it in prayer. King Edward refused, anxious to engage while his army was still fresh, although most combatants showed Christian respect by carrying sprigs of palm or yew, blessed by a priest. As dawn broke on that fateful day, mass was sung in each camp before the trumpets heralded the start of the bloodiest day on English soil. As the Yorkist army advanced towards Tadcaster, they faced a Lancastrian force deployed in three battle arrays along a plateau with the deep and steep sided River Cock to their right. Around 60,000 men were now primed

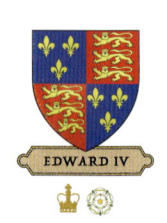

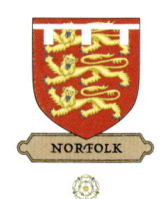

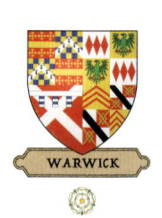

72 LIONS OF THE RED ROSE

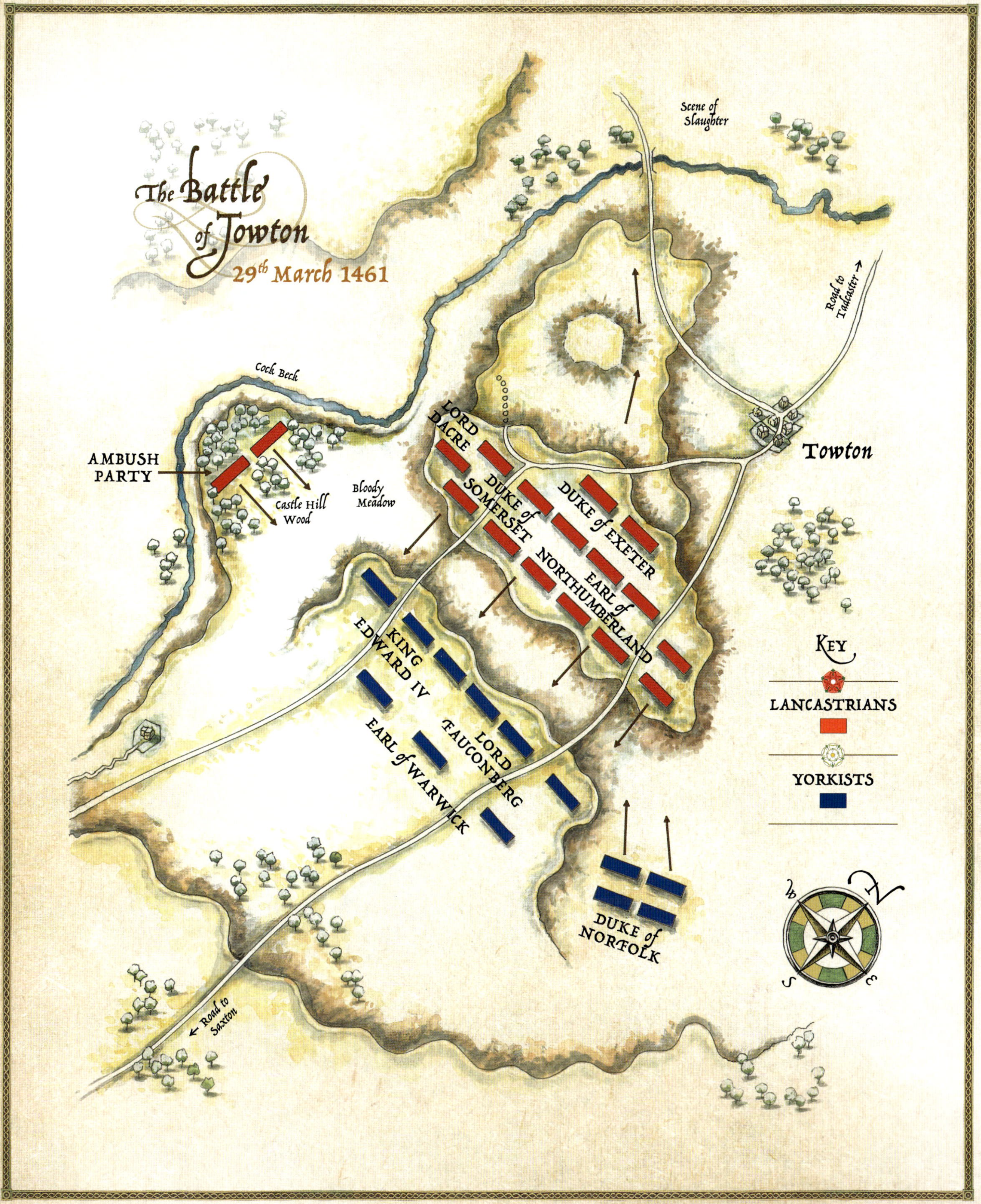
The Battle of Towton
29th March 1461
Cock Beck
Scene of Slaughter
Road to Tadcaster
Towton
AMBUSH PARTY
Castle Hill Wood
Bloody Meadow
LORD DACRE
DUKE of SOMERSET
DUKE of EXETER
EARL of NORTHUMBERLAND
KING EDWARD IV
LORD FAUCONBERG
EARL of WARWICK
DUKE of NORFOLK
Road to Saxton
KEY
LANCASTRIANS
YORKISTS
N
S
E
W

Typical Horse Armour of the period

to fight to decide which king would continue to rule. The Duke of Somerset commanded the right flank, facing Edward; the Earl of Northumberland commanded the left, facing the Earl of Warwick and Lord Fauconberg. King Henry and the Duke of Exeter were in the rear with the reserves.

The battle commenced with a great volley of arrows from both sides. The Lancastrians were at a huge disadvantage as they faced a strong, blustery wind and driving snowstorm that blinded them to the fact that their arrows were falling short of the enemy lines. The diminutive but tactically astute Lord Fauconberg added to this advantage by ordering his archers to fall back after each volley of Yorkist arrows so that the Lancastrian shafts continued to fall short. As their own arrows started to run out, the Yorkists collected Lancastrian arrows that had fallen harmlessly in front of them and returned them 'winged with death into the ranks of their owners'. The Duke of Somerset, uncharacteristically positive and effective, then surged forward crying 'King Henry,' and attacked King Edward's unprepared wing, which quickly broke and was chased down by Somerset's cavalry. If the Earl of Northumberland had been able to charge into King Edward's right, the Lancastrians would probably have carried the day, but the snow and mud forced him to lead his heavy infantry on foot at an enemy they could barely see. For several hours carnage ensued as swords, axes and maces reaped a bloody harvest on the field of battle.

The Earl of Northumberland's force was gradually pushed back. He slipped in the icy quagmire and was struck by an enemy weapon, leaving him badly wounded. His men

Archer in action, with some typical arrowheads of the period.

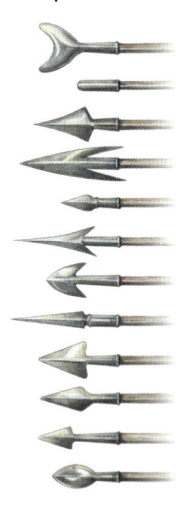

LIONS OF THE RED ROSE

The Battle of Towton, by Richard Caton Woodville, 1922.

dragged him to the rear through the slush and mud and the Duke of Norfolk's Yorkist reserve then hit this weakened and leaderless flank which subsequently collapsed. The Lancastrian army dissolved into chaos and many of the defeated troops attempted to escape down the steep, slippery slope and across the River Cock to Tadcaster. They had earlier destroyed the bridge to deter a Yorkist attack from the rear and many were now slaughtered on the banks of the swollen river or drowned as they tried to cross it, dragged down by heavy clothing, chain mail and armour. Bodies washed down the river, collecting in places and creating bridges of corpses.

The 3rd Earl of Northumberland's will, in which he specified that six years' income from his estates should pay off his debt, then four years' worth to 'spend on my sepulture in the Chapel of St Ninian the Bishop within the Cathedral Church of York near or next to the tombs of my ancestors there [Harry Hotspur and the 1st Earl], and on the foundation of three perpetual chantries within the same Chapel...' This did not come to pass after Towton. A further two years' income was for 'the marriages and betrothals of Alianor, Margaret and Elizabeth, my most dear daughters'. Only fragments of the seal remain, which are protected by a leather pouch.

The 39 year old 3rd Earl of Northumberland died in the carnage, either succumbing from his wounds on the battlefield, or later in the City of York where noble survivors gathered. He was buried in the Church of St Denys in Walmgate, York, with his brother, Sir Richard Percy, another of Towton's casualties. Lords Clifford and Neville were amongst the Lancastrian peers killed in the battle. The Earls of Wiltshire and Devon were captured and beheaded in York, Devon's head replacing Richard, Duke of York's on the Micklegate Bar. Between 20,000 and 38,000 men are thought to have died at Towton, most of them Lancastrians, leaving the snowbound fields thick with corpses and tinted pink with blood.

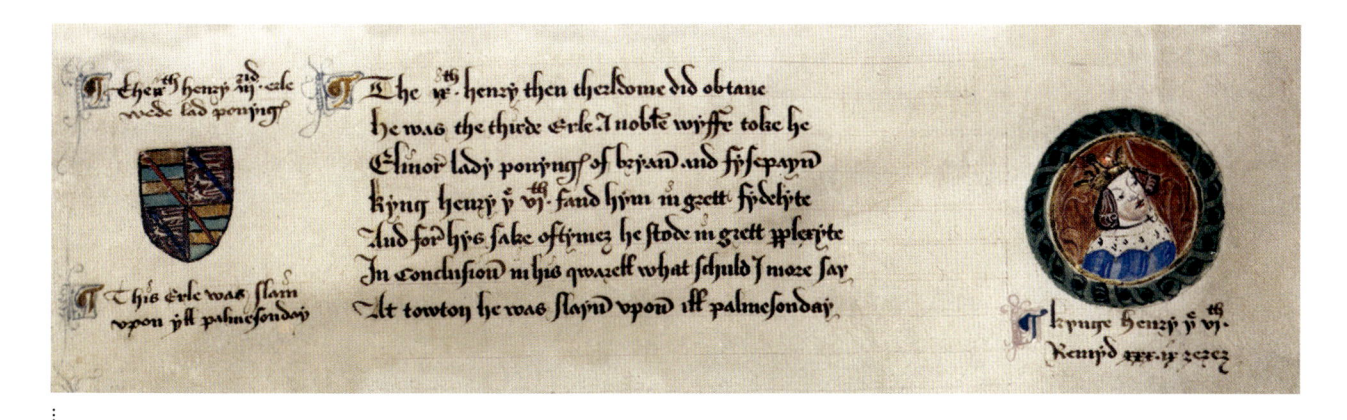

Excerpt on the 3rd Earl from William Peeris' pedigree roll.

"The ixth Henry then therldome did obtane,
He was the thirde Erle A noble wyffe toke he,
Elinor lady ponynges of bryan and fysepayn,
Kyng Henry the vjth fand hym in grett fydelyte,
And for hys sake oftymes he stode in grett perplexyte,
In Conclusion in his qwarell what schuld I more say,
At towton he was slayn upon ill palmesonday."

10 / 'UPON ILL PALM SUNDAY'

11 War in the North

Although the Battle of Towton was an utter disaster for the Lancastrians, it did not herald a conclusion. As Winston Churchill said of another war, 'it marked the end of the beginning', and the conflict moved to the North. King Henry, Queen Margaret, Prince Edward, the Dukes of Somerset and Exeter and a few other Lancastrian stalwarts, fled to Newcastle and then to Alnwick Castle where they sent an urgent message to the Bishop of St Andrews, Regent of Scotland, requesting safe passage to enter Scotland. As they headed north, they were besieged at Wark Castle, on the banks of the River Tweed, by a Yorkist force under Sir Robert Ogle, but the deceased Earl of Northumberland's retainers raised 5-6000 men to relieve the siege and allow the royal party to ride on to Berwick. King Edward did not pursue them at this stage as the North was still strongly Lancastrian, and the Earl of Northumberland's vengeful supporters made it too dangerous.

On 28th June 1461, with popular acclaim, Edward IV was crowned in Westminster Abbey. On the same day, he honoured his brother George, then 12, by creating him Duke of Clarence. His youngest brother, Richard, was just eight years old and remained under his mother's care. In the first parliament of the new reign, in November, King Edward attainted both Dukes of Somerset and Exeter, who went into exile on the Continent, as well as many other Lancastrian nobles both alive and dead. The release of their properties into his hands allowed him to reward his own loyal barons: Henry Tudor's Earldom of Richmond, for instance, was given to the King's brother, the new Duke of

Coronation of Edward IV, from an illuminated history of the 15th century.

Dunstanburgh Castle, Northumberland

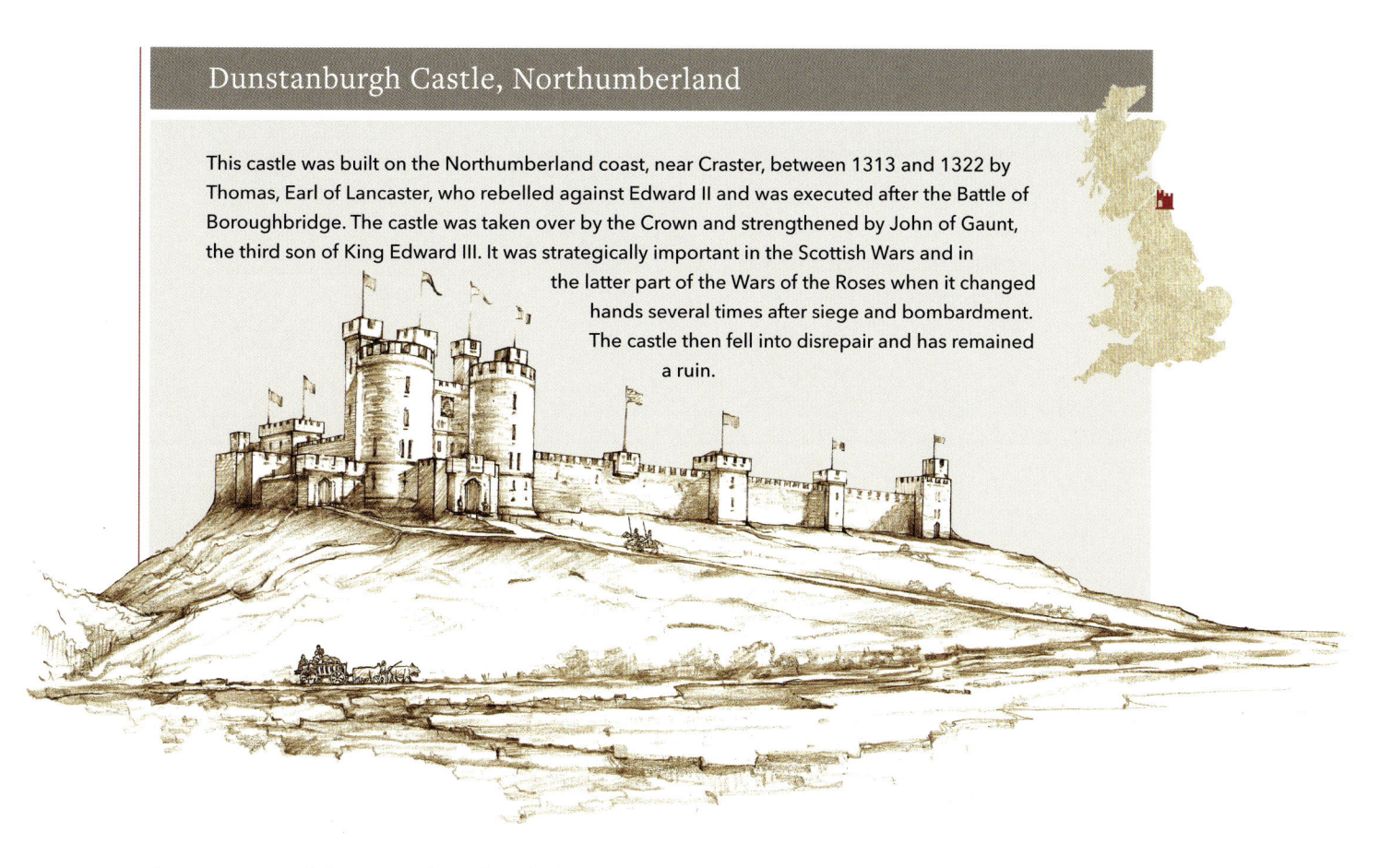

This castle was built on the Northumberland coast, near Craster, between 1313 and 1322 by Thomas, Earl of Lancaster, who rebelled against Edward II and was executed after the Battle of Boroughbridge. The castle was taken over by the Crown and strengthened by John of Gaunt, the third son of King Edward III. It was strategically important in the Scottish Wars and in the latter part of the Wars of the Roses when it changed hands several times after siege and bombardment. The castle then fell into disrepair and has remained a ruin.

Clarence. Meanwhile Henry, the 3rd Earl of Northumberland's 12 year old son, was placed in the Tower of London while King Edward worked out what to do with him.

In Wales, William Herbert defeated Jasper Tudor, Earl of Pembroke, and the Duke of Exeter near Caernarvon, and all resistance was mopped up there by the autumn of 1461. In the North, the Earl of Warwick had been granted wardenship of both Marches for 20 years. Lord Fauconberg, his uncle, was elevated to Earl of Kent and acted as his lieutenant, but died two years later and was replaced by Warwick's brother, John Neville, Lord Egremont's former adversary, who had been given the title Lord Montagu. By mid-September 1461, most Northern strongholds fell into Warwick's hands. Alnwick Castle submitted peacefully, followed by Dunstanburgh Castle of which Sir Ralph Percy, the last of the four brothers who fought for Henry VI, was constable, a position granted him by Queen Margaret in 1456. As far as this pragmatic Percy was concerned, submission to Yorkist rule was imperative not just for the sake of his wife and four children but for his nephew, the rightful heir to the soon to be attainted Earldom of Northumberland. For Edward IV, the risks of keeping a Percy in office in the family's heartland were outweighed by the calming effect it could have on the Northern population, potentially persuading the gentry to lay down their arms and accept the new regime, as long as Sir Ralph acquiesced. He was allowed to retain his position as constable of Dunstanburgh Castle and he apparently carried out his duties loyally.

In his 1902 history, Brenan recounts a different tale, removing any hint of treachery against the red rose in Sir Ralph's behaviour:

Naworth Castle

'Having seen Queen Margaret and her son safely into Scotland... he shut himself up in the castle of Dunstanburgh, and prepared to defend that fortress to the bitter end... attempts were made to dislodge him, but without success; and by dint of moonlight ridings into the surrounding country, he succeeded in keeping his little garrison sufficiently well supplied with food. To such a pitch did he harass his neighbours of the opposite party – attacking their hinds when they sought to garner the first peaceful harvest of years; carrying off their cattle and fat wethers (and if tradition tells truth, their daughters as well); and ever choosing a time for his attacks when they deemed themselves most secure – that the Yorkists resolved in the end to make terms with this 'Gledd (kite) of Dunstanburgh.' Accordingly, by the King's grace, Sir Ralph was granted leave to hold Dunstanburgh Castle as governor; and a pardon was drawn up in his name, although it does not appear that he made formal submission to King Edward. Indeed he became more active than ever in the cause of the Red Rose... and began to increase the force at his command by bringing bands of Scots from across the border.'

Other die-hard Lancastrians were as hard or harder to tame and by the New Year, Sir William Tailboys had retaken Alnwick Castle and Lord Dacre had recaptured his family castle of Naworth in Cumberland. Various minor insurrections, mostly emanating from across the Border, were dealt with by the Earl of Warwick but, in July, Queen Margaret led a Scottish force under the Earl of Angus into north-west England to try and capture Carlisle. They were driven back by Lord Montagu but managed to penetrate further south, as far as Durham, before being repulsed by Warwick. Edward needed to deal with this threat from the North, but without invading and attempting to subjugate Scotland in a lengthy war of attrition.

Margaret had persuaded the Scottish government to conclude a treaty providing for the marriage of Prince Edward to Margaret Stewart, James III's sister. Moreover, the Bishop of St Andrews would become Archbishop of Canterbury, and England would enter a tripartite alliance with Scotland and France, her traditional enemies. Berwick was formally ceded to the Scots on 25th April 1461 and was firmly in their hands by the end of the year, provoking fury among the English and giving Edward IV a powerful propaganda weapon. However, it lost him a vital bridgehead for invading Scotland, gave the Scots and French a powerful advantage and the Lancastrians an ideal centre from which to launch raids into England.

Early in 1462, the 12th Earl of Oxford, one of Margaret's chief agents in England, corresponded with the exiled royal family in Scotland whilst planning a Lancastrian invasion. Unfortunately his courier was a Yorkist double agent and the letters were taken to King Edward, revealing that as the King marched north to deal with the Lancastrian 'rebels', Oxford intended to follow with a large army, pretending to support the King but, at an opportune moment, planned to attack and kill him. Meanwhile the Duke of Somerset, then in Bruges, would return to England, Henry VI would lead an army of Scots over the Border and Jasper Tudor invade the South coast from Brittany. The exposure of the Lancastrian plan was a major blow for Queen Margaret, but for the Earl of Oxford and various other conspirators, it was very much worse. The unfortunate Earl was disembowelled, castrated and burned alive.

In March 1462, Queen Mary of Scotland financed a trip to Paris by Queen Margaret to negotiate support from the new French King, Louis XI. Despite his previous Yorkist sympathies, this King's hatred of Burgundy and delight at a divided England dictated French foreign policy. While the Queen was away, Yorkists under Lord Hastings, Sir John Howard and Sir Ralph Grey took back Alnwick Castle from Tailboys, Lord Montagu ejected Lord Dacre from Naworth Castle, and the Earl of Warwick took Bamburgh Castle. In May, to show that King Edward meant business, Warwick even led an army across the Border and seized a Scottish castle. This encouraged Queen Mary of Scotland to meet the Earl of Carlisle and sign a truce to last until 24th August. The Earl of Warwick hoped that this might lead to a more permanent peace and close Scotland off to the Lancastrians.

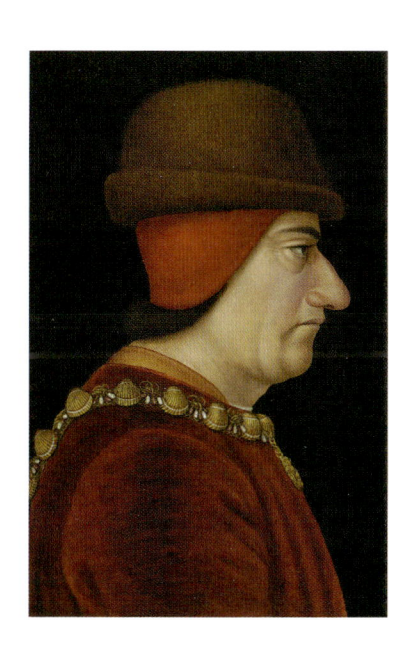

Queen Margaret achieved some modest success in France and the resulting Truce of Tours involved a plan for King Louis to occupy Calais and send over

Left: King Louis XI of France, oil painting, c. 1469.

Alnwick Castle, Northumberland

The original wooden structure, situated on an outcrop of whinstone in Northumberland, was rebuilt in stone after Yvo de Vescy was granted ownership by William II in 1096. The castle stood firm against Scottish attacks before and after the Percys bought it and the surrounding lands from Anthony Bek, the Bishop of Durham, in 1309. The castle was strengthened and played a pivotal role in the Scottish Wars until the union of the crowns in 1603. During the Wars of the Roses, between 1462 and 1464, Queen Margaret occupied Alnwick and other Northern castles, but it changed hands several times over this period. It was taken by the Yorkists but eventually restored to the 4th Earl of Northumberland by King Edward IV. Plots and rebellions kept the Percys in the South for much of the late 16th and 17th centuries and the castle fell into disrepair, exacerbated by passing armies and billeted troops during the Civil War. It was restored by the 1st Duke and Duchess of Northumberland in the 18th century and remains home to the Percy family to this day.

The Barbican, Alnwick Castle.

LIONS OF THE RED ROSE

an invasion force under the great 'seneschal' (king's representative) of Normandy, Pierre de Breze. In reality, King Louis didn't dare to cross Burgundian territory to get to Calais and the invasion force turned out to be a small force of 2000 French soldiers and mercenaries which sailed from Honfleur, in Normandy, in a dozen ships with Queen Margaret, Prince Edward and de Breze. Sometime earlier, Sir Richard Tunstall, one of Queen Margaret's champions, successfully plotted to wrest Bamburgh Castle from his Yorkist brother William, and install a Lancastrian garrison there in anticipation of a Lancastrian invasion from France. While this was successful, the Yorkist garrison at Tynemouth prevented the French fleet from landing, and strafed them with cannon, whereupon their ships were scattered in a violent storm and some were lost. As the seas calmed, the remaining ships sailed up the coast and landed near Alnmouth where they received a warning that the Earl of Warwick was on his way with 40,000 troops. This news terrified the mercenaries who subsequently abandoned the Queen, Prince Edward and de Breze on a beach, and sailed off with the fleet. A local fisherman eventually agreed to take them up the coast to Bamburgh where the little fishing boat was smashed on the rocks in a squall. All their baggage and provisions were lost, but they scrambled over the rocks to Bamburgh Castle, expecting loyal Lancastrians to rally there. Queen Margaret's sparse forces, however, did not inspire confidence and failed to encourage enough local men to join her. Undaunted, she reinforced Tunstall's garrison at Bamburgh Castle with the few French troops that had sailed up the coast to join them. They took charge of Dunstanburgh Castle and then laid siege to Alnwick Castle which, with few provisions, quickly capitulated. Warkworth Castle followed soon after but, despite her successes, few Englishmen wanted to rally to Margaret's cause as they resented the French garrisons. Nonetheless, the castles were stocked with enough provisions to withstand a siege and Margaret travelled north to Berwick to join up with King Henry, the Dukes of Somerset and Exeter and Lords Pembroke, Roos, Hungerford and Morton.

The widowed Queen Mary of Scotland, whom Somerset ungallantly claimed to have seduced on his last Scottish interlude, was tiring of her Lancastrian allies and their expensive and unproductive campaigns. She provided few resources for the next one but King Henry and Queen

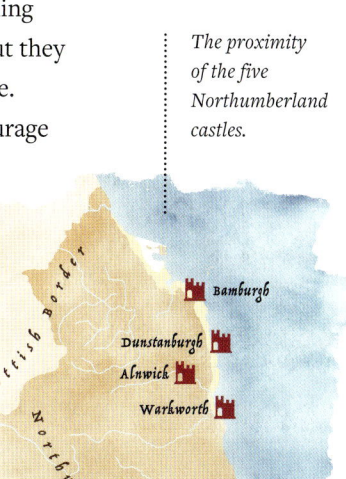

Tynemouth Castle

The proximity of the five Northumberland castles.

Margaret still set out to invade England with their retinue and 800 remaining troops. In response, the Earl of Warwick was sent north to besiege Berwick and, early in November, King Edward marched north with a large army including 31 peers, a record gathering of noble leaders. Many of those noblemen had unsurprisingly transferred their allegiance from the tragic and pathetic Henry VI to the new King Edward who encapsulated their ideals of kingship.

When Margaret heard the news of this approaching army, she placed the Duke of Somerset in command of Bamburgh Castle, supported by Lords Roos and Pembroke, and Sir Ralph Percy who pledged his loyalty to the Lancastrian King once more. Meanwhile the Lancastrian army failed to recruit sufficient troops, partly because it had managed to offend the local people by demanding money from Hexham and Durham Priories. On 13th November, realising that her army was far too small to face Edward IV's Yorkist host, Queen Margaret fled north by sea, taking King Henry, Pierre

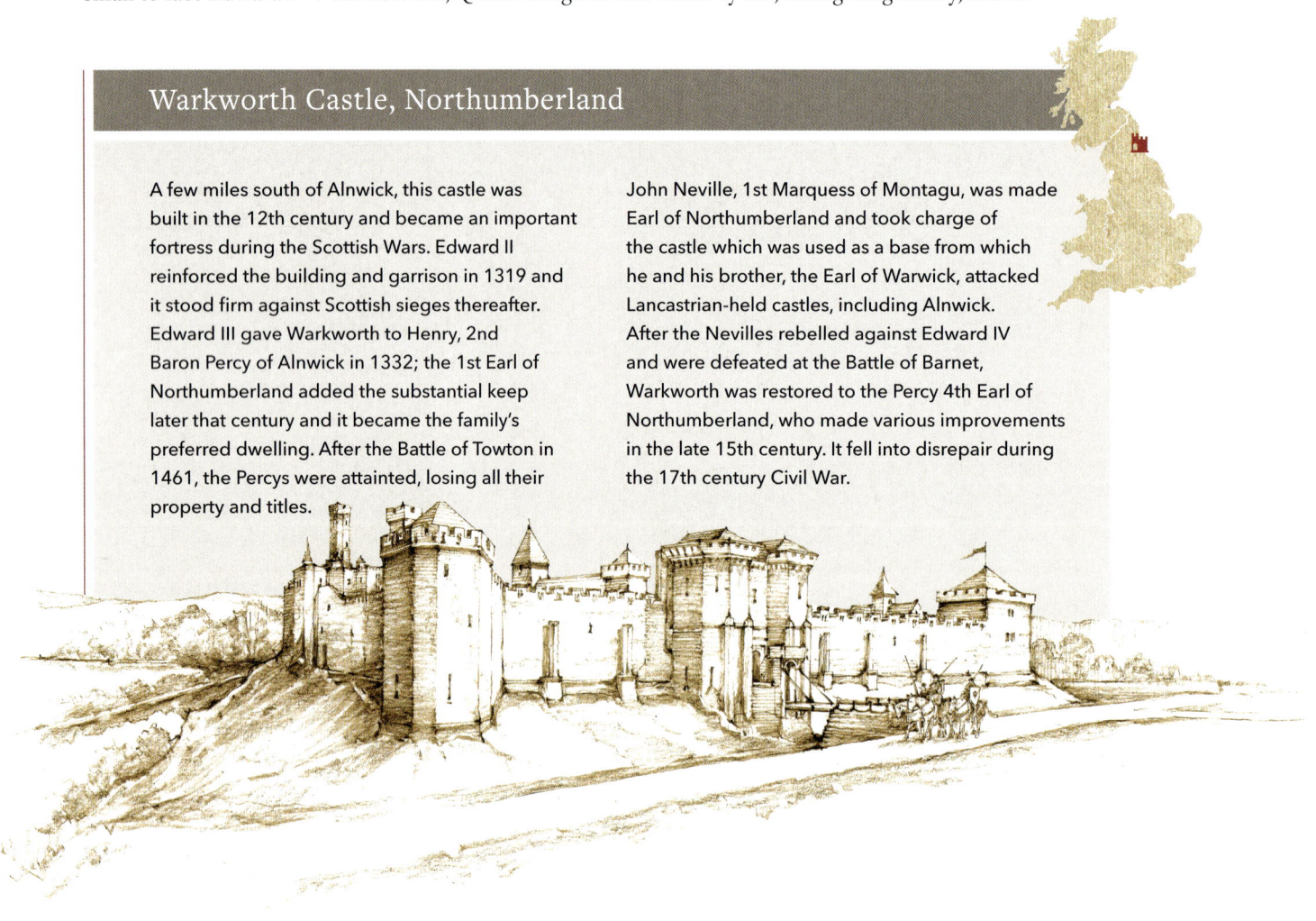

Warkworth Castle, Northumberland

A few miles south of Alnwick, this castle was built in the 12th century and became an important fortress during the Scottish Wars. Edward II reinforced the building and garrison in 1319 and it stood firm against Scottish sieges thereafter. Edward III gave Warkworth to Henry, 2nd Baron Percy of Alnwick in 1332; the 1st Earl of Northumberland added the substantial keep later that century and it became the family's preferred dwelling. After the Battle of Towton in 1461, the Percys were attainted, losing all their property and titles.

John Neville, 1st Marquess of Montagu, was made Earl of Northumberland and took charge of the castle which was used as a base from which he and his brother, the Earl of Warwick, attacked Lancastrian-held castles, including Alnwick. After the Nevilles rebelled against Edward IV and were defeated at the Battle of Barnet, Warkworth was restored to the Percy 4th Earl of Northumberland, who made various improvements in the late 15th century. It fell into disrepair during the 17th century Civil War.

de Breze and 400 men from Bamburgh with her. To add to her troubles, a storm blew up and the royal party was forced to land and then walk several miles to Berwick. Most of their men were stranded on Holy Island, where they were captured by local Yorkists and summarily executed or taken prisoner.

Edward IV intended to pursue Queen Margaret but was struck down by measles and confined to his bed in Durham. The Earl of Warwick, meanwhile, had captured Warkworth Castle which became his headquarters before he laid siege to Bamburgh Castle. The garrison there held out until Warwick offered Somerset a generous pension if he surrendered. He agreed on the condition that Sir Ralph Percy was granted custody of Bamburgh Castle, that the lords with him would be restored to their estates and the lives of those in the garrison would be spared. Warwick agreed and, on Christmas Eve, the Duke of Somerset handed over the keys of the castle, formally pledged his allegiance to Edward IV and rode to assist Warwick at the siege of Alnwick Castle which, together with Dunstanburgh Castle, surrendered on 6th January 1463. It is hard to fully understand the reasons for Somerset's actions, but his relationship with Queen Margaret had become increasingly strained and King Edward welcomed him as if he was his closest friend. Perhaps, like Sir Ralph Percy, he was following the best course for survival. Jasper Tudor, Earl of Pembroke, on the other hand, refused to make a deal with Warwick or King Edward, and returned to Scotland.

The county of Northumberland and all its strongholds were now in King Edward's hands but Queen Margaret wasn't finished yet and, just before Lent 1463, she marched south again with de Breze and a force of French and Scottish mercenaries. Sir Ralph Percy allowed the Queen to take Bamburgh and Dunstanburgh castles which were both under his control while, on 1st May, Sir Ralph Grey opened Alnwick Castle's gates to the Lancastrian invaders. Queen Margaret now held the county of Northumberland once more, setting up her headquarters at Bamburgh Castle. The Northern population, however, had begun to feel the benefits of Yorkist rule and was far from delighted at this return to war and strife under the Lancastrian yoke. Meanwhile, in London, there was horror at the speed and success of the Lancastrian invasion. The Earl of Warwick was sent north again and, on 1st June, his brother, Lord Montagu was made Warden of the Eastern March, the position traditionally held by a Percy.

Cannon balls found at the bottom of Alnwick Castle's Well in the Keep during restoration work in the 1760s, thought to have been jettisoned there by a fleeing garrison during the turbulent 1460s.

12　The Last Brother

Queen Margaret became aware that Edward IV was attempting to negotiate a treaty with Louis XI which would close France to Lancastrian exiles and diminish her military support. A possible tripartite treaty between France, Burgundy and King Edward would spell disaster and she determined to negotiate with Duke Philip of Burgundy to gain his support. Both King Louis and Duke Philip were offering potential brides to King Edward but he did not respond to either, although, given a choice, he was inclined towards friendship with France.

In June, Lord Montagu repelled a Lancastrian attack on Newcastle, and French ships laden with vital supplies for Queen Margaret were intercepted by Yorkist sailors. As the Yorkist army reasserted their supremacy, Lancastrian and Scottish forces besieging the Bishop of Durham's Castle at Norham, on the English side of the River Tweed, were put to flight after 18 days by the Earl of Warwick and Lord Montagu.

The Queen and her party were forced to flee across land through hostile territory back to Bamburgh. During this desperate escape, Margaret and her son were separated from the rest of the party and violently attacked by a band of robbers who stole her jewellery and threatened to torture and kill them. The Queen managed to persuade the robbers to spare them, whereupon 'Black Jack', the leader of the gang, was so moved by her story that he pledged his loyalty to her and led the royal party to a secret cave where they sheltered for two days until de Breze and his squire, Barville, found them. After bidding farewell to the gang, and pardoning them for the offences they had committed, the Queen's little group rode to Carlisle and then across the Border to Kircudbright. Unfortunately, an English spy called Cork, arranged to kidnap the Queen, de Breze and Barville there, put them in a boat

Bamburgh Castle, Northumberland

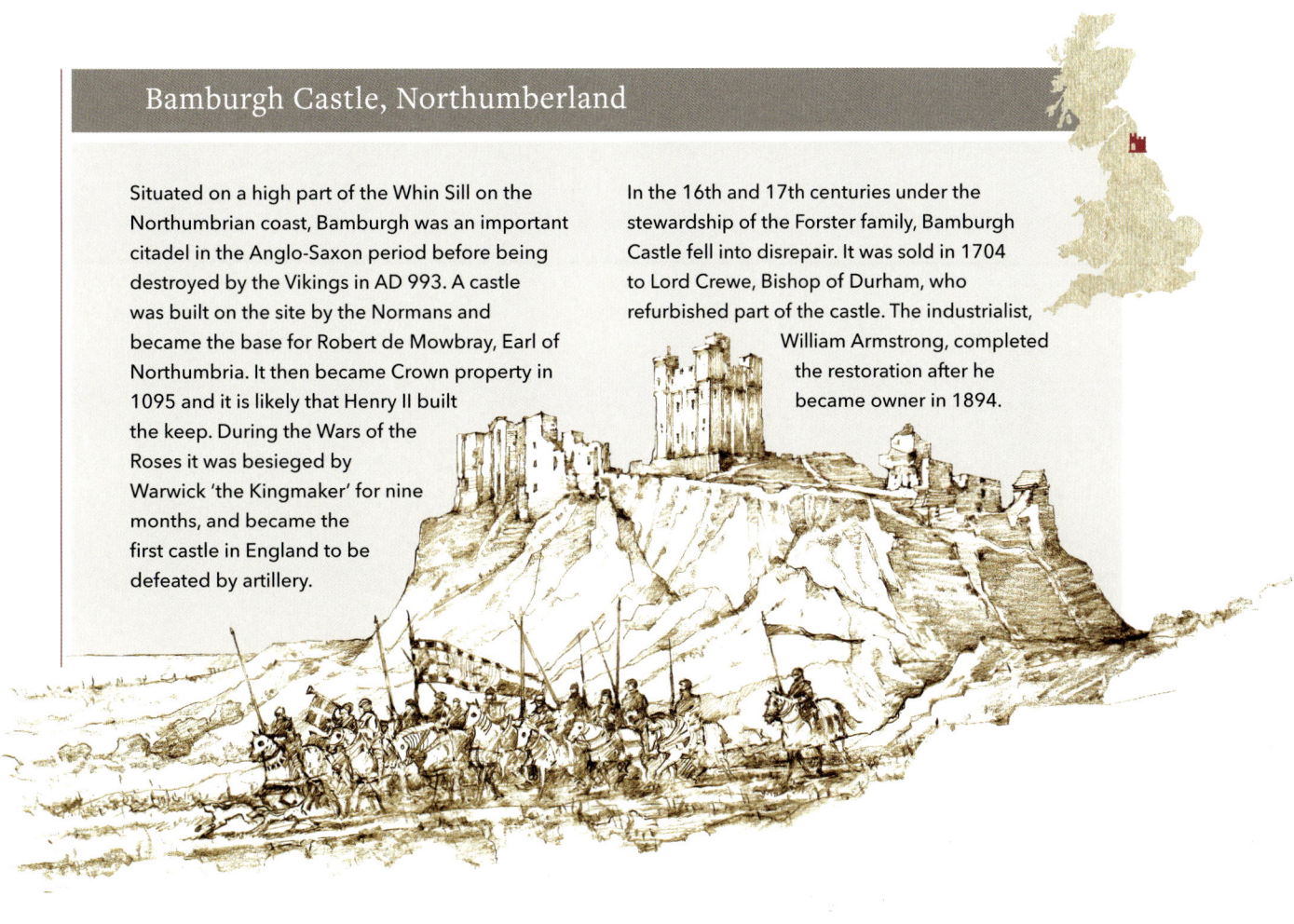

Situated on a high part of the Whin Sill on the Northumbrian coast, Bamburgh was an important citadel in the Anglo-Saxon period before being destroyed by the Vikings in AD 993. A castle was built on the site by the Normans and became the base for Robert de Mowbray, Earl of Northumbria. It then became Crown property in 1095 and it is likely that Henry II built the keep. During the Wars of the Roses it was besieged by Warwick 'the Kingmaker' for nine months, and became the first castle in England to be defeated by artillery.

In the 16th and 17th centuries under the stewardship of the Forster family, Bamburgh Castle fell into disrepair. It was sold in 1704 to Lord Crewe, Bishop of Durham, who refurbished part of the castle. The industrialist, William Armstrong, completed the restoration after he became owner in 1894.

and put to sea. Somehow, the Queen managed to free de Breze who knocked Cork senseless and seized the oars. The boat was eventually beached at Kircudbright Bay and de Breze gallantly carried the Queen ashore.

While in Scotland, Queen Margaret met Queen Mary who informed her that the promised betrothal of Prince Edward to Margaret Stewart had been cancelled at Burgundy's request. The only aid that Queen Mary would now offer was to help the impoverished Queen of England return to the county of Northumberland. The destitute and starving group arrived at Bamburgh Castle, but the redoubtable Queen was soon sailing off to France with de Breze, the Duke of Exeter, Lord Fortescue, the Scottish Earl of Morton and 200 men, in four fishing vessels, to try and garner support from Duke Philip of Burgundy. King Henry VI, meanwhile, made his way to Berwick.

Queen Margaret's desperate adventures continued with the vessels being badly damaged in a storm before landing at Sluys in Flanders. She sent a messenger to Duke Philip who was initially reluctant to see her, perhaps considering her to be an expensive embarrassment. However, he eventually met up with Queen Margaret and supplied her with enough money to survive. Her father, the impoverished King Rene of Anjou, persuaded her that a return to England was too dangerous and lent her his castle of Koeur-la-Petite where she established a court of exiles and set about the education of her son, the last hope for a Lancastrian revival.

In early December 1463, Edward IV made a truce with James III of Scotland, one of the conditions being that Scotland would no longer give any help to the Lancastrians. On 8th December, the unwelcome Henry VI crossed the Border once more and took up residence in Bamburgh Castle, where he ruled over a few Northumbrian castles. Meanwhile, having had his attainder reversed, the Duke of Somerset was given a senior place at court by Edward IV. He seemed to immerse himself in Yorkist England but, frustrated at Edward's failure to pay the pension that had been promised, and guilty of his own abandonment of Queen Margaret and King Henry, he suddenly deserted Edward and made his way to Newcastle. He was almost captured in Durham and was forced to flee and make his way to Queen Margaret's court in Northern France, where he was welcomed and readily forgiven by the Queen.

The early months of 1464 saw renewed Lancastrian activity, with Jasper Tudor, Earl of Pembroke, trying to rouse support in Wales, while the Duke of Somerset and Sir Ralph Percy stirred up rebellion in Northumberland. A raiding party from Alnwick Castle ventured south into Yorkist territory and took Skipton Castle, while Henry VI rode successfully into Lancashire to raise support there. The Lancastrians were soon strong enough to launch successful raids on Bywell, Langley and Hexham castles

Bywell Castle

and there were minor risings in East Anglia, Gloucestershire, Cheshire, Lancashire, Staffordshire and Wales, all brutally suppressed by King Edward.

Queen Margaret now attempted to get the Duke of Brittany to support her, and the Earl of Pembroke persuaded him to provide ships and men for an invasion of Wales. However, the suppression of all Lancastrian risings forced Pembroke to turn back and abort the invasion. Meanwhile, the Earl of Warwick persuaded King Edward that, for him to establish order in the North, he had to convert the Scottish Truce into a permanent peace. In April, Lord Montagu headed north to meet Scottish envoys at Norham and escort them to the City of York but Sir Ralph Percy, the Duke of Somerset, Lords Roos and Hungerford, Humphrey Neville and Sir Ralph Grey tried to ambush him, hiding men with spears and bows in a wood near Newcastle. Montagu had been alerted to the danger, however, by his scouts; he avoided the trap and continued on his journey.

Norham Castle

On St Mark's Day, 25th April, at Hedgeley Moor near Alnwick, Lord Montagu's route was blocked by the Lancastrians' relatively small army and a fierce battle ensued. Before long, however, Lords Roos and Hungerford, seeing that the battle was going badly, panicked and fled with their men, followed swiftly by the Duke of Somerset who galloped off to Alnwick. Though greatly outnumbered by the encircling foe, Sir Ralph Percy and his men remained, fighting bravely to the end. According to Brenan: 'In compact files they calmly awaited the Yorkist onfall, protecting by this heroic stand the wild flight of Somerset and his army...'

Tradition recounts that Percy charged his foe, urging his horse to make a prodigious leap of nearly 30 feet, perhaps across a defensive ditch. In the battle Sir Ralph was mortally wounded, uttering in his dying breath his famous last words, 'I have saved the bird in my bosom', taken to mean that by his death in battle for the Lancastrians, he had kept his original oath of allegiance to Henry VI.

Thus died the last of the four Percy brothers that had fought valiantly for Henry VI and his Queen. Sir Ralph's acquiescence with Yorkist rule may have marred his reputation but his heroic death certainly restored it.

Percy's Leap Survey drawing, c. 1806. The location was marked for posterity by two large whinstones. Road widening at the end of the 18th century caused the destruction of one of the stones, but a surviving fragment was set into a wall, preserving the distance. By 1819, however, the wall was removed and the great whinstone was 'in a great measure blasted to pieces.' Today a walled enclosure with information panels stands at the site by the side of the A697.

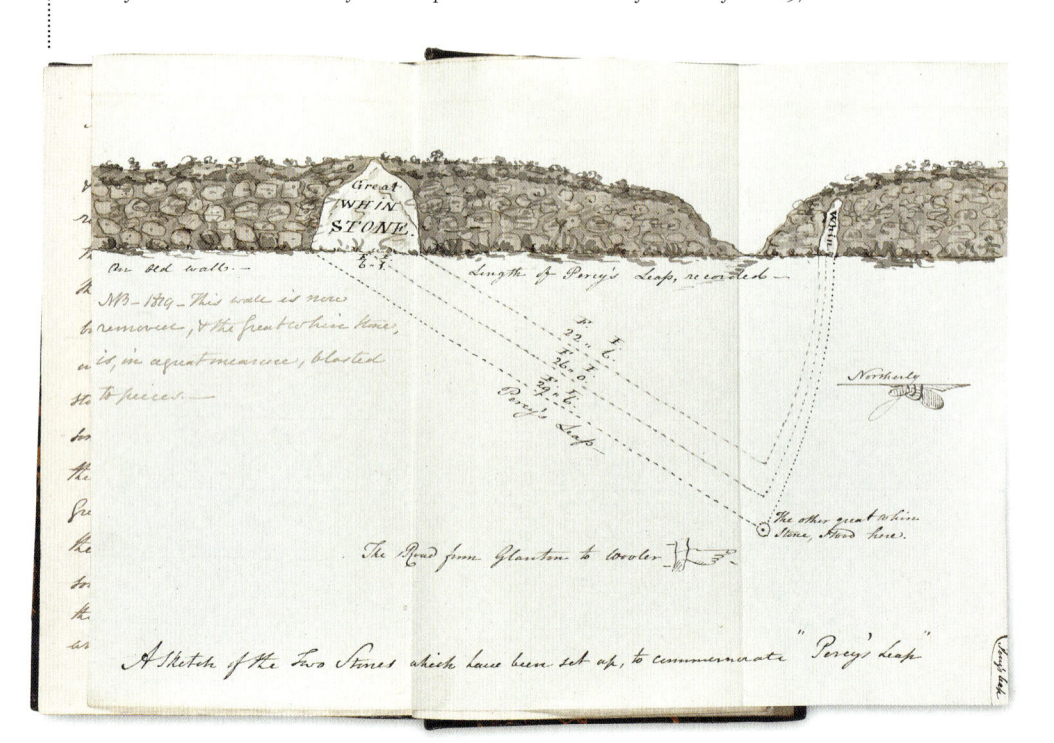

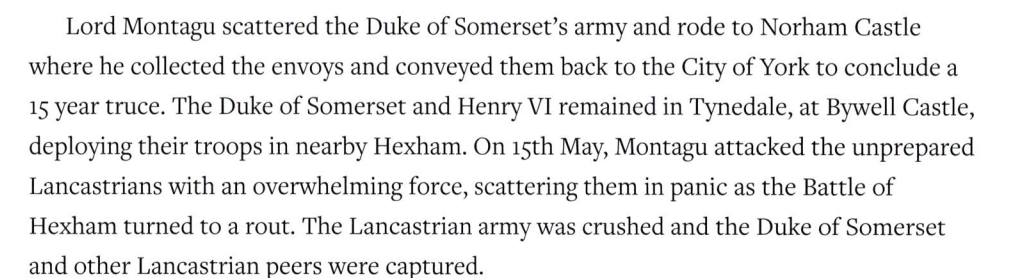

SOMERSET

PERCY

HUNGERFORD

ROOS

MONTAGU

Lord Montagu scattered the Duke of Somerset's army and rode to Norham Castle where he collected the envoys and conveyed them back to the City of York to conclude a 15 year truce. The Duke of Somerset and Henry VI remained in Tynedale, at Bywell Castle, deploying their troops in nearby Hexham. On 15th May, Montagu attacked the unprepared Lancastrians with an overwhelming force, scattering them in panic as the Battle of Hexham turned to a rout. The Lancastrian army was crushed and the Duke of Somerset and other Lancastrian peers were captured.

In accordance with King Edward's wishes, Somerset was beheaded immediately after the battle and his remains interred in Hexham Priory. Hungerford, Roos and three others were executed on 17th May. Other Lancastrian nobles were executed at Middleham, York and Hexham over the next few weeks.

King Henry VI was nearly captured by the Yorkists after the Battle of Hexham but, as

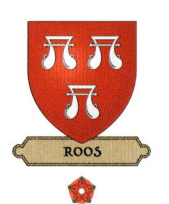

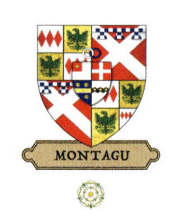

Left: Helmet said to have been worn by the Duke of Somerset at the Battle of Hexham, now in the Hexham Gaol Museum.

90 LIONS OF THE RED ROSE

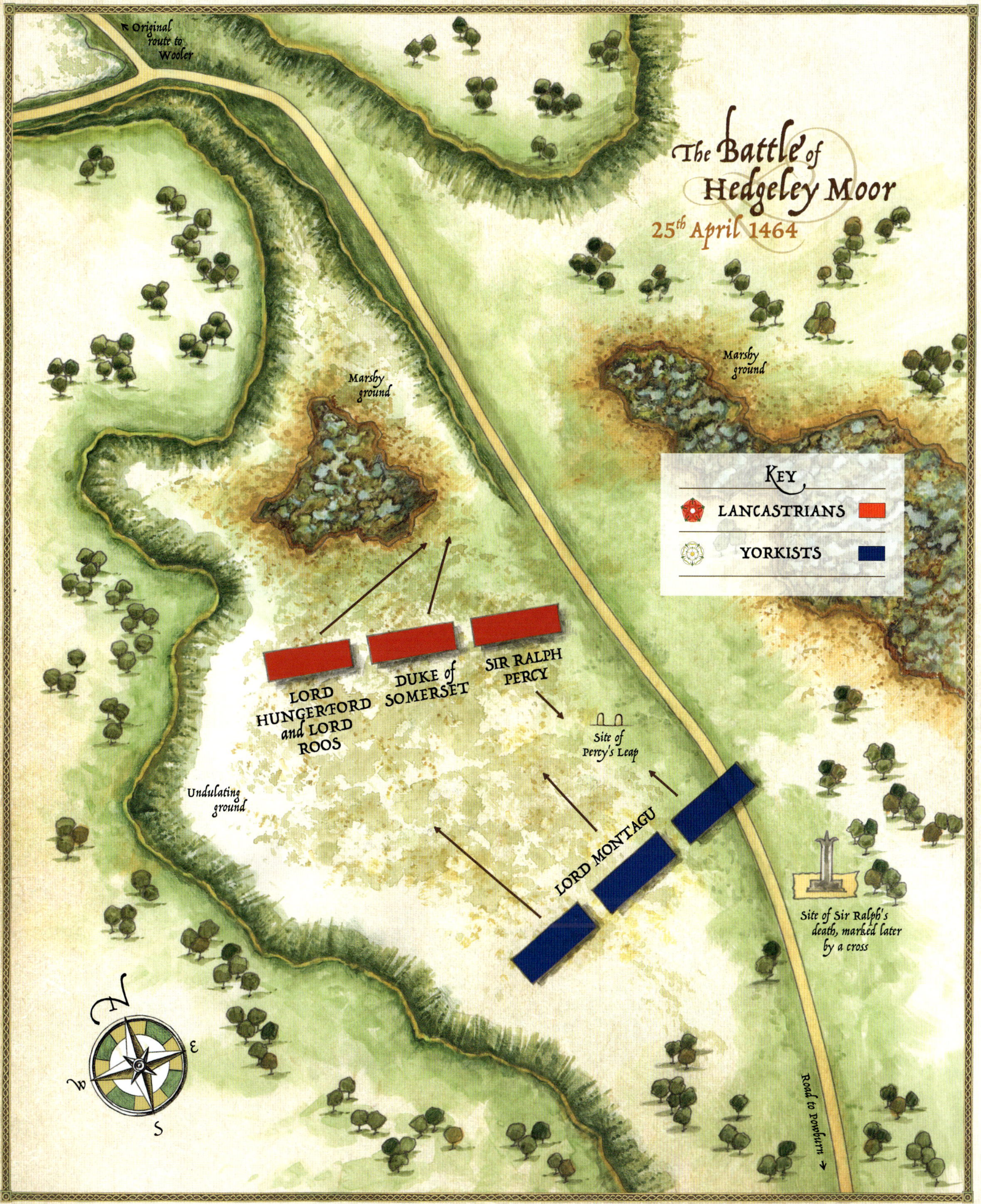
The Battle of Hedgeley Moor
25th April 1464
Original route to Wooler
Marshy ground
Marshy ground
KEY
LANCASTRIANS
YORKISTS
LORD HUNGERFORD and LORD ROOS
DUKE of SOMERSET
SIR RALPH PERCY
Site of Percy's Leap
Undulating ground
LORD MONTAGU
Site of Sir Ralph's death, marked later by a cross
Road to Powburn
N
E
S
W

soldiers rushed to grab him at Bywell Castle, he fled, leaving his helmet, sword and armour behind. He remained a fugitive for more than a year, hiding in safe houses in Lancashire, Yorkshire and Westmorland. In recognition of military success, King Edward gave Lord Montagu the Earldom of Northumberland and granted him most of the Percys' ancestral lands, although Alnwick Castle remained Lancastrian until 23rd June when the Earl of Warwick appeared before its gates and demanded its surrender. The garrison capitulated and thereby saved their lives, but Alnwick Castle and much of the Percy lands and titles were now in the hands of the Nevilles. Sir Ralph Grey refused to surrender Bamburgh Castle, but it was breached by Warwick's artillery and Grey was taken prisoner and later beheaded. All of England was now in Edward's hands, thanks mainly to the Earl of Warwick and his brother John, now Earl of Northumberland, who had simultaneously and effectively destroyed their Northern rivals.

While England enjoyed five years of peace after the Battle of Hexham, there were simmering signs of dissent in the Yorkist court. King Edward's secret marriage to Elizabeth Woodville, apparently the only woman to refuse his advances without a wedding ring on her finger, infuriated Warwick, who had been close to arranging a marriage between Edward IV and Princess Bona of Savoy, and exasperated other English diplomats who were also striving to forge marital alliances. Offers of marriage came from various quarters including France and Castile, with important potential benefits to England, but they were all thwarted by the King's apparent lust for this attractive but 'unsuitable' bride. Elizabeth's mother was the daughter of the French Count of St Pol but her father, the relatively humble Sir Richard Woodville, was the son of the Duke of Bedford's chamberlain. King Edward gave his new father-in-law the title Earl Rivers and, since the King had lost his own father while still a teenager, he welcomed paternal advice. Between them they planned to marry the King's 19 year old sister Margaret to Charles of Charolais, Philip of Burgundy's heir, sealing an alliance with England's largest overseas market.

The Earl of Warwick considered himself to be Edward IV's principal foreign adviser but he was not privy to these negotiations and was following a different diplomatic path, involving the marriage of Princess Margaret to Philip of Savoy, the brother-in-law of Louis XI, an arrangement that would come with lucrative trade deals and a potentially long peace with England's oldest enemy.

Portrait of Elizabeth Woodville, late 16th century copy of an earlier painting.

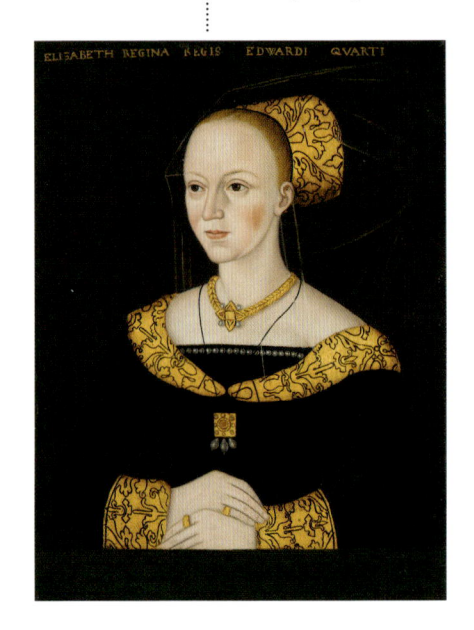

He became aware that he had been sent to negotiate with France to get him out of the way while King Edward and Earl Rivers entertained Burgundian envoys, and when the King announced a strengthened alliance with Burgundy and a pact with Castile, another enemy of France, Warwick felt humiliated and rode north to his Yorkshire estates in a blind fury. Warwick's anger was probably justified as the King's risky foreign policy slowly unravelled. The wedding of Princess Margaret to Charles of Charolais was postponed while King Edward desperately tried to raise the downpayment on the vast dowry. His truces with Scotland, Burgundy and Brittany, which gained him the hearty approval of Parliament and enough tax money to launch an invasion of France, were thwarted by King Louis who made peace with Brittany and Burgundy. An invasion was now impossible and King Edward's expensive navy was left aimlessly drifting about in the English Channel.

The divergence in foreign policy between Edward IV and the Earl of Warwick created terminal friction between the two men. The King continued to negotiate with Burgundy and Brittany while Warwick maintained his relationship with King Louis of France who had no intention of allowing the King of England to form alliances with his foes. However, he was losing faith in Warwick's ability to control King Edward.

Percy's Cross, marking the spot where Sir Ralph Percy died uttering his famous last words about the 'bird in his bosom' (the earliest instance cited for use of this phrase, meaning an 'oath', 'secret' or 'one's conscience'). Shown in its original form with decorative top, the cross was probably erected by Sir Ralph's nephew, the 4th Earl of Northumberland, and according to tradition, annual sports of football and cudgel playing were held there. Drawing, 26 October 1819.

12 / THE LAST BROTHER

13 The Kingmaker Turns

Elizabeth Woodville was crowned in Westminster Abbey by the Archbishop of Canterbury on Whit Sunday 1465. Her influence over King Edward was overwhelming and it wasn't long before the favoured Woodvilles, and those close to them, rose dramatically in rank, to the dismay of the Earl of Warwick and many barons who saw their own influence decline as that of the Queen's family increased. The Queen's brother, Anthony, was already titled Lord Scales thanks to marriage to an heiress while her younger brothers, Lionel and Edward, began their climb to high office. Her sister Margaret was engaged to Lord Maltravers, son and heir of the Earl of Arundel and, in January 1465, her 19 year old brother John married the dowager Duchess of Norfolk, a thrice married woman of around 67 (who still managed to outlive her young husband by 14 years). King Edward arranged for the Queen's sister Katherine to marry Henry Stafford, the young Duke of Buckingham, who was less than thrilled at the prospect of marrying so far beneath him. Other sisters also married nobles: Anne married Viscount Bourchier, Eleanor married Lord Grey de Ruthin's son, Mary married William Herbert, heir to Lord Herbert, Jacquetta married Lord Strange and Martha married John Bromley. The marriage market was thus dominated by Woodvilles, increasing Warwick's resentment as he needed to find suitable husbands for his two daughters, Isabel and Anne. The King's brothers, George and Richard, would have been Warwick's choices, but King Edward forbade these matches, preferring to forge more useful international alliances.

In the spring of 1466, Edward dismissed the Earl of Warwick's uncle, Lord Mountjoy, from the role of Treasurer of England, replacing him with Earl Rivers. For Warwick this was bad enough but, in October that year, Thomas Grey, the Queen's son from her previous marriage, was married to Anne Holland, daughter

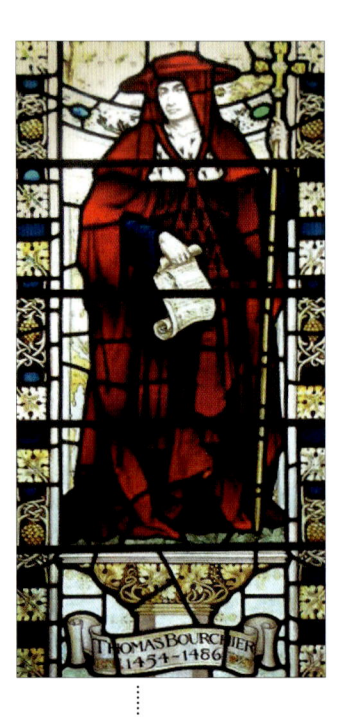

Thomas Bourchier, Archbishop of Canterbury and Cardinal, depicted wearing a cardinal's hat. 1909 stained glass, Sevenoaks Church, Kent.

of the Duke of Exeter and his duchess, the King's sister, Anne Plantagenet. Edward had paid the Duchess 4000 marks to break a previous betrothal between Anne and the son of Warwick's brother John, now Earl of Northumberland, infuriating both Nevilles. The Woodvilles resented the Neville Earls of Warwick and Northumberland, mainly because of the influence they still held over the King, and the Queen did all she could to undermine their positions. Although they had the King's full support, the Woodvilles were resented by both nobles and commoners for their arrogance and undeserved ascent from relative obscurity. Even the court jester dared to joke, in Edward's presence, that 'the Rivers run so high that it is impossible to get through them.'

Meanwhile, the deposed King Henry had been on the run with his loyal companion, Tunstall, moving from one safe house to another in the north of England. In July 1465, they stayed with Sir Richard Tempest at Waddington Hall in Lancashire, close to the Yorkshire border. Although Sir Richard was fervently loyal to King Henry, another guest in the house, a 'black monk of Abingdon', recognised Henry and told Sir Richard's brother John, a loyal Yorkist, who rode to his brother's house with two companions and challenged the deposed Lancastrian king to reveal himself. A scuffle broke out and Tunstall and Henry ran from the house, only to be hunted down by John Tempest's men and captured whilst trying to ford the River Ribble. When Edward IV heard this news while in Kent, he ordered that a service of thanksgiving be held in Canterbury Cathedral. On 24th July, Henry VI, escorted by the Earl of Warwick, rode into London on a small horse, with his legs bound with leather thongs to his stirrups, a rope lashing him to his saddle, and a straw hat on his head. Crowds gathered, hurling abuse and pelting him with rubbish and stones until he reached his destination, the Tower of London. News of his capture came as a terrible blow to Queen Margaret whose hopes for a Lancastrian revival, even if she could persuade France or Burgundy to support her, were overwhelmed by the desire to protect King Henry, whose life now depended on her good behaviour.

Perhaps to appease the Earl of Warwick, his brother, George Neville, was created Archbishop of York by King Edward, although neither he nor his queen attended the enthronement on 28th September 1465, adding to speculation of a rift between the King and Warwick. In January,

Fotheringhay Castle, Northamptonshire

This castle in Northamptonshire was built in the 12th century and fell into King John's hands in the early 13th century. In 1385, Edward III gave it to his son, Edmund of Langley, Duke of York, who spent considerable time there. It descended to Richard, 3rd Duke of York, and became his favourite residence; it was the birthplace of King Richard III. After York's death, his wife Cecily continued to live there and Elizabeth Woodville, Edward IV's queen, resided there in 1469. In 1482 Edward IV made a treaty there with the Duke of Albany to overthrow the Duke's brother, James III of Scotland. Fotheringhay Castle became a state prison and Mary, Queen of Scots spent her last days there before her execution in the castle's Great Hall in 1587. The castle became a ruin and was demolished in the 17th century.

LIONS OF THE RED ROSE

Warwick became desperate about his future relationship with King Louis and he wanted the French King to believe that his influence with Edward IV was still strong enough to turn the latter away from Burgundy and restore friendly relations with France. As a last resort, he forged a letter from King Edward to Louis, denying any intention of invading France or hindering the King in his suppression of rebellion in Normandy. This was a clear act of treason. Fortunately for Warwick, the King was unaware and rode to Fotheringhay Castle to attend the reinterment of his father, Richard of York, and his brother, the Earl of Rutland who had both fallen at Wakefield, as well as Edward, Duke of York who had been killed at Agincourt.

Soon after, in Westminster, King Edward's queen gave birth to a girl, and Warwick, surprisingly, was made godfather.

In April, King Edward sent Warwick to Calais to meet Duke Charles of Burgundy and discuss the proposed alliance, but since Warwick strongly opposed it, the meeting was somewhat strained. Warwick then met King Louis of France and signed a two year truce, under which King Louis agreed not to support Queen Margaret and Edward IV promised not to support Burgundy or Brittany against the French. The King had agreed to this treaty as a sop to Warwick but had no intention of honouring it, and almost immediately offered safe conduct to the envoys of Francis II of Brittany, enabling them to come to England.

In October 1465, King Edward and Philip of Burgundy reached a private agreement to sign a treaty of friendship. On hearing this, Queen Margaret decided, despite her grave mistrust of Warwick, to seek his support for a Lancastrian invasion, perhaps helped with funding from France. However, the messenger that she sent was caught near Harlech by William Herbert's men and her letter was discovered. Under torture, the man revealed that the Queen sought the Earl of Warwick's help although Warwick fervently denied having any dealings with 'the foreign woman.' However, as King Edward grew closer to Burgundy, Warwick's relationship with the King, Queen Elizabeth and her family, reached breaking point and he threw in his lot with King Louis.

Until Edward IV produced a son, his brother George, Duke of Clarence, was heir presumptive. The King gave him the County of Chester and a generous income of around £3700 per annum, but Clarence was a petulant teenager, irritated by his brother's controlling hand which dictated much of his life, including marriage to a foreign princess, possibly Mary of Burgundy. The equally petulant Earl of Warwick was irritated that his daughter Isabel was being saved for a despised Woodville. He was aware of Clarence's jealousy, ambition and discontent, and planned to encourage those sentiments. In 1467, as Queen Elizabeth produced another daughter, Warwick started to nurture a conspiracy to put the 17 year old Duke of Clarence on the throne and, against the specific orders of the King, to marry Clarence to his daughter Isabel. In 1468 King Edward and Charles, the new Duke of Burgundy, signed the treaty providing for Charles's marriage to Margaret of York. The King then concluded an alliance with Brittany, finally dashing Warwick's remaining hopes for an alliance with France. The final straw for Warwick was the elevation of Lord Herbert, a friend of the Woodvilles, who had defeated Jasper Tudor and taken Harlech Castle during the abortive Lancastrian uprising in Wales. The King's gift of Tudor's former title, the Earl of Pembroke, to Herbert, was a clear and present danger to Warwick's power and influence.

The Earl of Warwick and the Duke of Clarence fomented discontent, spreading anti-Woodville propaganda and undermining Edward IV's rule which had clearly failed to live up to its early promise. In the spring of 1469, Louis XI promised to give Warwick the principalities of Holland and Zealand if he could bring about a coup that would overthrow King Edward. In May and June 1469, as the King's tax policies became increasingly unpopular, a rebellion erupted in Yorkshire under a leader called 'Robin of Redesdale,' the pseudonym of Sir William Conyers, brother of Sir John Conyers, the Earl of Warwick's deputy for his Yorkshire estates. Redesdale (the valley of the River Rede) was a barren, lawless, English region close to the Scottish Border, and the 'rebels' were

Portrait of George Plantagenet, Duke of Clarence, oil painting by Lucas Cornelisz de Kock, 16th century.

Left: Portrait of Margaret of York, sister of Edward IV and wife of Charles of Burgundy. Oil painting c. 1470.

ostensibly aggrieved at the government's misrule. The rebellion was, in reality, an insurgence instigated and probably funded by Warwick. John Neville, Earl of Northumberland, gave the appearance of stamping out this rebellion in Yorkshire, but the rebels fled to Lancashire where they were joined by another disenchanted group of rebels under 'Robin of Holderness' who championed, among other things, the restoration of a Percy earl. Since John Neville held this position, the likelihood of a Percy restoration was negligible, but subsequent events may have altered that perception and sown a seed in the King's mind that a loyal Percy earl would be a powerful Northern ally against an increasingly disloyal Neville faction. King Edward moved north to deal with what he considered to be a minor insurrection but, in Newark, on 10th July, discovered that a force of 'Redesdalers' three times the size of his own army was heading towards Coventry. Having requested Warwick's assistance, with no response, the King realised he had fallen into a trap and quickly retreated to the City of Nottingham, ordering the Earls of Pembroke and Devon to summon their substantial Welsh and West Country levies.

While this was going on, the Earl of Warwick had managed to purchase a dispensation from the Pope allowing his daughter Isabel to marry Clarence, so he announced the betrothal and sailed to Calais with the Archbishop of York who officiated at the wedding ceremony on 11th July. The following day, Warwick issued a manifesto from Calais, proclaiming that he and the Neville Archbishop of York had been urged by the King's true subjects to save his Grace from the 'deceivable and covetous rule and guiding of certain seditious persons', that he would petition the King for the removal of the 'evil counsellours', the Woodvilles, Pembroke and Devon, and urge him to pay heed to 'true lords of his blood'. In addition, it menacingly observed that favouritism had caused the deposition of Edward II, Richard II and Henry VI, implying that a similar fate could befall Edward IV. The manifesto ended with a plea for armed support from all true subjects of the King.

The wedding party returned to Canterbury on 16th July, where they were met by a significant force of armed supporters, ready to enact the Earl of Warwick's and the Duke of Clarence's coup. Clarence's mother, the Duchess of York, got wind of this treachery and desperately tried to dissuade her son from taking part, but he was obstinate and determined to see it through. Warwick's force secured London then marched north towards Coventry to rendezvous with the 'Redesdalers', now led by Sir John Conyers, while the King was obliged to wait at Nottingham for

Isabel Neville, as depicted in the armorial roll chronicle known as the 'Rous Roll', c. 1483.

Warwick Castle, Warwickshire

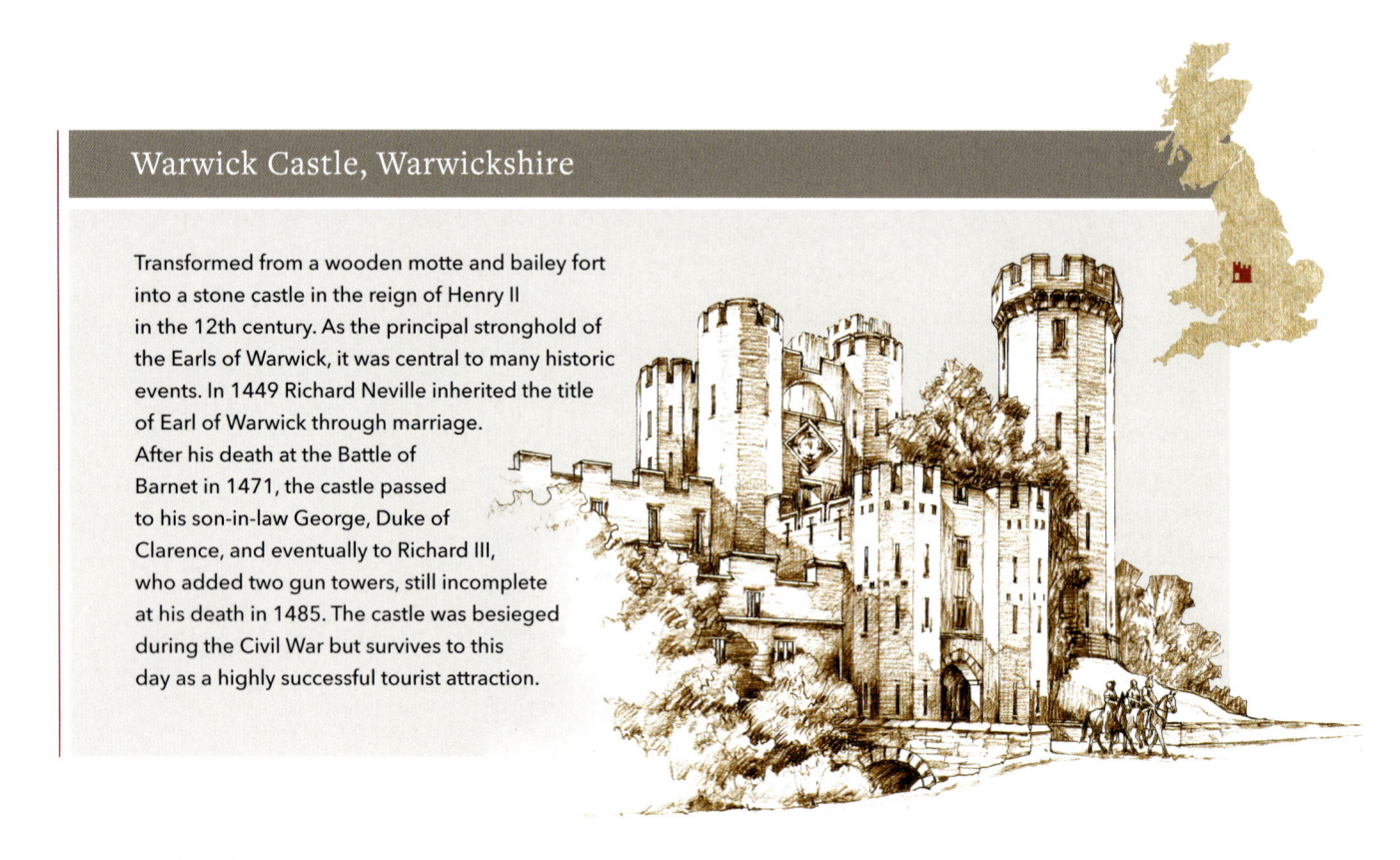

Transformed from a wooden motte and bailey fort into a stone castle in the reign of Henry II in the 12th century. As the principal stronghold of the Earls of Warwick, it was central to many historic events. In 1449 Richard Neville inherited the title of Earl of Warwick through marriage. After his death at the Battle of Barnet in 1471, the castle passed to his son-in-law George, Duke of Clarence, and eventually to Richard III, who added two gun towers, still incomplete at his death in 1485. The castle was besieged during the Civil War but survives to this day as a highly successful tourist attraction.

the Earls of Pembroke and Devon to reinforce his meagre army. On 24th July, they arrived at Banbury but quarrelled over who should have the best lodgings at the inn. The Earl of Devon arrived first, chose the best rooms, and seduced the innkeeper's daughter. On his arrival, the Earl of Pembroke, the senior commander, demanded that he should have those same lodgings so Devon marched off in a huff, with all his men. The next day, Pembroke rode back to Edgecote Hill, where his army was encamped. On 26th July, Warwick and Clarence attacked Pembroke's army and a vicious battle ensued. The Earl of Devon had rejoined Pembroke but, on seeing a force of 15,000 men from Kent and Calais heading towards Edgecote, he and his archers fled. As Warwick's reinforcements arrived, Pembroke's force was overwhelmed, and the Earl and his brother were captured and beheaded the next day.

King Edward waited, desperate for news of reinforcements, and finally left Nottingham on 29th July, only to be deserted by his entire army at Northampton, following news of the Earl of Pembroke's defeat. He dismissed all his lords except his brother Richard, Duke of Gloucester, and Lord Hastings who remained with him. King Edward was captured in the village of Olney near Northampton by George Neville, Archbishop of York, and sent to Warwick Castle. Two weeks later, the Earl of Devon was captured by the people of Somerset and Bridgwater, who removed his head, and then Warwick ordered the execution of Earl Rivers and John Woodville who had been hunted down and captured. By mid-August, Warwick 'the Kingmaker' was master of England and the Nevilles were in control. The temptation to execute the King must have been strong but Warwick and Clarence were not in a powerful enough position to do so without fear of reprisals, and they had not gathered enough support to depose Edward IV and put Clarence on the throne. Moreover, they could not keep the King imprisoned as this would be an act of treason, and the country could not be governed without a king.

Warwick and Clarence attempted to resolve this dilemma by keeping King Edward confined at Warwick Castle and trying to rule in his name, but they miscalculated the mood of the people and the majority of nobles who had no intention of seeing the Earl of Warwick extend his power even further. Fearing a rescue attempt, Warwick moved Edward at night to Middleham Castle, in the heart of Neville country, though even the Nevilles felt that 'the Kingmaker' might have overplayed his hand. The King, however, went along with this game, doing what he was told, signing everything that Warwick set before him, treating his captors with good humour whilst seething underneath. Within a few weeks, Warwick's authority was crumbling and the country was dissolving into anarchy in the absence of royal authority. Sir Humphrey Neville, who had been hiding in the Lake District since the Battle of Hexham, took the opportunity to raise Henry VI's standard and summon substantial numbers of Lancastrians to the cause. The Earl of Warwick rode north to suppress this rising but was unable to do so as his men threatened to desert unless they were assured of Edward IV's safety, and the magnates would not support him without the King's authority.

Warwick had no choice but to free the King, under certain conditions, and the effect was extraordinary. In the City of York, crowds turned out to cheers and fanfares and lords thronged around, eager to renew homage to their king. At Warwick's request,

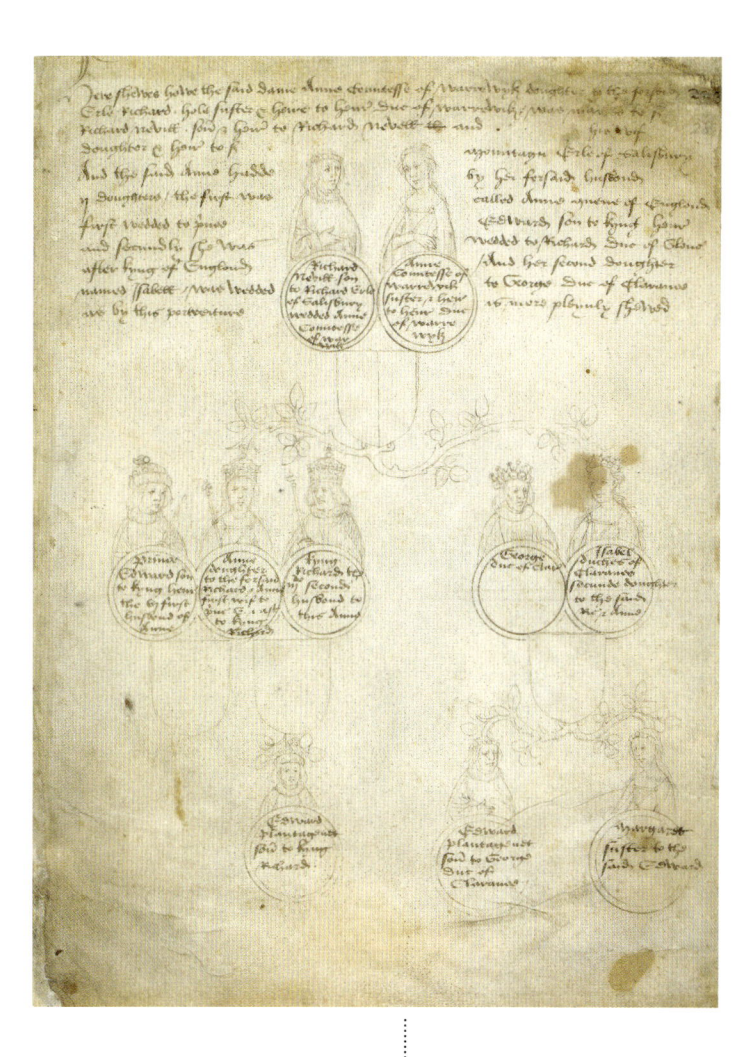

Drawing, c. 1483 of Anne, Countess of Warwick with her husband Richard Neville. Below is their elder daughter Anne, with her first husband Prince Edward, second husband King Richard III, and their son Edward; the younger daughter Isabel, with her husband the Duke of Clarence, and their children Edward and Margaret.

13 / THE KINGMAKER TURNS

York Castle

Edward IV summoned his lieges to arms and received an enthusiastic response. The royal army, commanded by Warwick, then crushed Sir Humphrey Neville's rebellion; the leader was captured and brought to the City of York where he was beheaded on 29th September. Inevitably, Warwick had to allow King Edward greater freedom, and the King subtly started shifting powers and responsibilities away from his captors. The Earl of Pembroke's Welsh offices were given to Richard, Duke of Gloucester, Edward IV's loyal youngest brother, and the Earldom of Wiltshire was given to John Stafford, the 1st Duke of Buckingham's younger son.

Henry Percy, under royal control since his father's death, became a pawn in the power struggle between Warwick and King Edward. The King had treated him well, wisely seeing him as a potential buffer against Neville dominance in the North, and Percy responded to this treatment, no doubt hoping that acquiescence might one day lead to the restoration of his titles and lands. He was 12 years old when his father was killed at the Battle of Towton and, though a prisoner, he had been immersed in Yorkist society since then. In 1467-8 Edward placed him into the care of William Herbert, Earl of Pembroke, who was also responsible for the young Henry Tudor. Pembroke's reports on Henry Percy would dictate the young man's future and it was clear that Percy was ostensibly loyal to the Yorkist regime. King Edward could never be quite sure that this last survivor of a slaughtered dynasty didn't retain some residue of Lancastrian sympathy, but others had no doubt as to his loyalty to Edward, particularly the Woodvilles who stood surety for his performance of fealty on 27th October 1469, when the 20 year old Percy swore the oath:

'I faith and truth shall bear to you as my sovereign liege lord...
of life and limb and of earthly worship,
for to live and die against all earthly people.'

At the beginning of March 1470, Lord Welles, a supporter of the Earl of Warwick, ignited some trouble in Lincolnshire which the King, Henry Percy, the Earl of Arundel and Lord Hastings easily extinguished. At Empingham, Edward IV overcame Sir Robert Welles, Lord Welles' son and, during the brief battle, war cries from the rebels, 'A Clarence!' and 'A Warwick!' revealed the true identity of

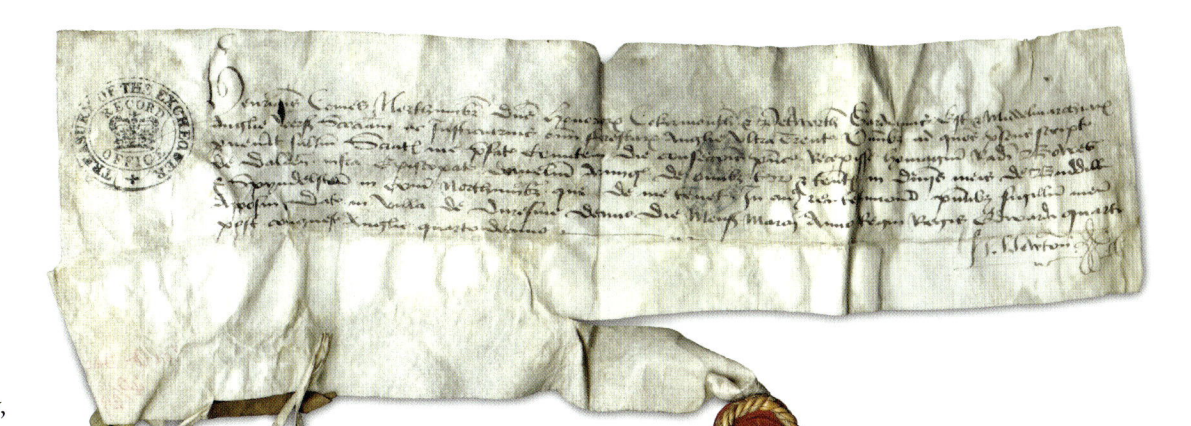

Receipt of homage by Henry, Earl of Northumberland, Lord of the honours of Cockermouth and Petworth, Warden of the East and Middle Marches, and Justice of all the Forests of England, from Ralph Bowes for tenements in Budle and Spindlestone. Dated at Durham, 10th March 1474. The seal has an edging of plaited straw to protect it.

the instigators. Sir Robert's capture, in Warwick's livery, clearly confirmed it. Furthermore, a casket was found on an envoy, containing correspondence between the Duke of Clarence and Sir Robert, detailing the Earl of Warwick's latest plan to trap King Edward at Leicester. Before his head was removed, Sir Robert confessed that Clarence and Warwick had put him up to it.

King Edward summoned Warwick and Clarence on 14th March but they ignored him and sped north, with the King in pursuit. He offered leniency but no pardon if they presented themselves to him before 28th March. If they failed to do so, they would be treated as traitors. While awaiting a response from Warwick, on 25th March, King Edward restored the Earldom of Northumberland to Henry Percy. He had laid the foundations for this momentous restoration by transferring substantial lands in south-west England to John Neville, whom he had previously made Earl of Northumberland. Neville was forced to surrender his claim to the Earldom and the Percy estates, and was compensated with the senior title of Marquess of Montagu. Henry Percy also received ancestral Percy lands held by the Duke of Clarence, without the latter's knowledge or consent. On 24th June, the new Earl of Northumberland was invested as Warden of the Eastern March for an initial five year contract. This clearly signified that, after a long period in the wilderness, the Percys were back.

John Neville, Marquess of Montagu, had fought the Percys for much of his life and was deeply unhappy with Edward's settlement which, in effect, retired him to a lush life in the South and allowed his enemies to take power in his homeland. He complained that the King had given him 'a magpie's nest' although Edward was completely unaware and believed that he had solved a thorny problem. Even the creation of Montagu's son, George, as Duke of Bedford, did not mollify Montagu, although resentment was assuaged by Edward's offer of the hand of his own eldest

The Earl of Warwick's ships anchored off Calais.

daughter, Elizabeth of York, as a bride for the new Duke. Should the Queen fail to produce a son, this could put Bedford on the throne when Edward died.

Warwick and Clarence failed to meet King Edward's deadline and, instead, they travelled to Southampton where one of Warwick's great ships, *The Trinity*, was expected to dock. King Edward had anticipated this and sent Lords Rivers and Howard to intercept them. They captured *The Trinity* and all Warwick's other ships and crews, forcing the fugitives to travel on to the Port of Exeter where they met up with the heavily pregnant Isabel, the Duchess of Clarence, and her mother, the Countess of Warwick. The Earl of Warwick commandeered a ship and they sailed for Calais on 3rd April. When the King discovered their escape, he took his fury out on the men who had been captured on Warwick's ships; 20 were hanged, drawn and quartered and, once dead, their corpses beheaded and mutilated.

Warwick's party arrived outside Calais where, to their surprise, they were fired upon by Warwick's deputy, Lord Wenlock, who was actually trying to warn them away from Calais as the Duke of Burgundy was lying in ambush, intending to capture the group and hand them over to King Edward. Being forced to remain at anchor outside Calais was terrible for Isabel who went into labour on 16th April, and although her mother saved her life after a difficult birth, the child died. Lord Wenlock sent wine over to the ship, containing a secret message advising Warwick that if he sailed along the coast, landed in Normandy and obtained aid from Louis XI, he and the Calais garrison would support him. Eventually they followed this advice and landed at Honfleur where they were granted refuge by King Louis, who sent the Admiral of France and the Archbishop of Narbonne to welcome them. King Louis sent messages of support for a campaign which would allow the Earl of Warwick to recover England and drive a wedge between England and Burgundy, but this would involve restoring Henry VI to the throne, a step too far for Warwick at this stage. When King Louis invited him and Queen Margaret to join him at Angers, Warwick initially refused. However, he realised that there was no rational alternative to throwing in his lot with the Lancastrians, supported by the might of France and, on 22nd July 1470, Warwick met the 'foreign woman', the queen that he had dethroned and abused, and begged her forgiveness. She made him kneel for fifteen minutes and pledge to do the same publicly in Westminster Abbey. Three days later, Warwick's second daughter, Anne, was betrothed to Prince Edward of Lancaster.

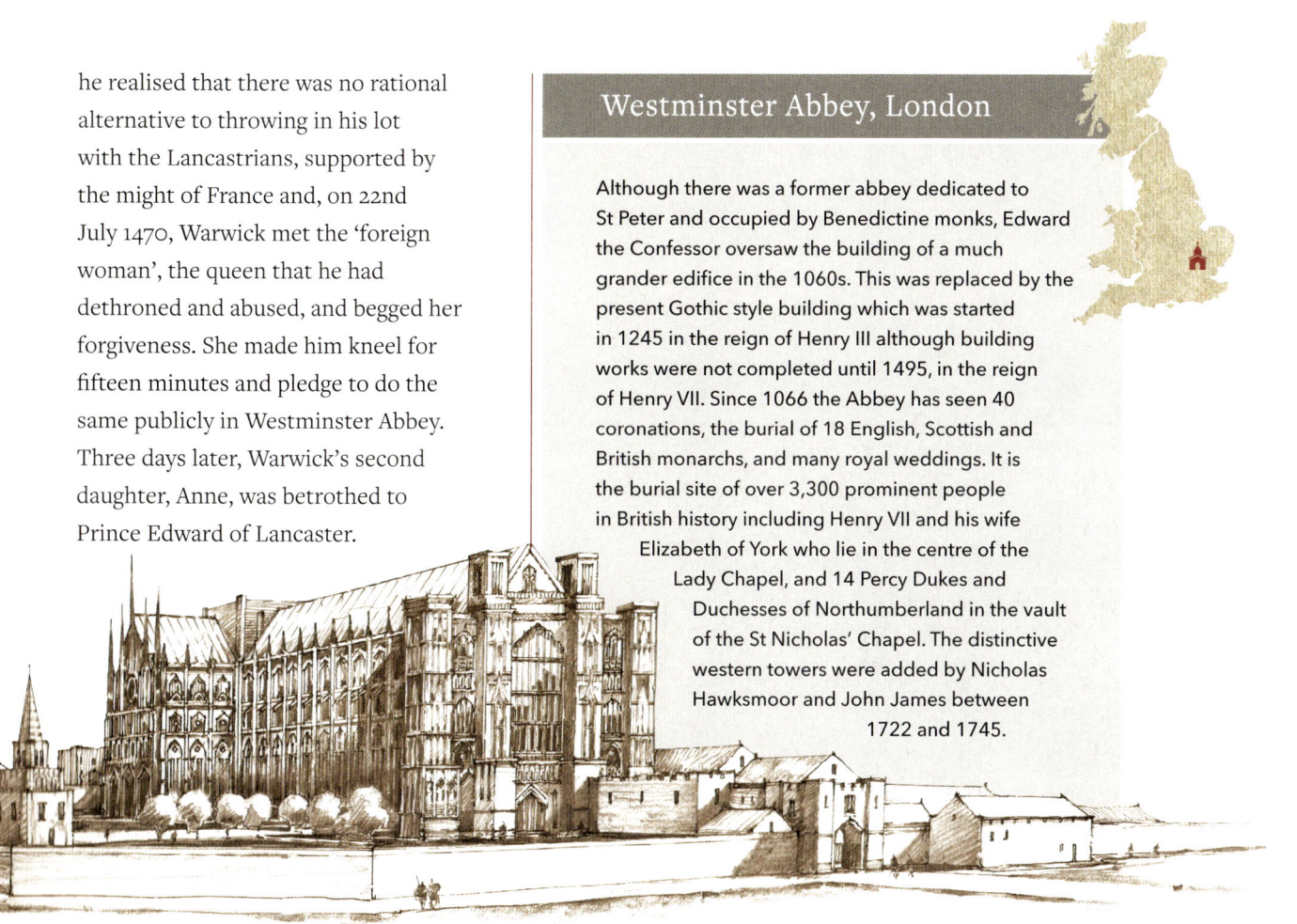

Westminster Abbey, London

Although there was a former abbey dedicated to St Peter and occupied by Benedictine monks, Edward the Confessor oversaw the building of a much grander edifice in the 1060s. This was replaced by the present Gothic style building which was started in 1245 in the reign of Henry III although building works were not completed until 1495, in the reign of Henry VII. Since 1066 the Abbey has seen 40 coronations, the burial of 18 English, Scottish and British monarchs, and many royal weddings. It is the burial site of over 3,300 prominent people in British history including Henry VII and his wife Elizabeth of York who lie in the centre of the Lady Chapel, and 14 Percy Dukes and Duchesses of Northumberland in the vault of the St Nicholas' Chapel. The distinctive western towers were added by Nicholas Hawksmoor and John James between 1722 and 1745.

Initially, the Duke of Clarence did not appreciate that the plot to replace King Edward IV with King Henry VI more or less removed him from his royal ambitions, preferring to believe that Warwick was loyal to him and would quickly get rid of King Henry, Queen Margaret and Prince Edward when the time was right. Queen Margaret, who trusted Warwick so little that she refused to sail with her son on the same ship as him, planned to ditch him as soon as he had served her purpose, while King Louis was happy to use all of them as pawns to overthrow the English government.

14 The End of the Nevilles and Murder of a King

The plan for the Lancastrian restoration was hardly original: first a rebellion would be started in the North to lure King Edward out of London, then the Lancastrians would land in the South-West, gain support from those like Jasper Tudor who remained loyal to the cause and powerful in their region, then march north-east towards Warwick's strongholds in the Midlands while the Northern army marched south to catch and crush King Edward in a vice. In late July, Warwick instigated rebellions in Yorkshire and Cumberland using veteran 'Redesdalers' and previous retainers of the Marquess of Montagu who were now without a chief or income. Edward IV took this threat seriously and though he suspected a simultaneous invasion from France, he rushed north to deal with it. As he appeared, the rebels dispersed, but he stayed in the North for a few weeks to ensure the rebellion really was extinct, and to support the inexperienced and somewhat shaken Henry Percy, 4th Earl of Northumberland.

The King appeared relaxed about potential invasion from the continent as the Burgundian fleet was blockading the Earl of Warwick's ships. However, a violent storm dispersed the blockade and Warwick

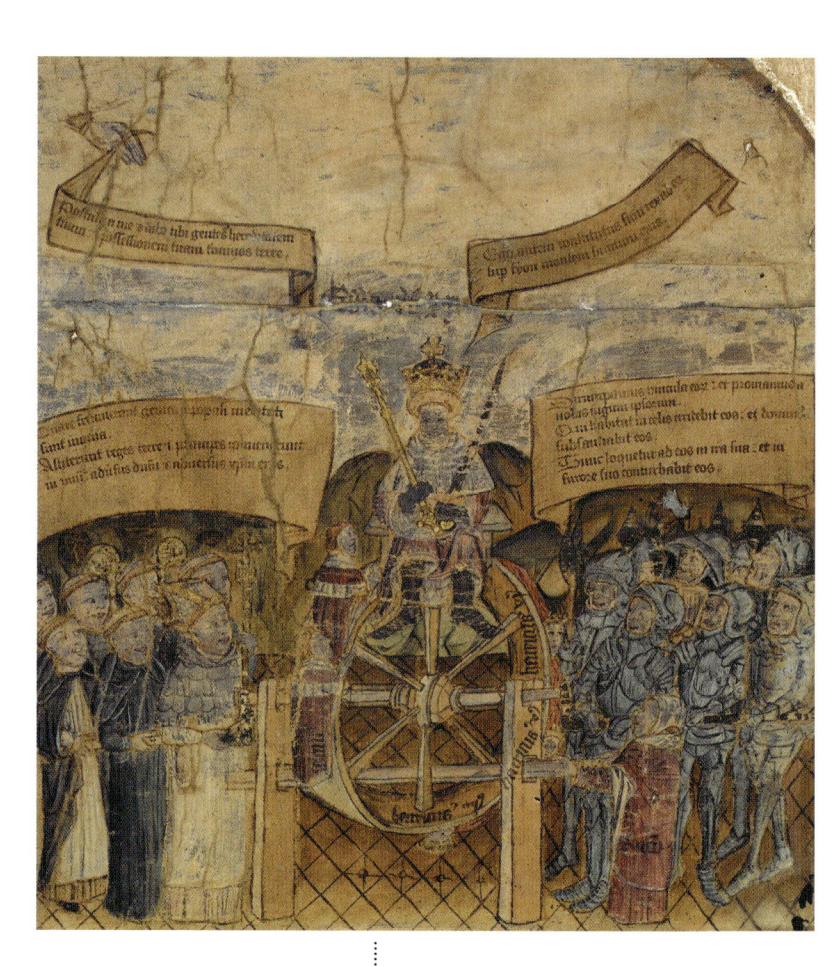

King Edward IV on Fortune's Wheel, flanked by the Dukes of Clarence and Gloucester and representatives of the Church and Army. From an illuminated manuscript of the 1460s.

was able to launch his invasion from Normandy. A royal fleet sent out to prevent him from landing was scattered in the storm and, on 13th September, Warwick unexpectedly landed in Devon and immediately marched north towards the Midlands with the Duke of Clarence, Jasper Tudor, the Earl of Oxford and Thomas Neville, collecting Lord Stanley and the Earl of Shrewsbury on the way. King Edward naively counted on Montagu's support, asking him to raise the Northern levies and follow him to fight Warwick, but Montagu declared support for his brother and turned his army on the King. With two armies now bearing down on him, King Edward knew that defeat was inevitable and capture meant likely execution, so he released his army with great sadness and fled east with some of his commanders. In Bishop's Lynn they boarded two heavily laden Dutch hulks that were lying at anchor, ready to sail. In return for 'a goodly gown furred with martens', as King Edward carried no money, the master of the ships took them aboard and sailed to Holland, and into the welcoming arms of Charles, Duke of Burgundy. Queen Elizabeth, meanwhile, was still in London where she sought sanctuary in Westminster Abbey. She was given fine rooms by the Abbot, Thomas Mylling, and there she gave birth to her first royal son, another Edward. This encouraged the Earl of Warwick to write to Queen Margaret urging her and her son to come to England, as the birth of Elizabeth's son was an existential threat to the security of the restored Lancastrian dynasty, or 'Readeption' as it was known.

Tower of London

On 6th October, King Henry VI was released from the Tower of London. This sad and pathetic figure was cleaned up and placed on the throne of England once more, as Warwick's limp and trembling puppet. Henry may have been weak but he showed great kindness to Edward IV's queen, sending beef and mutton to her sanctuary. On 26th November the Readeption parliament disinherited and attainted Edward IV and the Duke of Gloucester, and reversed attainders on Lancastrian nobles such as Jasper Tudor, the Dukes of Exeter and Somerset and the Earl of Ormond.

Edward was not going to renounce his crown so soon, and sought Burgundy's vital support for an invasion. But Duke Charles of Burgundy argued that the Anglo-Burgundian Alliance was with the King of England and that, for the moment, was Henry VI, so he initially baulked from supplying Edward with the help that he required. However, Duke Charles's attempts to negotiate with Warwick were rebuffed and, on 10th December, King Louis XI of France repudiated his treaty of friendship with Burgundy and planned to crush Duke Charles, with Warwick's help. Duke Charles therefore began privately funding Edward's campaign and enabled him to set sail from Flushing harbour on 2nd March 1471, with 36 ships, about 1000 Englishmen and 300 Flemish mercenaries, who were experts with handguns. After delays due to adverse weather, they were unable to land on the East Anglian coast, as planned, as the Earl of Oxford's men were waiting for them. They headed further north but, while at sea, another storm separated the fleet and Edward IV's lone vessel landed at Ravenspur on the Humber on 14th March, at the same place where Henry Bolingbroke had stepped ashore in 1399 to take the Crown from Richard II. Fortunately, the other vessels landed safely nearby and the men joined together at Ravenspur where Edward burned his boat to make clear that there was no going back. It wasn't long, however, before a small army rose against him under a local vicar, supported by a captain called John Westerdale and another fellow called 'Martin of the Sea'. Edward managed to persuade this motley leadership that, like Bolingbroke 72 years earlier, he sought only the duchy held by his father, not the Crown. Aware that he was close to Percy territory, where loyalties now lay almost exclusively with the Earl of Northumberland, he claimed that he enjoyed the support of the Earl, and

Portrait of Henry Percy, 4th Earl of Northumberland, English School, mid-18th century.

displayed letters under the Earl's seal, which invited him to return to England.

Since many locals had recently suffered under Yorkist rule, just as they had previously experienced deprivation from Lancastrian armies, his popularity could not be guaranteed, so this low-key return was sensible. The Earl of Northumberland could have levied an army and destroyed Edward's dreams of restoration if revenge for his father's death was on his mind, but he made no move, one way or the other. Instead, he hedged his bets and waited for a result, perhaps suspecting that the Duke of Clarence had put spies into the households of his and other suspected sympathisers of his brothers, Edward and Richard. Moreover, a Yorkist restoration could mean further reward for the Earl of Northumberland, even if that just meant the removal of a few Neville heads. If Edward failed, Northumberland could honestly state that he played no part in the rebellion. On 25th March, the small Yorkist army crossed the Trent, heading for the Midlands. At the City of Leicester, Lord Hastings arrived with 3000 soldiers. Soon after, two wealthy knights arrived with 600 heavily armed troops and, a week later, leading a force of about 6000 men, Edward IV publicly declared himself King of England once more.

Meanwhile, the Earl of Warwick was in the City of Coventry, awaiting assistance from the Earl of Oxford and Duke of Clarence. The Yorkist army bypassed Pontefract, where the Marquess of Montagu was lying in wait, and reached Coventry, where Warwick refused to come out and fight, so King Edward marched south and took Warwick Castle, where he formally proclaimed himself King. Hearing that the Earl of Oxford and Duke of Clarence were on their way to Coventry, King Edward sent an army which defeated the Earl of Oxford's force on 3rd April. Clarence, eventually realising that he was superfluous to Warwick's plans, then threw in his lot with his brothers who welcomed him and his 12,000 men. Together they then made a final challenge to Warwick who wisely refused to fight this vast array, so the Yorkist army marched on London to get there before Queen Margaret, who had been delayed by bad weather in the English Channel. The Earl of Warwick brought his forces out of Coventry and followed the Yorkist army south, staying a safe two days' march behind. He sent messages to London's city authorities to resist King Edward, and urged his brother, Archbishop Neville, to stir up the city against the Yorkist pretender and make King Henry VI ride around London to try and gather Lancastrian support. Unfortunately the feeble, languid and scruffy King did little to inspire Londoners, many of whom longed for King Edward's arrival. On 10th April, Edward IV advanced to St Albans while London's officials decided to throw open the gates to him. Since most of the Lancastrian lords were heading to the West Country to greet Queen Margaret, there was no one powerful enough to resist King Edward anyway. Even the Archbishop saw the writing on the wall and sought Edward IV's mercy by undertaking to deliver Henry VI into his hands.

On 12th April, King Edward and his brothers marched into London through open gates and rejoicing crowds. In St Paul's Cathedral the Archbishop gave thanks for his restoration and declared Henry VI deposed. In the Bishop's Palace, Edward IV was presented to Henry who embraced him with the words, 'My cousin of York, you are very welcome. I know that in your hands my life will not be in danger'. King Edward then went to greet his wife and baby son at Westminster.

On Easter Day, 14th April 1471, despite a considerable numerical disadvantage, King Edward rode out to meet the Earl of Warwick and Marquess of Montagu. At Barnet the two forces clashed and, in thick morning mist, compounded by the smoke from Warwick's night-time bombardment, a chaotic battle ended with an overwhelming victory for the King. Montagu was killed in the confused heat of battle, quite possibly by someone on his own side. Despite a royal order to save Warwick's life, a group of Yorkists caught him as he tried to escape the battlefield, killed him, stripped his body of its armour and left it lying naked. After the battle, the bodies of Warwick and Montagu were displayed in a single coffin at St Paul's Cathedral for three days in order to prove their demise, and were then taken to Bisham Abbey in Berkshire and interred next to their father, Richard, Earl of Salisbury.

The Battle of Barnet. From an illuminated manuscript, 1471.

The Battle of Barnet finally rid the Earl of Northumberland of the Nevilles, the men who had plagued his family for three generations. But he was absent from that battlefield, busy suppressing minor insurrections in the North.

LIONS OF THE RED ROSE

King Edward still needed to deal with the threat posed by Queen Margaret and Prince Edward who were now marching from the west. On Easter Monday, Margaret and her retinue arrived at the Benedictine abbey at Cerne in Dorset, where they stayed for ten days and were joined by the Earls of Pembroke and Devon, the Duke of Somerset (Edmund Beaufort, brother of the duke executed after the Battle of Hexham), and his brother John, who broke the news of Warwick's defeat and death. The Queen was deeply shocked and wanted to take her son back to France, but the lords persuaded her to remain, recruit an army and prevail against Edward IV without having the treacherous Earl of Warwick breathing down her neck. Their strategy was to send the Earl of Pembroke to Wales to recruit there, and link up with him on their way north to Lancashire where they could raise a large force of archers and recruit lords and commoners alike in the Lancastrian heartlands.

Battered and bruised after the Battle of Barnet, King Edward heard the news of Queen Margaret's landing on 16th April 1471. On the 24th, he led 3000 foot soldiers west, hoping to overtake the Lancastrian army before it could cross the River Severn and link up with Jasper Tudor in Wales. As Queen Margaret moved west to the City of Exeter then north to Taunton, Glastonbury, Wells and Bristol, many men came to swell her army but, when she reached the City of Gloucester, she discovered that the King's messenger had bypassed her in the night and ordered the town's governor, Sir Richard Beauchamp, to close the gates to her army. She then made for Tewkesbury, ten miles to the north, where she could cross into Wales. However, King Edward's army arrived there on 3rd May, blocking Queen Margaret's army and forcing her to confront his forces before she could join up with those of Jasper Tudor.

Battle commenced the following day. The Lancastrians were commanded by the Duke of Somerset who led the right wing. The Earl of Devon led the left wing and Prince Edward, under the tutelage of Lord Wenlock, a seasoned commander, led the centre. Wenlock was supposed to attack the Yorkists from the front while Somerset came in from the right, but King Edward took the offensive, leading his

The Battle of Tewkesbury. From an illuminated manuscript, 1471.

centre uphill into the Lancastrians' position prior to the Duke of Gloucester's attack with his left flank. The Yorkists pounded the enemy with arrows and ordnance, much of which had been captured at the Battle of Barnet, before the Duke of Gloucester sounded the retreat, luring the Duke of Somerset into a trap. He charged down the hill, shouting at Wenlock and the Prince to follow him but Wenlock declined and Somerset was surrounded on every side by the Yorkist forces which cut his men to pieces. The remnants returned to the Lancastrian lines where Somerset publicly branded Wenlock a traitor before smashing his head in with a battle mace. The inexperienced Prince Edward was now in command of the Lancastrian centre which was subjected to a vicious onslaught from the Duke of Gloucester and, though Prince Edward tried bravely to resist, his line broke and his men fled. There followed a desperate rout, men being slaughtered as they ran. Others were forced into the River Severn where they drowned. Some tried to reach refuge in Tewkesbury Abbey but were cut down near the Abbey mill.

Tewkesbury Abbey

Over 2000 Lancastrians were killed in the battle, including Prince Edward who either died in the field or was killed afterwards, perhaps by Richard of Gloucester. King Edward had won a final, devastating victory and all hopes of a Lancastrian revival died with the young prince. Other Lancastrian leaders were dragged out of Tewkesbury Abbey, where they had sought sanctuary, and were killed on

Left: The Bastard of Fauconberg besieges London and is repulsed by Edward IV. From an illuminated manuscript, 1471.

LIONS OF THE RED ROSE

the spot. The Duke of Somerset was executed in the marketplace at Tewkesbury on 6th May, leaving Margaret Beaufort, mother of the 14 year old Henry Tudor, the future Henry VII, as the only senior surviving Beaufort. Twelve other leaders suffered the same fate as Somerset.

For a while, Jasper Tudor created some trouble for Edward in Wales while the Earl of Northumberland remained in the North to deal with a small Lancastrian uprising before it could get out of hand. Thomas, 'Bastard of Fauconberg', who still had control of Warwick's ships, landed in Kent and raised a signifcant army of rebels. By mid May, he was beseiging the City of London, having burnt Southwark. In the end, however, he was repulsed, and eventually captured and executed. There was just one matter outstanding before King Edward could feel completely secure and, before he arrived back in London on 21st May, Henry VI was murdered in the Tower of London. Richard of Gloucester, being in charge of the Tower at the time, appears to be the likely suspect, but Edward IV probably issued the order. In 1910, King Henry's body was exhumed and the back of his skull was found to be smashed, perhaps by a mace swung by the Yorkist King's loyal but ruthless brother.

Apart from a failed uprising by the Earl of Oxford in 1473, King Edward enjoyed 12 years of welcome domestic peace, although there remained a score to settle with Louis XI of France who had given succour and support to his enemies. In September 1472, Edward IV forged alliances with Burgundy and Brittany in the Treaty of Chateaugiron which initiated a military campaign in France. His allies, however, baulked at confrontation and ratified a treaty with King Louis which forced the campaign to be postponed. Duke Charles of Burgundy had ambitions to be elected Holy Roman Emperor and his army was bogged down in Alsace fighting the Swiss, so he was little use to Edward until 1474. In the Treaty of London that year, Duke Charles recognised Edward IV as King of France, in return for some conquered

Beheading of Edmund Beaufort, 4th Duke of Somerset at Tewkesbury, watched by Edward IV. From an illuminated manuscript, 1471.

14 / THE END OF THE NEVILLES AND MURDER OF A KING

territory, while Duke Francis of Brittany agreed to send 8000 troops for the campaign. In July 1475, King Edward's army of around 12,000 troops was transported to Calais, including a significant force under the Earl of Northumberland for whom this was the first overseas campaign. He was given a senior commanding role and brought a larger force than either of the Dukes of Norfolk or Suffolk. Charles of Burgundy, however, treacherously obstructed their progress and they were forced to negotiate with King Louis who, thankfully, was willing to pay for the English to leave as soon as possible. With this fee, an annual payment to refrain from invading, and marriage of his daughter to the Dauphin, King Edward just needed to seal the treaty by a meeting with King Louis.

On a specially-made bridge over the River Somme at Picquigny near Amiens, the two kings and their retinues met in the centre at a trellised barrier which allowed them to speak but not fight, while their armies waited on either side of the river. Edward was accompanied by the Duke of Clarence, Earl of Northumberland, Lord Hastings (the Chancellor) and various other lords. The kings got on surprisingly well and the barrier was soon removed so that they could embrace and conclude the deal.

King Edward achieved most of what he desired in the resulting Treaty of Picquigny and, in a secret coda to the Treaty in September, the former Queen, Margaret of Anjou, was ransomed to her cousin, King Louis, for a sum of £10,000. Forced to release all English and French claims, and given a modest allowance by Louis, Margaret lived quietly alone for another seven years. She died on 25th August 1482 and was buried in Angers Cathedral. In life she had inspired thousands of men to die for the House of Lancaster, and caused the deaths of thousands of her enemies. Now, mourning a lost son, husband and kingdom, she ended her life as a sad and harmless woman at the age of 52. Even in death however, she could not lie in peace; Angers Cathedral was ransacked during the French Revolution and her remains were removed and scattered.

Opposite: Document recording that William Johnson, a Scot, swore an oath of fealty to Edward IV at Warkworth Castle, 10th April 1475, sealed by the 4th Earl of Northumberland under his March Warden's seal.

14 / THE END OF THE NEVILLES AND MURDER OF A KING

15 Power in the North

The Earl of Northumberland had inherited substantial debts, mainly thanks to war, although his father's attainder, like a bankruptcy, quashed some of those liabilities. Relative peace from 1471, even on the Border, allowed him to recoup and restore most of his wealth, but his life then became intertwined with that of Richard, Duke of Gloucester, who adopted the North as his home. In June 1471, Edward IV gave his youngest brother much of the Neville inheritance that had been confiscated through the attainder on John Neville, Marquess of Montagu. In July 1472 Gloucester married Warwick's 16 year old daughter, Anne, widow of Edward Prince of Wales, slain at Tewkesbury. Richard thereby absorbed half of the Warwick inheritance, much to the annoyance of his brother George, Duke of Clarence. After a few legal issues with Clarence were resolved, Gloucester acquired Warwick's lands in the North and Wales whilst Clarence received the main estates in the Midlands. Richard of Gloucester, still in his early twenties, thereby rose to become the wealthiest and most powerful man in the North.

The disgruntled Clarence then made a serious error. When his wife, Isabel, died in December 1476, two months after giving birth to a short-lived son, he planned to marry Mary, the Duke of Burgundy's extremely wealthy heir, a union which was forbidden by the King who saw it as a waste of bargaining power. The outraged Clarence foolishly launched an abortive revolt whilst simultaneously casting aspersions on King Edward's own legitimacy. The King finally lost patience with his unstable and treacherous brother and, after a trial in which he acted for the prosecution, Clarence's execution was ordered. On 18th February 1478, Clarence was privately executed in the Bowyer Tower at the Tower of London, allegedly by drowning in a vat of Malmsey wine, his favourite tipple.

Gloucester disposed of his properties in Wales and the West Country, and expanded his Northern holdings, obtaining the Lordships of Barnard Castle, Scarborough and Richmond as well as holdings in Skipton-in-Craven and Helmsley that had been

Anne Neville as depicted in the armorial roll chronicle known as the 'Rous Roll', c. 1483.

Left: The execution of the Duke of Clarence in a vat of Malmsey wine.

confiscated from the Scropes and Cliffords. He also acquired various important roles including wardenship of the Western March, which gave him even greater powers. This empire required a significant workforce, which made it harder for lesser magnates, like the Earl of Northumberland, to recruit good employees, be they foresters, bailiffs, stewards, grooms or soldiers. The disgruntled Earl raised this matter with the royal council who took his lament more seriously than they might because of his recent marriage, around 1474, to William Herbert's daughter, Maud. Her close relationship to the Woodvilles was helpful enough, but her brother, now 2nd Earl of Pembroke, had married the Queen's sister, thereby further enhancing the relationship. The King promised to have a word with his brother but things didn't improve until a legal indenture was eventually signed, essentially making the Earl of Northumberland subservient to the Duke of Gloucester in return for guarantees that Gloucester would not 'poach' men in the county of Northumberland. In other traditional Percy areas no such guarantee was made, but at least it ensured that the Earl of Northumberland's dominance continued in the far North towards the Eastern March.

In fact the relationship between the two men remained good and they both observed the limits of their sphere of influence whilst working together where and when required. Although Northumberland was undoubtedly the grandest magnate in the North, he was now under Gloucester's control, and by the end of the 1470s all Northern lords, such as the Earl of Westmorland and Lords Greystoke, Scrope and Dacre, had followed suit.

Edward IV arranged an Anglo-Scottish truce in 1474 which was supposed to last until 1519 and involved the marriage of James III's heir, another James, to King Edward's daughter, Cecily. This had kept the Border quiet for a while but the Scottish King's brother, Alexander, Duke of Albany, Earl of March and Warden of the Marches on the Scottish side, was a fervent nationalist

15 / POWER IN THE NORTH

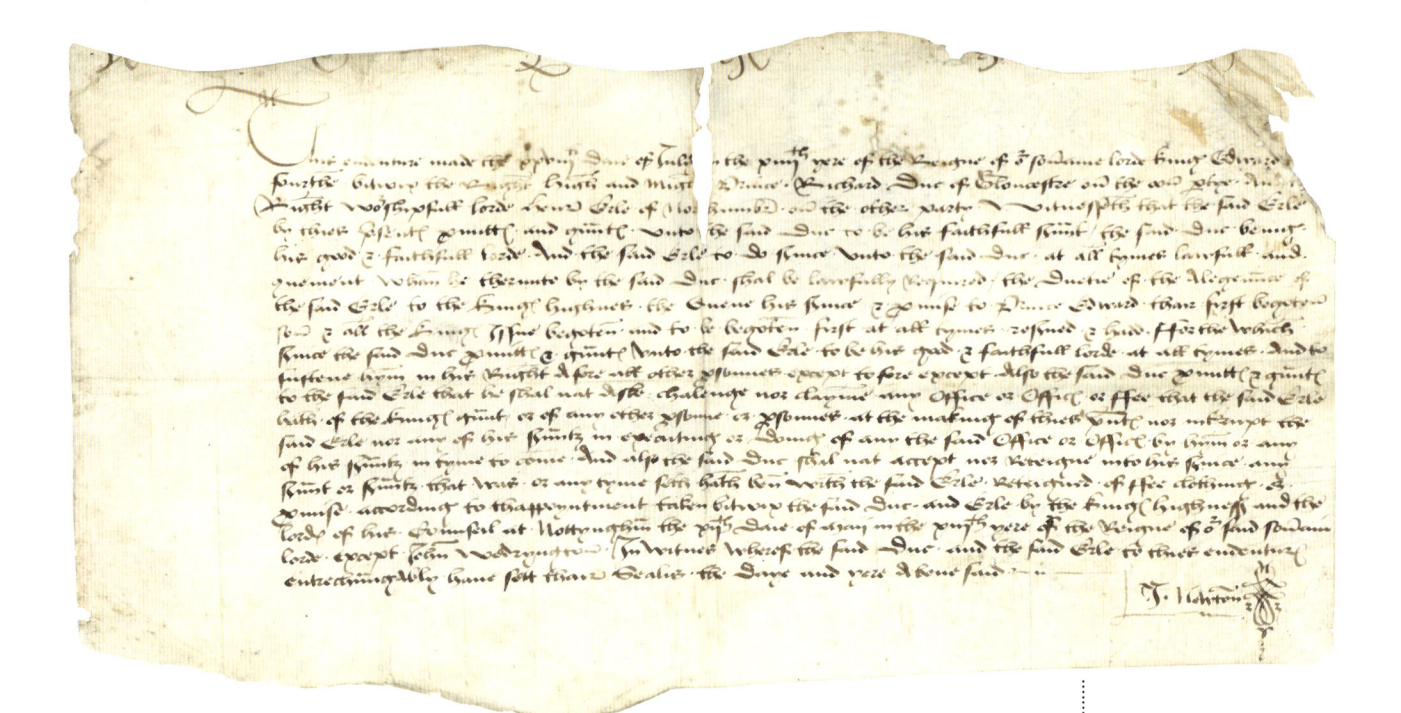

who loathed the truce and the planned marriage, and did all he could to scupper it. In 1479 he launched border raids and sabotaged 'Truce Days', when wardens were supposed to sort out grievances on both sides of the Border. During one violent episode, Robert Lisle, a Percy retainer, was murdered and the Earl of Northumberland's cousin and lieutenant, Henry Percy, was taken prisoner. Since James III had been receiving instalments of Cecily's dowry for six years and was keen to keep the money flowing, he needed to restrain his brother, so Albany was arrested, charged with treason and later exiled, bringing relative peace to the region for a while. Scottish politics invariably involved France, and the balance of power on the Continent had changed in 1477 when Duke Charles of Burgundy was killed during the Battle of Nancy, leaving his daughter Mary as heir. Louis XI of France then invaded Burgundy, seeing his chance to finally extinguish its independence. This left Edward IV in a quandary for, while he was getting on well with King Louis, he couldn't allow the French to gain full control of the North Sea coast and thereby threaten Calais. The devious French King continued to express the importance of his alliance with King Edward but, at the same time, he sent a Scottish academic at the Sorbonne, John Ireland, to persuade James III to make peace with his brother, Albany, and make war on England. A Scottish embassy was sent to King Louis under the Earl of Buchan to explore terms, which were thought to have included the potential marriage of King James's sister, Margaret, to the Dauphin.

King Edward was soon aware of the French King's duplicity and the dangers of a renewed 'Auld Alliance' and in early 1480, on Richard's advice, he sent King James an ultimatum. He accused the Scottish King of holding Berwick and Roxburgh illegally, demanded satisfaction over the planned marriage of Cecily and insisted on the restoration

Counterpart deed of agreement between the 4th Earl of Northumberland and Richard, Duke of Gloucester, 28th July 1474. The Earl agrees to be the Duke's 'faithfull servant', the Duke being his 'good and faithfull lorde'. The Duke also promises not to take into his service any of the Earl's servants, with the exception of 'John Wedryngton'.

of the Earl of Douglas to his estates. In essence though, he promised not to declare war on Scotland if Prince James was delivered to the Earl of Northumberland, and Berwick was returned to England. Neither happened, so the Duke of Gloucester and Earl of Northumberland were put on a war footing, though King Edward would not yet sanction an invasion. Much of 1480 saw raiding on either side of the Border and the Earl of Angus made a particularly successful incursion, ravaging the Northumbrian countryside, and burning the village of Bamburgh and other nearby settlements. In early September, Gloucester directed the Earl of Northumberland to join him in a 'return match'. Their significant army reached as far as Jedburgh but the Scots would not meet them in battle, choosing instead to raid as far south as York. However, with no proper satisfaction from King James, King Edward ordered preparation for war. During the winter of 1480, fearing a full-scale Scottish assault, the walls of Carlisle were repaired and men filled the garrisons along the Border. On the orders of the Crown, a military census took place under the Earl of Northumberland to assess the number of soldiers available for conflict, while the Duke of Gloucester spent time in London trying to persuade Edward IV of the merits of this war.

1480 Account Roll of John Harbottell, Receiver for the Baronies of Alnwick, Warkworth, Beanley and Rothbury, detailing the 4th Earl's expenditure for his attack on Jedburgh in Scotland. It includes money paid to tenants for providing 15 wagons for carrying accoutrements of war and victuals from Alnwick to Jedburgh, a surgeon's bill for treating a wounded French gunner (whose singed uniform was also replaced), Alan Reed was paid for herding sheep from Alnwick to Jedburgh for 'the Lord's great expedition there', while William Bower received 4d per bow for making 104 bows in a single month prior to the expedition.

King Edward feared a long, drawn-out campaign in Scotland and delayed an invasion partly due to a poor harvest and consequent financial constraints, and partly to try and resolve issues in France. To Louis XI's relief, Edward reconfirmed the Anglo-French treaty at Nottingham, and the planned marriage of Princess Elizabeth to the Dauphin. This was a relief to King Edward too, for he continued to receive a pension of £10,000 from King Louis, which he desperately needed. The French King subsequently ignored pleas for help from Scotland and Edward ignored pleas for help from Burgundy, hoping that the balance of power in France would soon shift as King Louis' health declined.

The now fat, slothful and lecherous King Edward was no longer the handsome, politically astute warrior king of the past, and his prevarications and delays infuriated the Duke of

15 / POWER IN THE NORTH   119

Gloucester and Earl of Northumberland. In October 1481 Richard rode to meet his brother at Nottingham, trying to get the campaign started, but King Edward decided that the weather would soon get worse so military action should be delayed until the following year. In late October, however, Gloucester and Northumberland besieged Berwick, which James III had recently reinforced with an extra 500 men and new artillery, only to be forced back across the Border by a counter-attack.

An invasion of Scotland was now inevitable and, as a prelude to the forthcoming campaign, Edward IV invited the exiled Duke of Albany to Fotheringhay Castle where, on 11th June 1482, he offered him the Crown of Scotland and asked Gloucester to help put him on the throne. Neither King Edward or his brother held high hopes of success in replacing James with Albany but they believed that the latter's supporters would add discord in Scotland and thereby help their campaign.

At the beginning of July, the Duke of Gloucester and Earl of Northumberland assembled an army at Alnwick Castle of around 19,000 men divided into several 'battles' and deployed separately by the main commanders, Gloucester, Northumberland, Earl Rivers and Lord Stanley. On 24th July, this sizeable army was marshalled outside Berwick. According to *Hall's Chronicle*, Northumberland commanded the vanguard with 6700 men. Gloucester and Albany were in the centre with 5000 men. Lord Neville commanded the rearguard of 3000 men while Lord Stanley led the right wing with 4000 men. A further 1000 men were in charge of the ordnance. Lord Gray, the Governor of Berwick and ally of Albany, opened the gates to the town without a shot being fired, thereby escaping destruction, but Berwick Castle, with a garrison of 500 men under Sir Patrick Hepburn (later Earl of Bothwell), remained defiant and Gloucester could not waste time and valuable resources besieging it. Leaving Lord Stanley to blockade Berwick with 4000 troops, the English army moved west and divided into two forces. Gloucester and Albany met King James' hastily assembled army at Lauder Bridge but, as the English force approached, the unpopular Scottish king was taken into custody by his own disaffected magnates, particularly Archibald, Earl of Angus, who was probably already in league with Albany. The King's ministers were dismissed, two were executed and King James was taken to Edinburgh and imprisoned in Edinburgh Castle.

The Duke of Gloucester marched directly to Edinburgh, occupying but not sacking the city for fear of alienating any support for Albany. The Earl of Northumberland, meanwhile, laid waste to farms and took castles and bastle

Portrait of King James III of Scotland accompanied by his son James, presented by St Andrew. Wing from a triptych attributed to Van de Goes, c. 1475.

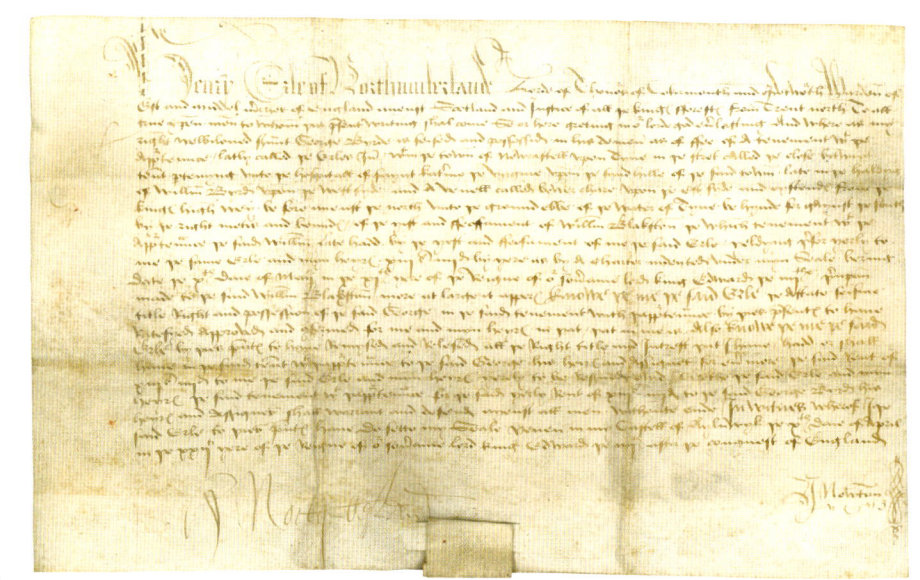

houses, including Kirk Yetholm, Bemersyde, Roxburgh, Jedburgh and Ednam. In early August he joined Gloucester in Edinburgh but, through lack of time, provisions and ordnance, they were unable to take Edinburgh Castle and impose terms on King James who was holed up inside, refusing to communicate. However, Gloucester gained a promise from the city to refund Cecily's dowry if the planned marriage didn't take place. The Duke of Albany failed in his bid to become King of Scotland but was issued with a pardon by the Scottish government and left to take possession of Edinburgh Castle where he became his brother's keeper for a while. Gloucester and Northumberland then marched south and faced a sizeable Scottish force in Haddington which fortunately declined to risk a battle and allowed the English to pass. The English army then besieged Berwick Castle until it surrendered to Lord Stanley in the last week of August. The Earl of Northumberland, as Warden of the Eastern March, took over custody of the town and castle for a fee of £438 per month. His cousin, the now freed Sir Henry Percy, deputised for him. Berwick was back in English hands and has stayed there ever since.

The Scottish campaign of 1482 wasn't a huge success, but it was a morale boost for England in the face of bad news from the Continent. King Louis, who still clung to life made the Treaty of Arras with Duke Maximilian of Burgundy, the husband of Mary, Duke Charles' heir. Their daughter, Margaret, was to marry the Dauphin, her dowry being Artois and Burgundy. Burgundy was now vassal to a supreme France and any hope of Burgundian support for England disappeared.

On 20th January Parliament heaped praise on the Duke of Gloucester, the Earl of Northumberland and Lord Stanley for their roles in the Scottish campaign. Gloucester was permanently granted wardenship of the Western March and King Edward surrendered virtually all rights and fees throughout Cumberland to his brother, who was also allowed to keep any land he conquered in Scotland and given the right to make any Scots living within his empire 'denizens' of England. With regal powers and vast land holdings, Richard of Gloucester became a virtual king in the North. Before long that power was extended to the South as well.

Charter confirming George Byrd's possession of the Earl's Inn in Newcastle with a reserved annual rent of 13s 4d, signed by the 4th Earl of Northumberland at Alnwick Castle, 10th April 1482.

15 / POWER IN THE NORTH 121

16 The Rise and Fall of Richard III

Portrait of King Richard III, English School, 16th/17th century.

Late at night, on 9th April 1483, Edward IV died, aged 40. His sudden illness gave rise to rumours of foul play, perhaps poisoning, but Dominic Mancini, the Italian chronicler, gives the most likely explanation: that he succumbed to pneumonia after catching a bad cold while boating. Seeing the dangers of delay, the unpopular Woodville faction wisely determined to have the 12 year old Edward V crowned as soon as possible, on 4th May, after which they would surround and protect him, and their own interests, during his minority. However, at the end of April, while the young king and his uncle, Earl Rivers, were travelling from Ludlow to London, they were met by Richard of Gloucester and the Duke of Buckingham at Stony Stratford near the Woodvilles' estate in Northamptonshire. They spent a pleasant evening together but, the next morning, claiming that there was a conspiracy by the Woodvilles to assassinate the young king, Gloucester and Buckingham arrested Rivers, Richard Grey (the King's half-brother), and Thomas Vaughan (the chamberlain), and sent them to various Neville castles in Yorkshire. Assuring Londoners that he had saved the young king from harm, Gloucester placed Edward V in the Tower of London for his protection, pending a new date for the coronation and settlement of the protectorship. The Queen, meanwhile, sought sanctuary in Westminster Abbey once more, with her youngest son, Richard, her brother, Lionel Woodville, Bishop of Salisbury, and her daughters.

In early May, the council set 22nd June as the new date for the coronation of Edward V and recognised Richard of Gloucester as Lord Protector. With this, Gloucester moved fast to secure his position. He stripped the Woodvilles and their adherents of offices and grants, and replaced them with his own supporters. The Duke of Buckingham was given enormous power in Wales and the Marches, while the Earl of Northumberland was confirmed as Warden of the Eastern and Middle Marches for five months and made captain of Berwick until October. On 10th June, the Lord Protector sent a message asking Northumberland to assemble a force at Pontefract by the 18th as the Queen was threatening to seize the North and murder Gloucester. On 13th June, Lord Hastings, one of the architects of Gloucester's coup, expressed reservations to the Archbishop of York, the Bishop of Ely and Edward V's private secretary about the means and methods of the coup. Before Hastings was due to meet Gloucester for a council meeting in the Tower, he was arrested and summarily beheaded for treason while the men he had confided in were arrested and imprisoned. Richard of Gloucester's ruthlessness was never in question but paranoia now appeared to infect his mind. On 16th June, his soldiers broke into Westminster Abbey, grabbed the young Richard of York from his mother's arms and delivered him to the Tower of London, to join his brother.

On 22nd June, the Mayor of London's brother, a preacher called Ralph Shaw, gave a sermon claiming that Edward IV's sons were bastards. Two days later, the Duke of Buckingham revealed a marriage contract between the late King Edward and Lady Eleanor Butler which, if true, would have made Edward's children by Elizabeth Woodville illegitimate under canon law. Authenticity of this contract was debatable as the lady in question died in 1468, before the two boys were born. The information came from Robert Stillington, the Bishop of Bath and Wells, who had apparently witnessed the original pre-contract which had enabled Edward to seduce the lady, and kept it secret for 20 years. The Bishop had approached the

Anthony Woodville, 2nd Earl Rivers, younger brother of the Queen, presents his translation of 'Dictes and Sayings of the Philosophers' to King Edward IV and his family, as depicted in that book, c. 1477.

16 / THE RISE AND FALL OF RICHARD III

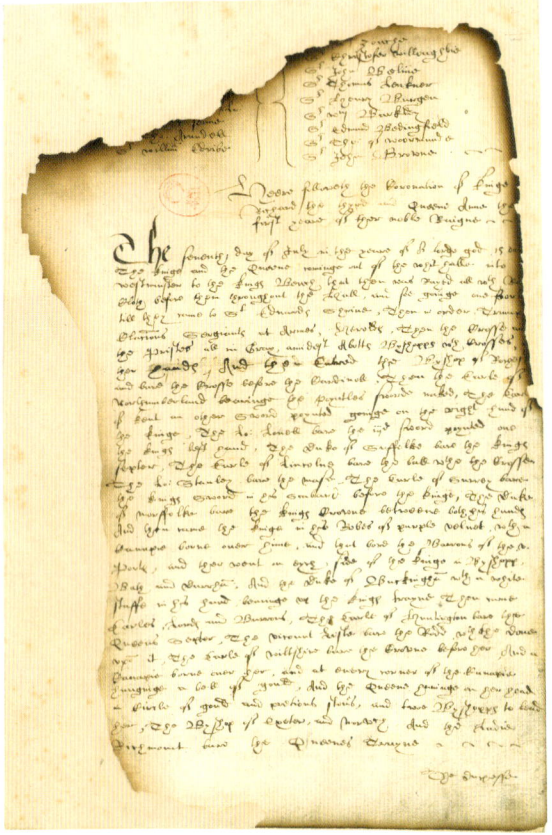

Duke of Gloucester with this information, handing him clear justification for claiming the throne. With this in mind, the citizens of London, nobles and commoners, wishing to avoid the dangers of another minority, opted for proven leadership and offered Richard the Crown, which he accepted on 26th June.

The previous day, Earl Rivers, Richard Grey and Thomas Vaughan were executed at Pontefract Castle on the charge of high treason against the Lord Protector, after appearing before a tribunal led by the Earl of Northumberland, who was now fully complicit in Richard III's usurpation of the throne. After the executions, the Earl of Northumberland marched his army to London for the coronation on 6th July, his force of feared Northerners being ready to defend the King against any treachery. At the coronation, Northumberland headed the list of earls, just below the three Dukes of Norfolk, Suffolk and Buckingham. He bore 'Curtana,' a sword without a point which, ironically after the recent purge, symbolised mercy. Wasting little time after Richard III's accession, Northumberland petitioned the new King for the complete restoration of all the estates owned by the 1st Earl before his attainder in 1405, complaining that subsequent acts had failed to fully revoke the effects of that attainder, and the forfeiture attaching to it. He pleaded that King Richard should revoke all grants of Percy lands to other recipients after the attainder, and thereby give him full restitution. The King agreed and, within a year, the petition was fully implemented.

Soon after the coronation, King Richard III and Queen Anne set out on a royal tour of the country, during which they endowed King's College and Queen's College, Cambridge. In September, however, a series of rebellions broke out, involving Margaret Beaufort and the former Queen Elizabeth's surviving family, the Marquess of Dorset and the Bishop of Salisbury, with the aim of removing King Richard and putting Edward V on the throne.

An eyewitness account of the coronation of King Richard III and Queen Anne, damaged by fire in the 18th century. The description includes the 4th Earl bearing the Sword of Mercy, 'Curtana', in front of the King.

After it became increasingly obvious that King Edward and his brother were probably dead, the conspiracy altered course with King Richard's former ally, the Duke of Buckingham, at its head. He proposed that Henry Tudor, Margaret Beaufort's son by Edmund Tudor, Earl of Richmond, should return from exile, take the Crown and marry Elizabeth of York, Edward IV's daughter.

Buckingham raised a substantial army from his Welsh estates and the Marches but, on seeing the King's mostly Northern army, led by the Earl of Northumberland, the Duke of Norfolk and Lord Stanley, the rebellion collapsed and Buckingham, who tried to escape in disguise, was captured, convicted of treason and beheaded in the City of Salisbury on 2nd November. Henry Tudor's ships ran into a storm and had to return to Brittany but Richard III made a deal with the Breton Treasurer, Pierre Landais, who had been funding Henry's campaign. He offered military support for Landais's weak regime, under Duke Francis II of Brittany, in return for handing over Henry Tudor. Henry fortunately got wind of this deal and fled to Paris where he was welcomed heartily by the French Regent, Anne of Beaujeu. Most of the leading figures in the rebellion escaped to Flanders or Brittany, but King Richard's sole and vengeful parliament attainted 100 men. The lands and offices of these mostly Southern traitors were handed out to the King's loyal Northern supporters whom

Royal letter patent under the Great Seal of Richard III (of which only a fragment remains), dated 5th May 1485. It recites the 4th Earl's petition for the return of lands and property yet to be restored, referring to 'Sir Herry Percy, Besaile to the now Earl'. 'Besaile' is an obsolete English word meaning Great-Grandfather. It also describes Henry IV and Henry V as kings 'in dede and not in right'.

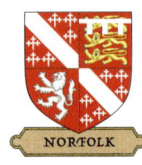

he believed to be more trustworthy. The Earl of Northumberland was high amongst them, and he was made Lord High Chamberlain on 30th November, filling a space vacated by the Duke of Buckingham. He was also given the role of Warden-General of the Eastern March. As Richard III saw the North very much as his main sphere of influence, Northumberland did not enjoy the same autonomy as his forebears but he appeared content to take and carry out orders without question. This probably helped to save the Percys and restore their wealth and estates, although coming events would challenge that achievement.

Following the death of his father, the Earl of Richmond, and the self-imposed exile of his uncle Jasper, Henry Tudor was put under the control of William Herbert, later Earl of Pembroke, with whom he would have met the teenage Henry Percy, also under Herbert's control. A plan was hatched for Tudor to be betrothed to Pembroke's daughter Maud; in fact she married Henry Percy sometime between 1473 and 1476, produced seven children and died a short time before the Battle of Bosworth in 1485. Henry Tudor's mother, Margaret Beaufort, claimed royal blood from John of Gaunt, making young Henry Tudor a magnet for disaffected Yorkists as well as Lancastrians. After Richmond's death, Margaret remarried: first to Henry Stafford, who died in 1471, and then to Lord Stanley, scion of the most powerful family in Lancashire.

Henry Tudor's focus on revenge and conquest was demonstrated on Christmas Day 1483, in Rennes Cathedral where he publicly pledged to marry the 17 year old Elizabeth of York and thereby merge the warring dynasties once and for all. His mother had helped to instigate rebellion against King Richard while her husband had loyally helped to put it down, so there was a serious conflict of loyalties within that family. Marriage to Stanley probably saved her from execution but Richard III stripped her of all titles and estates, including her son's inheritance, and Stanley was ordered to keep her in 'some secret place' without her servants. This may have been a lenient sentence by King Richard's ruthless standards but it tipped Stanley into covertly supporting the cause of his stepson. That cause became more imperative with the death of King Richard's only son in April 1484 and the death of his wife, Anne, 11 months later, leaving him bereft and, crucially, without an heir to trump Henry Tudor's claim.

Portrait of Margaret Beaufort, Countess of Richmond and Derby. English School.

126 LIONS OF THE RED ROSE

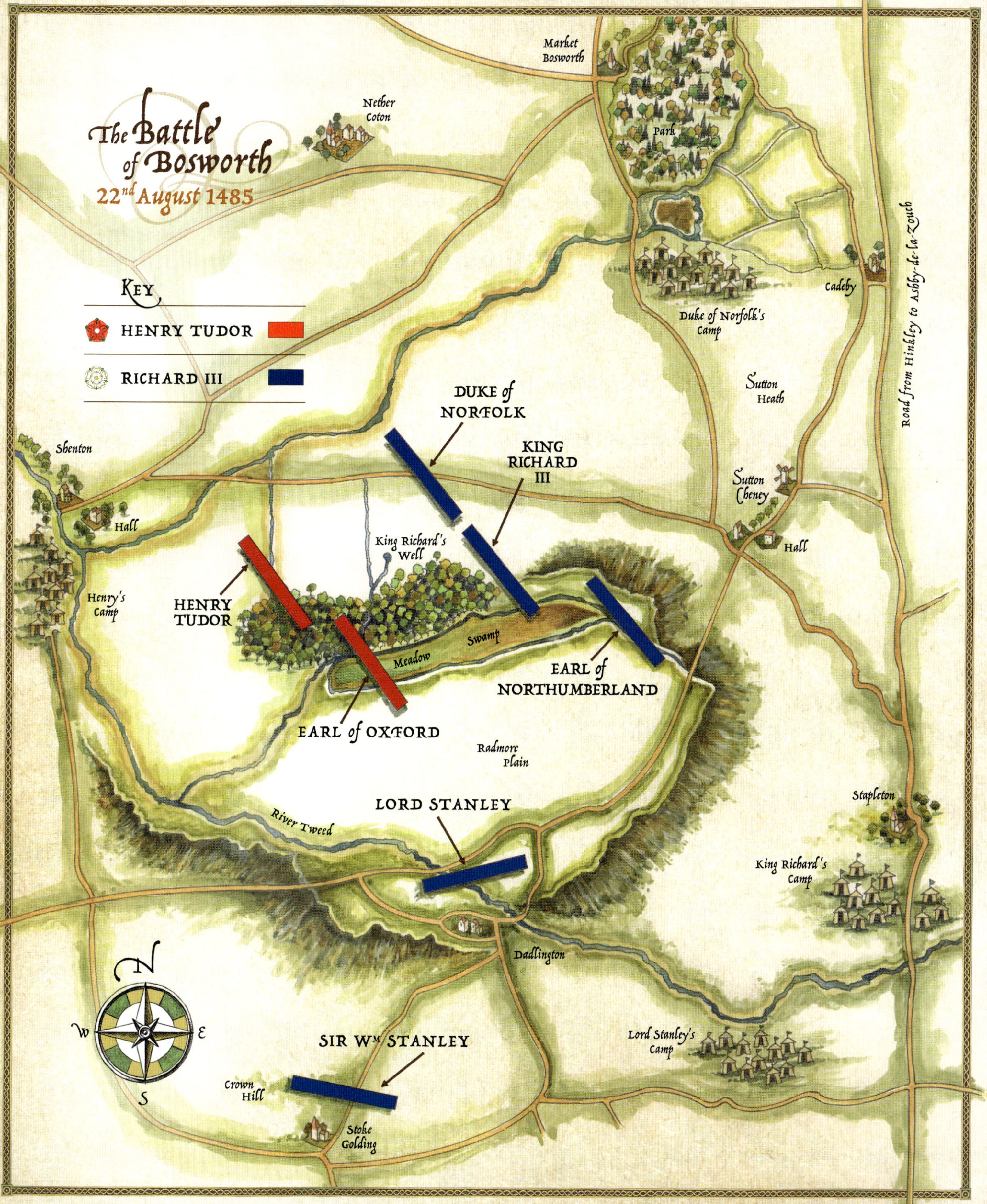
The Battle of Bosworth
22nd August 1485
KEY
HENRY TUDOR
RICHARD III
Market Bosworth
Nether Coton
Park
Duke of Norfolk's Camp
Cadeby
Road from Hinkley to Ashby-de-la-Zouch
Sutton Heath
DUKE of NORFOLK
KING RICHARD III
Shenton
Hall
Sutton Cheney
Hall
King Richard's Well
Henry's Camp
HENRY TUDOR
Swamp
Meadow
EARL of NORTHUMBERLAND
EARL of OXFORD
Radmore Plain
LORD STANLEY
River Tweed
Stapleton
King Richard's Camp
Dadlington
N
W
E
S
SIR W^M STANLEY
Lord Stanley's Camp
Crown Hill
Stoke Golding

On 7th August 1485 Henry Tudor landed at Milford Haven in South Wales, with 400 exiled Englishmen and around 3500 Norman soldiers. Over the next few weeks he marched through Wales and into the Midlands with his uncle, Jasper Tudor, and the Earl of Oxford by his side, aiming for the City of Nottingham, recruiting en route, facing no significant resistance. King Richard, meanwhile, assembled his forces and the Duke of Norfolk was already on his way to Nottingham with a significant force by the time the Earl of Northumberland, within weeks of his wife's death, belatedly heard the call to arms. He managed to raise an army and arrive in Nottingham just in time to join King Richard's forces at Bosworth Field.

On 22nd August, the royal army of more than 10,000 men faced a far smaller force of perhaps 5000 under Henry Tudor. King Richard's vanguard in the west was commanded by the Duke of Norfolk while the King commanded the main body in the centre and the Earl of Northumberland led the left flank, with a force of 4000 mainly mounted men. Henry Tudor, in contrast, had a more mobile force divided into two battle groups. The main force, under the Earl of Oxford, included the archers, while Henry Tudor's company of exiles and elite guardsmen followed on. To one side was Lord Stanley and his brother, Sir William Stanley, with around 5000 men, apparently still uncommitted and wavering, though Richard now strongly suspected treachery. He held Lord Stanley's son, Lord Strange, hostage and threatened to execute Strange on the battlefield unless Stanley immediately joined the attack on Henry Tudor. Stanley famously replied that he had other sons, but Lord Strange did, somehow, manage to survive the battle.

King Richard's vanguard, under the Duke of Norfolk, was pounded by the Earl of Oxford's cannon, so it attacked, only to be driven back by Oxford's men who had formed tight wedges, prickling with spears and poleaxes that Norfolk's men could not penetrate. Henry's cavalry wings under Sir John Savage and Gilbert Talbot then hammered into them killing many, including the Duke of Norfolk. Some of Norfolk's men fled and the King staked all on a charge across the battlefield, to attack the seemingly ill-protected Henry Tudor, calling desperately on the Earl of Northumberland for support. King Richard came very close to Henry Tudor, killing his standard bearer, Sir William Brandon but, as the King's charge faltered, the Earl of Northumberland could not or would not order his men to join the attack. Then the Stanleys intervened. Seeing the King separated from his army, Lord Stanley stood and watched as Sir William Stanley led his troops to help Henry Tudor, who had dismounted and hidden amongst his own men. In so doing, Stanley's men

Silver-gilt livery badge of a boar, symbol of King Richard III.

128 LIONS OF THE RED ROSE

killed many of Richard's knights and eventually surrounded the King who had dismounted and left his horse trapped in a bog. Fending off several of Stanley's men and screaming, according to Shakespeare, 'a horse, a horse, my kingdom for a horse,' Richard was killed, not by Henry Tudor, as in Shakespeare's version, but by a Welshman wielding a halberd. His brutalised body, recently discovered beneath a car park in Leicester, was found to have multiple wounds, many to the head, while the back of his head had been sliced away.

As news of the King's death spread, the Earl of Northumberland ignominiously fled the battlefield. Historians have many theories on the reasons for the Earl's lack of action that day. Had he done a deal with Henry Tudor and decided to turn on King Richard? Jean Molinet, the French chronicler, suggests that Northumberland did not intend for Henry to become King but had planned for a son of the Duke of Clarence to take the throne and marry one of the Earl's daughters. Perhaps he did not hear the order to charge, or was hidden behind the King's main force, unable to manoeuvre into a position whereby he could help. There are suggestions that marshy terrain in front of him made it impossible to lead his men to Richard's aid. Or did he just dither, too inexperienced in warfare, having only taken part in skirmishes before? Some accounts suggest that Northumberland actually turned his forces against Richard's men while others state that his men stood motionless as battle commenced, then left the field once the outcome was clear. Whatever his motives, Northumberland could have turned the battle in Richard's favour. Instead, his inaction contributed greatly to the end of the Plantagenet dynasty and the start of a Tudor one.

According to legend, Richard III's crown was discovered under a hawthorn bush and placed on Henry Tudor's head by Lord Stanley, later created Earl of Derby for his outstanding service. When the Earl of Northumberland presented himself to the new King and knelt in homage, Henry placed him in custody but did not attaint him, unsure of the Earl's battlefield motives but thankful that he didn't engage his forces. Lord Fitzhugh, the Kingmaker's nephew, took over Northumberland's roles in the North.

Remains of King Richard III as discovered in situ under a car park at the site of Grey Friars Priory, Leicester, 2012.

Left: Portrait of Henry VII, English School, 16th/17th century.

17 Restitution and Revolt

Henry VII was suspicious of the Earl of Northumberland and detained him until Clarence's son, Edward, Earl of Warwick, the focus of a conspiracy theory, was no longer a threat. There is no evidence of Northumberland's involvement in a plot involving the young Earl but there were rumours that concerned the King who seized the 10 year old Warwick, and placed him in the Tower of London. After a brief period in the same establishment, Northumberland pledged his loyalty, was forgiven by the new King, and released from custody. He was confirmed in all the offices he had held under Richard III and was called to the Council. Amongst other commissions, he was made Warden of the Eastern and Middle Marches, Bailiff of Tynedale for life, and commissioner of the Royal Mines in the north of England for 20 years, as well as Constable of Newcastle, Dunstanburgh and Bamburgh castles.

Henry Tudor was crowned in Westminster Abbey on 30th October 1485. He married Edward IV's daughter, Elizabeth of York, whom he hardly knew, on 18th January 1486, thereby uniting the houses of Lancaster and York, the red and the white rose, and starting a new Tudor dynasty. Henry visited the North later that year and was met by Northumberland at Barnsdale in Yorkshire, together with the Earl's retinue of 33 knights and 300 horsemen. At this time, Yorkist survivors of the Battle of Bosworth, including Francis, Lord Lovell, and Humphrey and Thomas Stafford, were plotting a rebellion. As De Fonblanque claims, 'Henry narrowly escaped from falling into the hands of his enemies, by whom during his progress he had found himself surrounded'. Apparently King Henry was praying on St George's day in York Minster and would certainly have been captured or killed had not the Earl of Northumberland come to his rescue.

In 1487 there was a Yorkist rebellion in support of a boy called Lambert Simnel

Above: Portrait of Henry VII with his three sons, Arthur, Henry and Edmund. Right: Portrait of Elizabeth of York, Queen of England with her four daughters, Margaret, Elizabeth, Mary and Catherine. After Anonymous Flemish Painter, c. 1510.

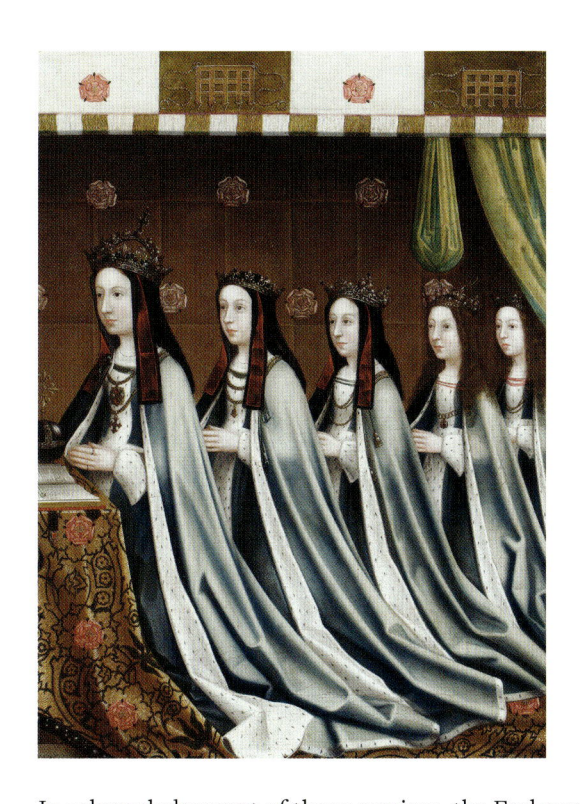

who claimed to be Clarence's son, the Earl of Warwick, who was last seen as a prisoner in the Tower of London. He claimed to have escaped from the Tower and attracted considerable Yorkist support. He was taken to Dublin and crowned as if he were King Edward V, before marching an army against Henry VII. Northumberland, according to De Fonblanque, 'took a prominent part in the fiercely-contested action at Stoke which resulted in defeating one of the most impudent attempts to win a crown by fraudulent personation recorded in history.'

In acknowledgement of these services, the Earl was given the wardenship of Berwick and, the following year, he was part of a commission which concluded a peace treaty with Portugal. He was also appointed Bailiff of Boroughbridge, giving him various lucrative rights. The Earl was now fully integrated into the Tudor regime.

Henry VII clearly recognised the importance of clemency towards, and resulting loyalty from, Northern nobles who had once supported Richard III. The Earls of Northumberland and Westmorland, the two Lords Scrope, Lord Greystoke, Lord Dacre, Lord Fitzhugh and Lord Lumley survived and benefitted from this policy. But it was not just political expediency that dictated the King's mercy. Lambert Simnel was, by the standards of the day, treated with considerable lenience. He was pardoned and put to work in the royal kitchens as a 'spit-turner', becoming a falconer in later life.

Henry VII may have been merciful but he was also financially astute with a reputation for hoarding and meanness. In 1489 Parliament voted him substantial tax increases, ostensibly for a military campaign in France and, as his agent, the Earl of Northumberland was responsible for collecting these unpopular dues. Traditionally the North was subjected to very few taxes owing to its economic problems

The Princes in the Tower

The disappearance of the two princes in 1483 gave rise to the general assumption that their ruthless uncle, Richard III, had murdered them and disposed of the bodies. Others have suggested that Henry Tudor, unsure of his own regal claim, was responsible for their murder. Recent analysis of contemporary documents by a team led by Philippa Langley, who famously discovered the remains of Richard III in a Leicester car park, casts doubt on those assumptions and gives compelling evidence that suggests that the princes escaped or were released from the Tower of London. There is also evidence that the two pretenders to the throne of Henry VII, Lambert Simnel and Perkin Warbeck, were in fact the two princes Edward and Richard, who raised armies to assert their claims and were defeated and captured in 1487 and 1497 respectively. The former was allowed to live and serve in the royal kitchens but the latter was executed at Tyburn in 1499.

1480 Quitclaim by Sir John Percy, illegitimate son and heir of Thomas Percy, Lord Egremont, to Thomas Styler for land in North Lambeth. Sir John signs himself 'Egremont'.

and Scottish deprivations, but King Henry refused to accept any exemptions from his taxation policy from a Northern population that had strong Yorkist leanings. On 20th April, significant unrest erupted at Ayton in Cleveland where a local chaplain and a few yeomen decided to march to Thirsk to raise a rebellion against taxes. Northumberland had travelled north from London where he had been attending Parliament and, hearing of the disturbance, called on local worthies for help.

At Cocklodge, the Earl's house near the ruined Percy castle of Topcliffe, Northumberland and his retinue were confronted by 700 angry rebels. The Earl bravely tried to placate them but tempers flared and he was dragged from his horse and killed by the ringleader of the rebellion, a Welsh forester who had recently moved to Yorkshire, called John Chamber. The Earl's retinue stood by and watched this vicious murder. Their failure to intervene has puzzled historians and foul play has been suggested. The Earl was in the midst of a bitter family tussle over Wressle Castle and estates with his cousin, Sir John Percy, the illegitimate son of the late Thomas, Lord Egremont, who had been killed at the Battle of Northampton in 1460. Sir John wasn't present at Cocklodge but several of his friends and associates were and, apart from Egremont's cronies, Northumberland's retinue was also packed with loyal supporters of the late King Richard. They would have known of Northumberland's perceived treachery at Bosworth and, perhaps, be inclined to stand and watch his murder just as he had stood and watched their beloved king be hacked to death.

John Chamber was executed for the 4th Earl of Northumberland's murder, the rebellion petered out and Egremont disappeared. At the order but not the expense of the King, the Earl was given a lavish burial in Beverley Minster, costing more than £1000. The ceremony was attended by 500 priests, 1000 clerks and 13,340 'poor people,' who each received two pennies for attending. His tomb lies in a specially built chapel at the east end of the Minster.

LIONS OF THE RED ROSE

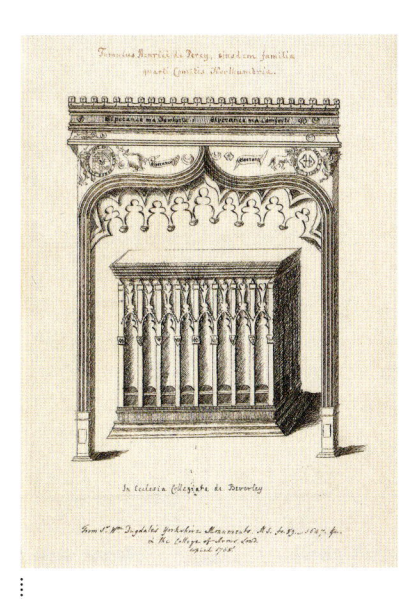

The 4th Earl's tomb in Beverley Minster with the original canopy, 18th century drawing.

Excerpt on the 4th Earl from William Peeris' pedigree roll.

"The xth Henry his sone aftir certayn yeres,
Aftyr m[an]y troble and grett adversite,
Succedid to therldome amonge the statly peres,
A lady he maryd of Auncient and he degre,
The lorde harbard doghter Mald of benyngnite,
Wysse, polytike, prudent and all way graciosse,
To hir trew servantes a lady most bountiuosse.

"This noble Erle in kyng henry the vijth tyme,
At Thriske was slayn in the cause of his kynge,
O horryble myscheff, o most cruell crime,
In owr days not seen so detestable athinge,
There own naturall lord the Commons so murderynge,
He gudly Commandyng them in the kinges nayme,
To doo ther dewte and kepe thamselfe fro blame.

"Both knyghtes and gentilmen that day with hym he led,
To whom he yave fees and was especiall lord,
Bott in his grett nede all sodenly from hym fled,
Some privy treson was the trewth to Record,
Alase in there Conscience they have Cause to Remord,
So to forsake hym wherby he lost hys lyffe,
In beverley mynstyr he lyeth and also Mald his wyffe."

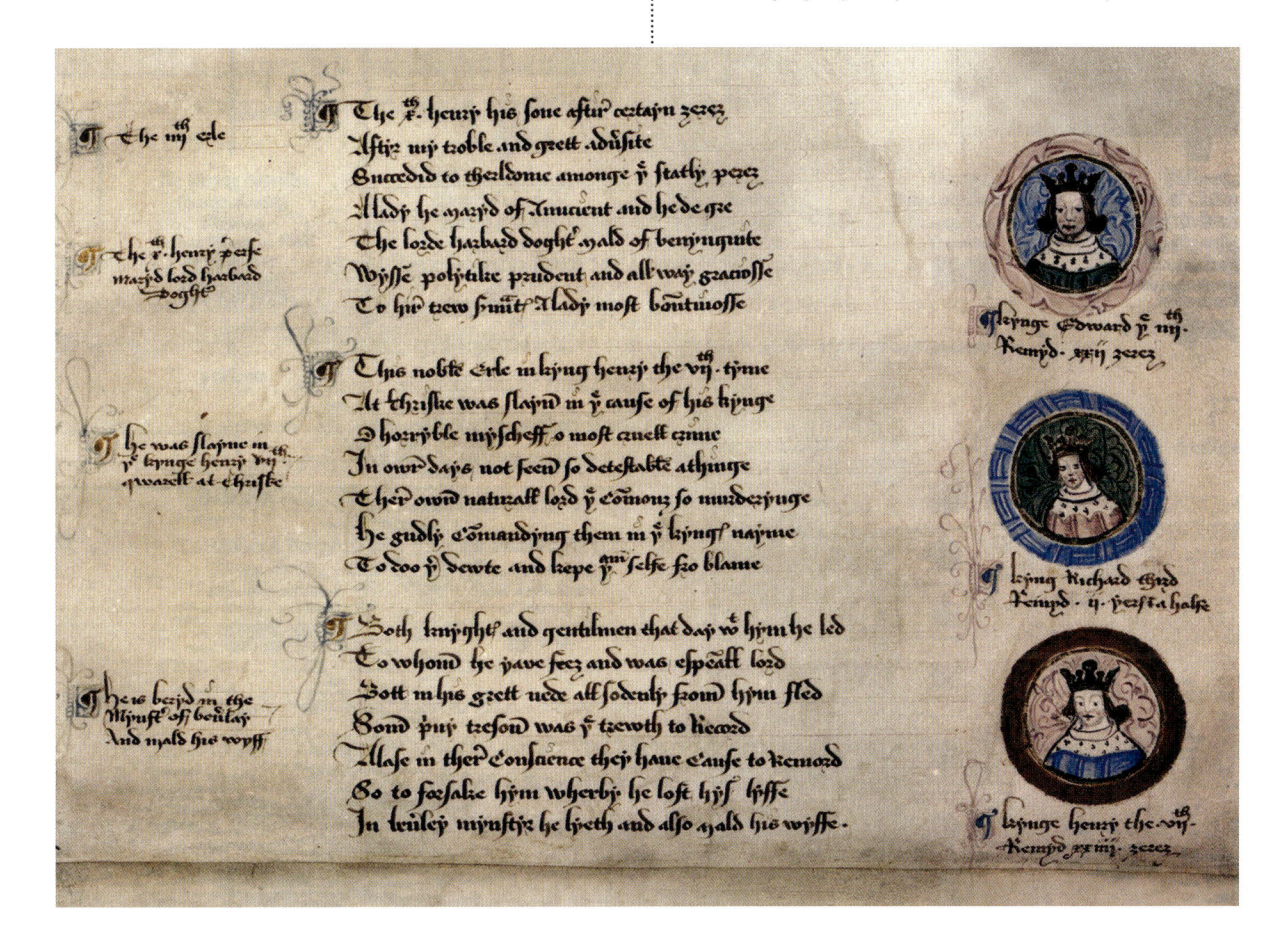

17 / RESTITUTION AND REVOLT   133

Epilogue

The birth of Tudor England heralded the conclusion of the Middle Ages, while the death of the 4th Earl of Northumberland brought an end to the semi-regal power of the Percys. Their titles and lands had nearly all been restored but their power was forever compromised by the centralisation of government, one of Richard III's legacies. They remained powerful servants of the Crown, though were not always loyal and continued to flirt with treason and rebellion over the next two centuries.

The 4th Earl and his countess had seven children. Their eldest son, Henry, succeeded as the 5th Earl and became a prominent figure at the court of Henry VIII. Known as 'The Magnificent', he saw himself as a Renaissance prince. He died in 1527, the first Earl of Northumberland to die of natural causes since the Earldom was created by King Richard II in 1377.

THE END

Portrait miniature of Henry Percy, 5th Earl of Northumberland, 1525-1527.

EPILOGUE

Appendices

Appendix A	Map of Land Ownership in England & Wales during the Wars of The Roses	137
Appendix B	Timeline, 1377-1527	138
Appendix C	The Royal Houses of York and Lancaster	142
	The Percy Family Tree – Earls of Northumberland	144
	The Neville Family Tree 1 – Earls of Westmorland	146
	The Neville Family Tree 2 – Earls of Salisbury and Warwick	148
Appendix D	Maps showing the loss of English-held or Allied Territory in Continental Europe, c. 1429-1453	150

Index	152
Acknowledgements; Select Bibliography	158
Picture Credits	159

Appendix A

Land Ownership in England & Wales during The Wars of The Roses

Key
- ECCLESIASTICAL (purple)
- ROYAL (orange)

Labels on map

- Berwick
- Palatinate of Durham
- PERCY
- Alnwick
- PERCY
- Newcastle
- ROYAL
- Palatinate of Durham
- NEVILLE
- NEVILLE · NEVILLE
- PERCY
- Isle of Man — STANLEY
- BEAUFORT
- NEVILLE · PERCY · NEVILLE · PERCY
- PERCY · ROYAL
- CLIFFORD · PERCY · York
- ROYAL · STAFFORD
- YORK
- MOWBRAY
- YORK
- ROYAL · PERCY
- NEVILLE · DE LA POLE
- ROYAL · ROYAL
- YORK · MOWBRAY
- NEVILLE
- STAFFORD
- BEAUFORT
- MOWBRAY · DE LA POLE
- Leicester
- STAFFORD · MOWBRAY · DE LA POLE
- NEVILLE · YORK · MOWBRAY
- YORK · ROYAL · DE LA POLE
- YORK · YORK
- Warwick
- NEVILLE · STAFFORD · YORK · MOWBRAY
- NEVILLE · NEVILLE · MOWBRAY · NEVILLE · DE LA POLE
- STAFFORD · ROYAL · PERCY
- YORK · STAFFORD · STAFFORD
- PERCY · MOWBRAY
- NEVILLE · YORK · STAFFORD
- Oxford · London
- ROYAL · NEVILLE · STAFFORD · NEVILLE · DE LA POLE · BEAUFORT
- MOWBRAY
- Bristol Channel
- BEAUFORT · ROYAL · STAFFORD
- PERCY · NEVILLE · NEVILLE · MOWBRAY · STAFFORD · Dover
- COURTENAY · ROYAL · Petworth · ROYAL
- BONVILLE · COURTENAY · ROYAL · PERCY · ROYAL
- ROYAL · COURTENAY · BEAUFORT
- Plymouth · Isle of Wight
- ROYAL
- Palatinate of the Isle of Ely

The Irish Sea · The German Ocean · The Wash · Thames Estuary · The English Channel

137

Appendix B

Timeline, 1377-1527

1377	Henry Percy is created 1st Earl of Northumberland.
1393	Birth of Henry Percy, grandson of the 1st Earl, who later became 2nd Earl of Northumberland.
1397	Financial institution The Medici Bank was founded in Florence, Italy.
1399	Henry Bolingbroke crowned as Henry IV after deposing Richard II.
1403	Sir Harry 'Hotspur' Percy, eldest son of the 1st Earl of Northumberland, rebels against Henry IV and is killed at the Battle of Shrewsbury. His uncle Thomas, Earl of Worcester, is executed on Henry IV's orders.
1405	The Archbishop of York and the 1st Earl of Northumberland lead a doomed further rebellion against Henry IV.
1406	As Beijing became the secondary capital of the Ming empire, construction began of what would become the Forbidden City.
1408	Sir Thomas Rokeby defeats the 1st Earl of Northumberland at the Battle of Bramham Moor, in which the Earl is killed.
1410	The Renaissance began to establish itself throughout Europe, bringing advancement in the arts, sciences, and banking.
1413	Death of Henry IV.
1414	Henry V lays claim to the crown of France as the heir of Edward III.
1415	Henry V lands in France with his army, captures Harfleur and wins the Battle of Agincourt.
1416	Henry Percy is restored as 2nd Earl of Northumberland by Henry V.
1419	Henry V captures Rouen, accompanied by the 2nd Earl of Northumberland.
1420	Henry V marries Catherine of Valois and makes peace with France. The Treaty of Troyes makes Henry and his heirs the lawful successors to the French throne.
	In China, the Ming dynasty completes the construction of the Forbidden City.
1421	Henry V returns to France. His son, the future Henry VI, is born in England while the King is undertaking a siege. Henry Percy, later 3rd Earl of Northumberland, is born.
1422	Death of Henry V at Vincennes. His infant son succeeds as King. The 2nd Earl of Northumberland is part of the Regency Council and becomes Ambassador to the Court of France.
	Thomas Percy, later Lord Egremont, is born.

Giovanni di Bicci de' Medici, founder of the Medici Bank.

The Forbidden City, Beijing.

A significant work of the Renaissance period, 'The Birth of Venus' by Sandro Botticelli.

1429	A French force led by Joan of Arc lifts the English siege of Orleans.
c.1430	Catherine, widow of Henry V, marries Owen Tudor.
1431	Joan of Arc is burned as a heretic.
1434	The 2nd Earl of Northumberland is granted a licence to enclose and fortify the town of Alnwick.
1437	James I of Scotland is assassinated.
1440	Johannes Gutenberg invents the moveable type printing press.
	Moctezuma I begins his rule over the Aztec Empire.
1445	Henry VI marries Margaret of Anjou.
1446	Eleanor Poynings, wife of young Henry Percy, inherits substantial lands. Percy inherits the title of Lord Poynings.
1449	Thomas Percy, younger brother of Lord Poynings, is created Lord Egremont.
1450	Jack Cade leads a rebellion against Henry VI. It fails and the ringleaders are hunted down and killed.
	Machu Picchu, the iconic citadel of the Inca Empire, was built at this time.
1453	French victory at Castillon ends the 'Hundred Years War' and all English territories in France are lost, with the sole exception of Calais and the Channel Islands.
	Prince Edward, son of Henry VI and Margaret of Anjou, is born. Henry VI's mental state collapses and he falls into a catatonic coma.
	Constantinople falls to the Ottomans, bringing the end of the Byzantine Empire.
1454	The Duke of York is made Lord Protector.
1455	York is removed as Protector after Henry VI's mental state improves.
	At the First Battle of St Albans the 2nd Earl of Northumberland is slain.
1456	Lord Egremont and Sir Richard Percy escape from Newgate Prison.
1460	Henry VI's forces are defeated at the Battle of Northampton and Lord Egremont is slain defending the King's tent. Queen Margaret raises an army and defeats the Yorkists at Wakefield. The Duke of York is killed in the battle. The Scottish King, James II, is killed by an exploding cannon at Roxburgh.

Johannes Gutenberg, whose moveable type press revolutionised printing.

The coronation of Moctezuma I, 1440.

Machu Picchu, iconic citadel of the Inca Empire.

The fall of Constantinople, 1453.

1461	The Yorkists are defeated at the 2nd Battle of St Albans.
	Edward, son of the Duke of York, defeats the Lancastrians at Mortimer's Cross and marches on London. He declares Henry to have forfeited the crown and is proclaimed King as Edward IV.
	The Lancastrians are defeated at the Battle of Towton, in which the 3rd Earl of Northumberland is slain.
	Edward IV is crowned at Westminster Abbey.
	The Earl of Warwick takes over Northern strongholds including Alnwick and Dunstanburgh castles. Berwick is ceded to Scotland. Queen Margaret seeks aid in France.
1462	Queen Margaret takes several Northern castles including Alnwick, Bamburgh and Warkworth.
1463	Alnwick and Dunstanburgh surrender to the Earl of Warwick; Queen Margaret regains them later in the year.
1464	Sir Ralph Percy is slain at the Battle of Hedgeley Moor in Northumberland. The Lancastrians are crushed at the Battle of Hexham.
	John Neville is made Earl of Northumberland. Henry Percy, son and heir of the 3rd Earl, remains in prison.
1465	Elizabeth Woodville, the wife of Edward IV, is crowned in Westminster Abbey.
1469	Rebellion against Edward IV in Yorkshire under a leader known as 'Robin of Redesdale'. Henry Percy, son of the 3rd Earl of Northumberland, swears fealty to Edward IV.
1470	Henry Percy is restored as 4th Earl of Northumberland. The Earl of Warwick offers his help to Queen Margaret and raises an army in aid of Henry VI.
1471	Edward defeats the Lancastrians at the Battle of Barnet and Warwick is killed in the battle. The Lancastrians are defeated again at the Battle of Tewkesbury.
	Death of Henry VI.
1472	Richard, Duke of Gloucester (later Richard III), marries Anne Neville, daughter of Warwick.
1474	Edward IV arranges a truce between England and Scotland. It is supposed to last until 1519.
c. 1475	William Caxton's *Recuyell of the Historyes of Troye* becomes the first book to be printed in English.
1475	The 4th Earl of Northumberland accompanies Edward on campaign in France.

William Caxton presenting a copy of his Recuyell of the Historyes of Troye *to Margaret of York.*

Ferdinand and Isabella, the Catholic Monarchs of Spain, 1475.

Vlad 'the Impaler', inspiration for Count Dracula.

Unification of Spain following the marriage of King Ferdinand II of Aragon and Queen Isabella I of Castile in 1469.

1476   Death of Vlad 'the Impaler', Prince of Wallachia and inspiration for Count Dracula.

1478   The Duke of Clarence, brother of Edward IV, is privately executed in the Tower of London.

Birth of Henry Percy, later 5th Earl of Northumberland.

1479   The Duke of Albany, brother of Scottish King James III, launches raids on the Border and sabotages 'Truce Days'.

1480   Raiding takes place on both sides of the Anglo-Scottish Border; settlements are burned and fortresses garrisoned.

1482   The Duke of Gloucester (later Richard III) and the 4th Earl of Northumberland capture the strategic port town of Berwick and bring it back into English possession.

Death of Margaret of Anjou.

1483   Death of Edward IV. Edward V succeeds to the throne, but is usurped by his uncle Gloucester, who is crowned as Richard III. The 4th Earl of Northumberland bears the sword 'Curtana' at the coronation.

1485   Henry Tudor lands at Milford Haven and proceeds to defeat Richard III at the Battle of Bosworth, where the 4th Earl of Northumberland and the Earl of Derby do not commit their forces. Richard III is killed in the battle and Henry Tudor is crowned as Henry VII.

1486   Henry VII marries Elizabeth of York, uniting the 'roses' of York and Lancaster.

1487   A Yorkist rebellion breaks out in support of Lambert Simnel, who purports to be the Earl of Warwick and to have a claim to the throne.

1489   The 4th Earl of Northumberland is murdered by a mob in Yorkshire led by John Chamber.

1492   Christopher Columbus lands in the Americas.

1498   Vasco da Gama reaches India by sea from Portugal.

1503   James IV of Scotland marries Henry VII's daughter, Margaret Tudor.

1506   Leonardo da Vinci paints the 'Mona Lisa'.

1509   Death of Henry VII. Henry VIII accedes to the throne.

1527   Death of Henry Percy, 5th Earl of Northumberland.

Columbus sets foot on the American mainland, 1492.

Vasco da Gama.

The 'Mona Lisa'.

Appendix C

The Royal Houses of York and Lancaster

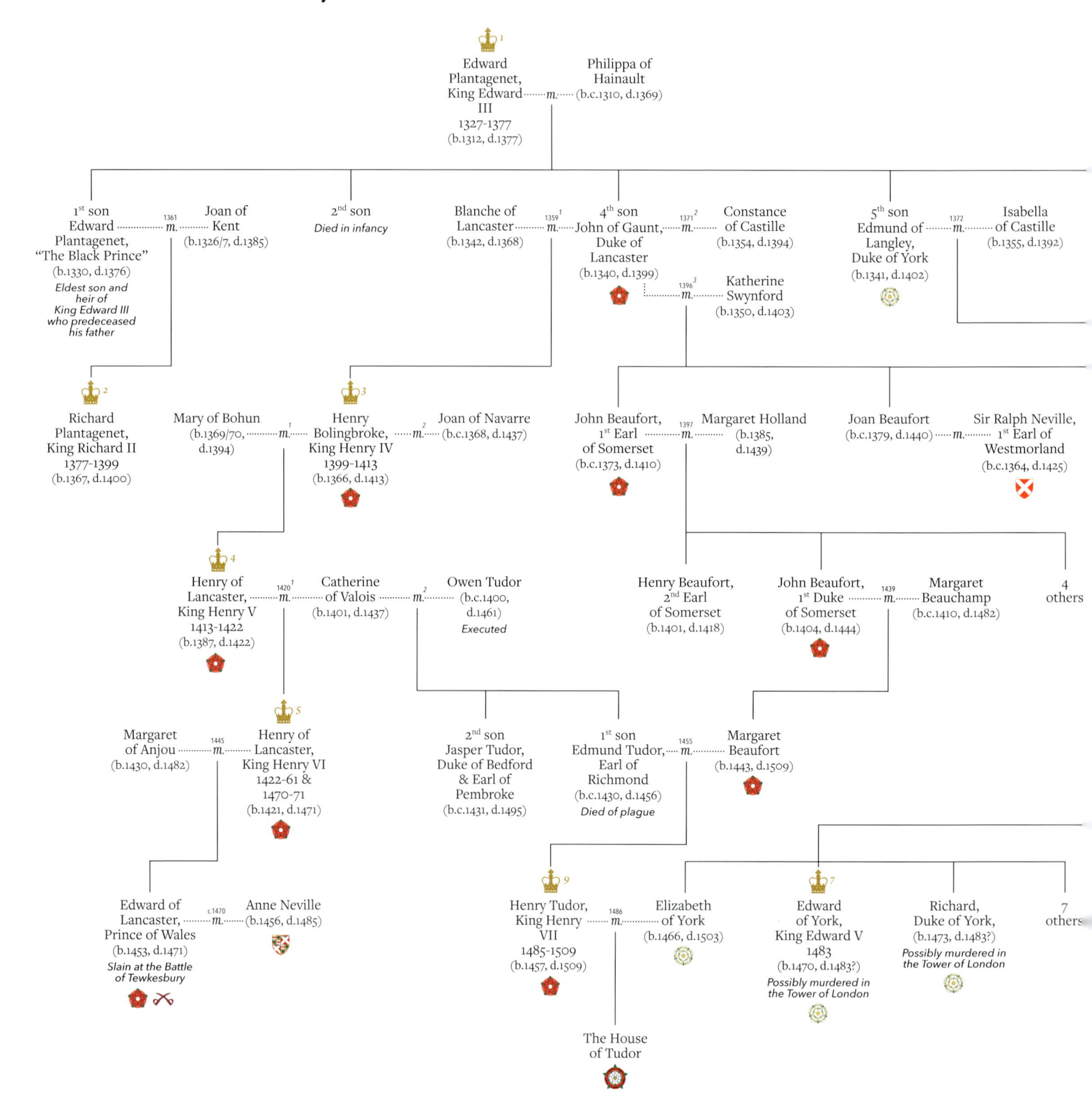

Edward Plantagenet, King Edward III (1327–1377, b.1312, d.1377)
m. Philippa of Hainault (b.c.1310, d.1369)

Children of Edward III and Philippa:

- **1st son: Edward Plantagenet, "The Black Prince"** (b.1330, d.1376) — Eldest son and heir of King Edward III who predeceased his father. m.1361 Joan of Kent (b.1326/7, d.1385)
- **2nd son**: Died in infancy
- **Blanche of Lancaster** (b.1342, d.1368) m.1359 (1st marriage) **John of Gaunt, Duke of Lancaster** (b.1340, d.1399); m.1371 (2nd) Constance of Castille (b.1354, d.1394); m.1396 (3rd) Katherine Swynford (b.1350, d.1403)
- **5th son: Edmund of Langley, Duke of York** (b.1341, d.1402) m.1372 Isabella of Castille (b.1355, d.1392)

Next generation:

- **Richard Plantagenet, King Richard II** 1377–1399 (b.1367, d.1400)
- **Henry Bolingbroke, King Henry IV** 1399–1413 (b.1366, d.1413); m.1 Mary of Bohun (b.1369/70, d.1394); m.2 Joan of Navarre (b.c.1368, d.1437)
- **John Beaufort, 1st Earl of Somerset** (b.c.1373, d.1410) m.1397 Margaret Holland (b.1385, d.1439)
- **Joan Beaufort** (b.c.1379, d.1440) m. Sir Ralph Neville, 1st Earl of Westmorland (b.c.1364, d.1425)

Next generation:

- **Henry of Lancaster, King Henry V** 1413–1422 (b.1387, d.1422) m.1420 (1st) Catherine of Valois (b.1401, d.1437); m.2 Owen Tudor (b.c.1400, d.1461) — Executed
- **Henry Beaufort, 2nd Earl of Somerset** (b.1401, d.1418)
- **John Beaufort, 1st Duke of Somerset** (b.1404, d.1444) m.1439 Margaret Beauchamp (b.c.1410, d.1482)
- 4 others

Next generation:

- **Margaret of Anjou** (b.1430, d.1482) m.1445 **Henry of Lancaster, King Henry VI** 1422–61 & 1470–71 (b.1421, d.1471)
- **2nd son: Jasper Tudor, Duke of Bedford & Earl of Pembroke** (b.c.1431, d.1495)
- **1st son: Edmund Tudor, Earl of Richmond** (b.c.1430, d.1456) — Died of plague; m.1455 **Margaret Beaufort** (b.1443, d.1509)

Next generation:

- **Edward of Lancaster, Prince of Wales** (b.1453, d.1471) — Slain at the Battle of Tewkesbury; m.c.1470 Anne Neville (b.1456, d.1485)
- **Henry Tudor, King Henry VII** 1485–1509 (b.1457, d.1509) m.1486 **Elizabeth of York** (b.1466, d.1503)
- **Edward of York, King Edward V** 1483 (b.1470, d.1483?) — Possibly murdered in the Tower of London
- **Richard, Duke of York** (b.1473, d.1483?) — Possibly murdered in the Tower of London
- 7 others

The House of Tudor

142 LIONS OF THE RED ROSE

Key to Symbols

- House of York
- House of Lancaster
- Kings numbered in order of their reigns
- Percy Family Tree, Earls of Northumberland
- Neville Family Tree 1, Earls of Westmorland
- Neville Family Tree 2, Earls of Salisbury and Warwick
- Slain in battle

3rd son Lionel of Antwerp, Duke of Clarence (b.1338, d.1368) —m.1352— Elizabeth De Burgh (b.1332, d.1363) — Others

Philippa, Countess of Ulster (b.1355, d.1382) —m.1368— Edmund Mortimer, 3rd Earl of March (b.1352, d.1381)

2 others

Sir Harry "Hotspur" Percy (b.1364/6, d.1403) —m.1379— Elizabeth Mortimer (b.1371, d.1417) *See Percy Family Tree*

Alianore Holland (b.1370, d.1405) —m.1388— Roger Mortimer, 4th Earl of March (b.1374, d.1398)

Sir Edmund Mortimer (b.1376, d.1409)

1 other

Edward of York, 2nd Duke of York (b.1373, d.1415) *No legitimate issue*

1 other

Richard, Earl of Cambridge (b.1385, d.1415) —m.— Anne Mortimer (b.1388, d.1411)

Edmund Mortimer, 5th Earl of March (b.1391, d.1425) *No legitimate issue*

2 others

Richard of York, 3rd Duke of York & 6th Earl of March (b.1411, d.1460) —m.c.1429— Cecily Neville, "The Rose of Raby" (b.1415, d.1495)
Slain at the Battle of Wakefield

Elizabeth Woodville (b.c.1437, d.1492) —m.1464— Edward of York, King Edward IV (6) 1461-1470 and 1471-1483 (b.1442, d.1483)

Edmund, Earl of Rutland (b.1443, d.1460) *Slain at the Battle of Wakefield*

George, Duke of Clarence (b.1449, d.1478) —m.1469— Isabel Neville (b.1451, d.1476) *Executed*

Anne Neville (b.1456, d.1485) *Widow of Edward of Lancaster, Prince of Wales* —m.1472— Richard, Duke of Gloucester, King Richard III (8) 1483-1485 (b.1452, d.1485) *Slain at the Battle of Bosworth*

8 others

Margaret Plantagenet, Countess of Salisbury (b.1473, d.1541) *Executed*

Edward Plantagenet, Earl of Warwick (b.1475, d.1499) *Executed, the last male heir of Plantagenet*

Edward of Middleham, Prince of Wales (b.c.1475, d.1484) *Predeceased his father*

APPENDIX C – THE ROYAL HOUSES OF YORK AND LANCASTER

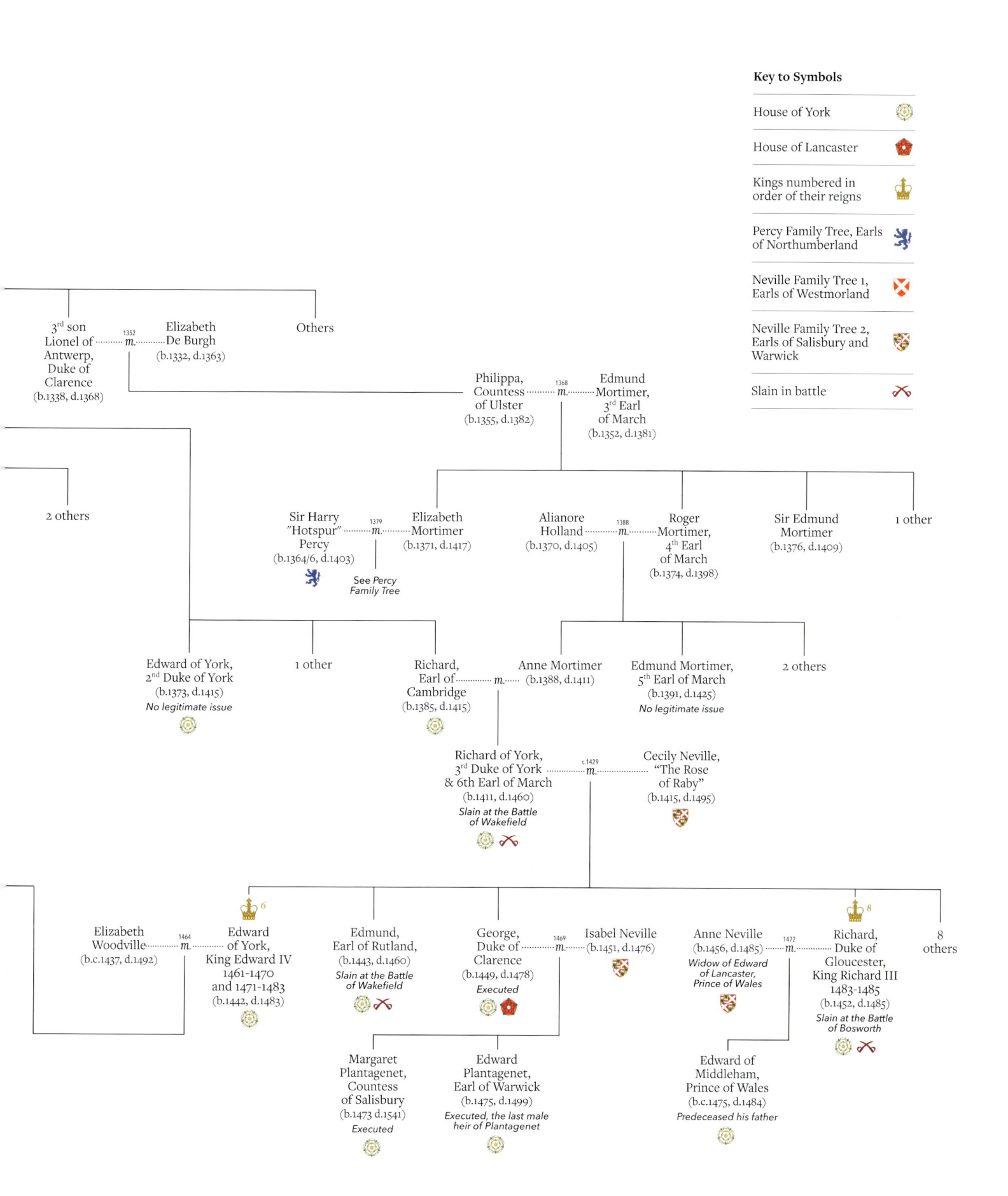

The Percy Family Tree
Earls of Northumberland

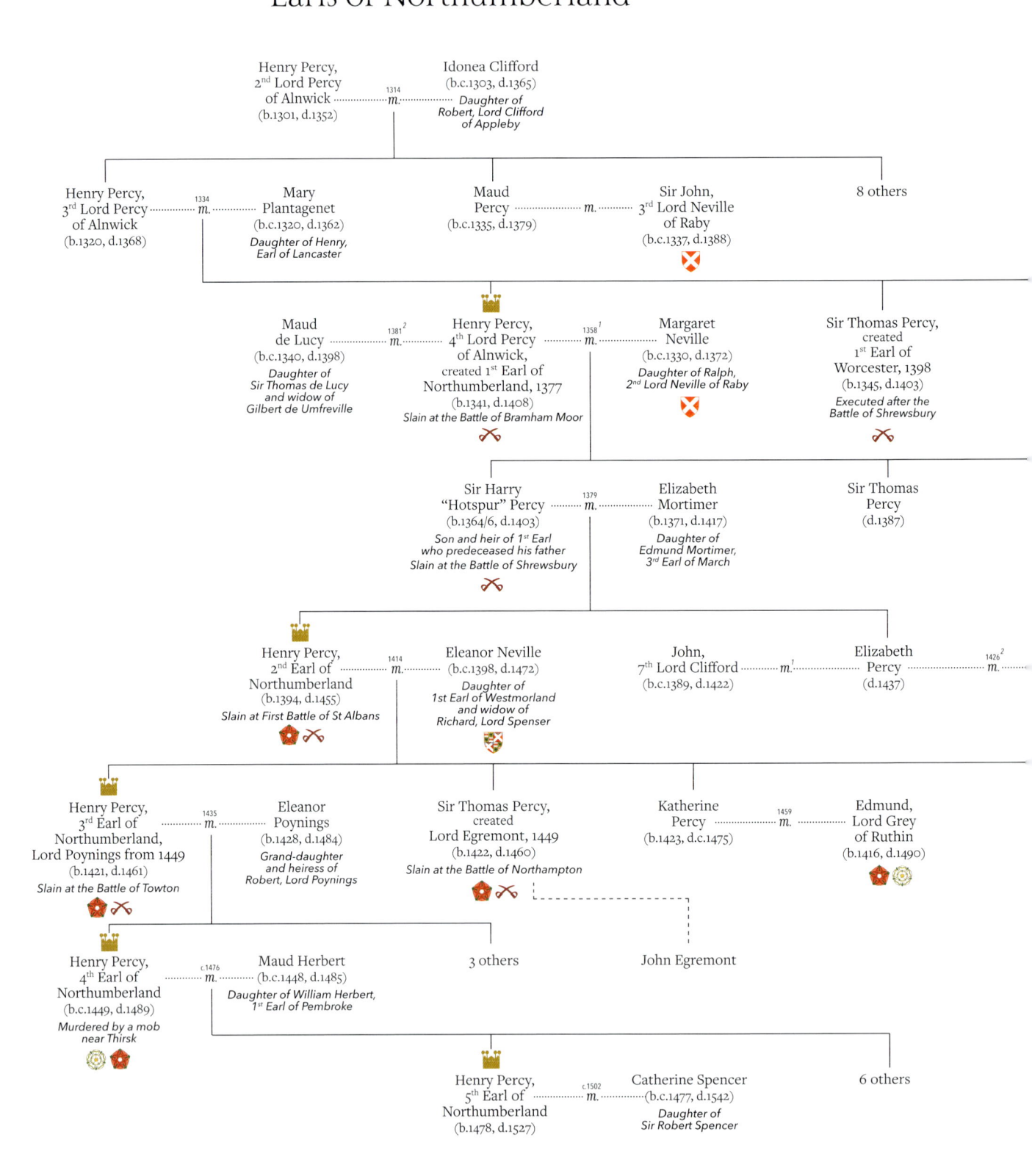

Henry Percy, 2nd Lord Percy of Alnwick (b.1301, d.1352) —m. 1314— **Idonea Clifford** (b.c.1303, d.1365), *Daughter of Robert, Lord Clifford of Appleby*

Children:

- **Henry Percy, 3rd Lord Percy of Alnwick** (b.1320, d.1368) —m. 1334— **Mary Plantagenet** (b.c.1320, d.1362), *Daughter of Henry, Earl of Lancaster*
- **Maud Percy** (b.c.1335, d.1379) —m.— **Sir John, 3rd Lord Neville of Raby** (b.c.1337, d.1388)
- **8 others**

Children of Henry Percy, 3rd Lord Percy, and Mary Plantagenet:

- **Maud de Lucy** (b.c.1340, d.1398), *Daughter of Sir Thomas de Lucy and widow of Gilbert de Umfreville* —m. 1381 (2)— **Henry Percy, 4th Lord Percy of Alnwick, created 1st Earl of Northumberland, 1377** (b.1341, d.1408), *Slain at the Battle of Bramham Moor* —m. 1358 (1)— **Margaret Neville** (b.c.1330, d.1372), *Daughter of Ralph, 2nd Lord Neville of Raby*
- **Sir Thomas Percy, created 1st Earl of Worcester, 1398** (b.1345, d.1403), *Executed after the Battle of Shrewsbury*

Children of Henry Percy, 1st Earl of Northumberland, and Margaret Neville:

- **Sir Harry "Hotspur" Percy** (b.1364/6, d.1403), *Son and heir of 1st Earl who predeceased his father. Slain at the Battle of Shrewsbury* —m. 1379— **Elizabeth Mortimer** (b.1371, d.1417), *Daughter of Edmund Mortimer, 3rd Earl of March*
- **Sir Thomas Percy** (d.1387)

Children of Sir Harry "Hotspur" Percy and Elizabeth Mortimer:

- **Henry Percy, 2nd Earl of Northumberland** (b.1394, d.1455), *Slain at First Battle of St Albans* —m. 1414— **Eleanor Neville** (b.c.1398, d.1472), *Daughter of 1st Earl of Westmorland and widow of Richard, Lord Spenser*
- **John, 7th Lord Clifford** (b.c.1389, d.1422) —m. (1)— **Elizabeth Percy** (d.1437) —m. 1426 (2)—

Children of Henry Percy, 2nd Earl of Northumberland, and Eleanor Neville:

- **Henry Percy, 3rd Earl of Northumberland, Lord Poynings from 1449** (b.1421, d.1461), *Slain at the Battle of Towton* —m. 1435— **Eleanor Poynings** (b.1428, d.1484), *Grand-daughter and heiress of Robert, Lord Poynings*
- **Sir Thomas Percy, created Lord Egremont, 1449** (b.1422, d.1460), *Slain at the Battle of Northampton*
- **Katherine Percy** (b.1423, d.c.1475) —m. 1459— **Edmund, Lord Grey of Ruthin** (b.1416, d.1490)

- **John Egremont**

Children of Henry Percy, 3rd Earl of Northumberland, and Eleanor Poynings:

- **Henry Percy, 4th Earl of Northumberland** (b.c.1449, d.1489), *Murdered by a mob near Thirsk* —m. c.1476— **Maud Herbert** (b.c.1448, d.1485), *Daughter of William Herbert, 1st Earl of Pembroke*
- **3 others**

Children of Henry Percy, 4th Earl of Northumberland, and Maud Herbert:

- **Henry Percy, 5th Earl of Northumberland** (b.1478, d.1527) —m. c.1502— **Catherine Spencer** (b.c.1477, d.1542), *Daughter of Sir Robert Spencer*
- **6 others**

144 LIONS OF THE RED ROSE

Key to Symbols

Yorkists	
Lancastrians	
Earls of Northumberland	
Neville Family Tree 1, Earls of Westmorland	
Neville Family Tree 2, Earls of Salisbury and Warwick	
Slain in battle	

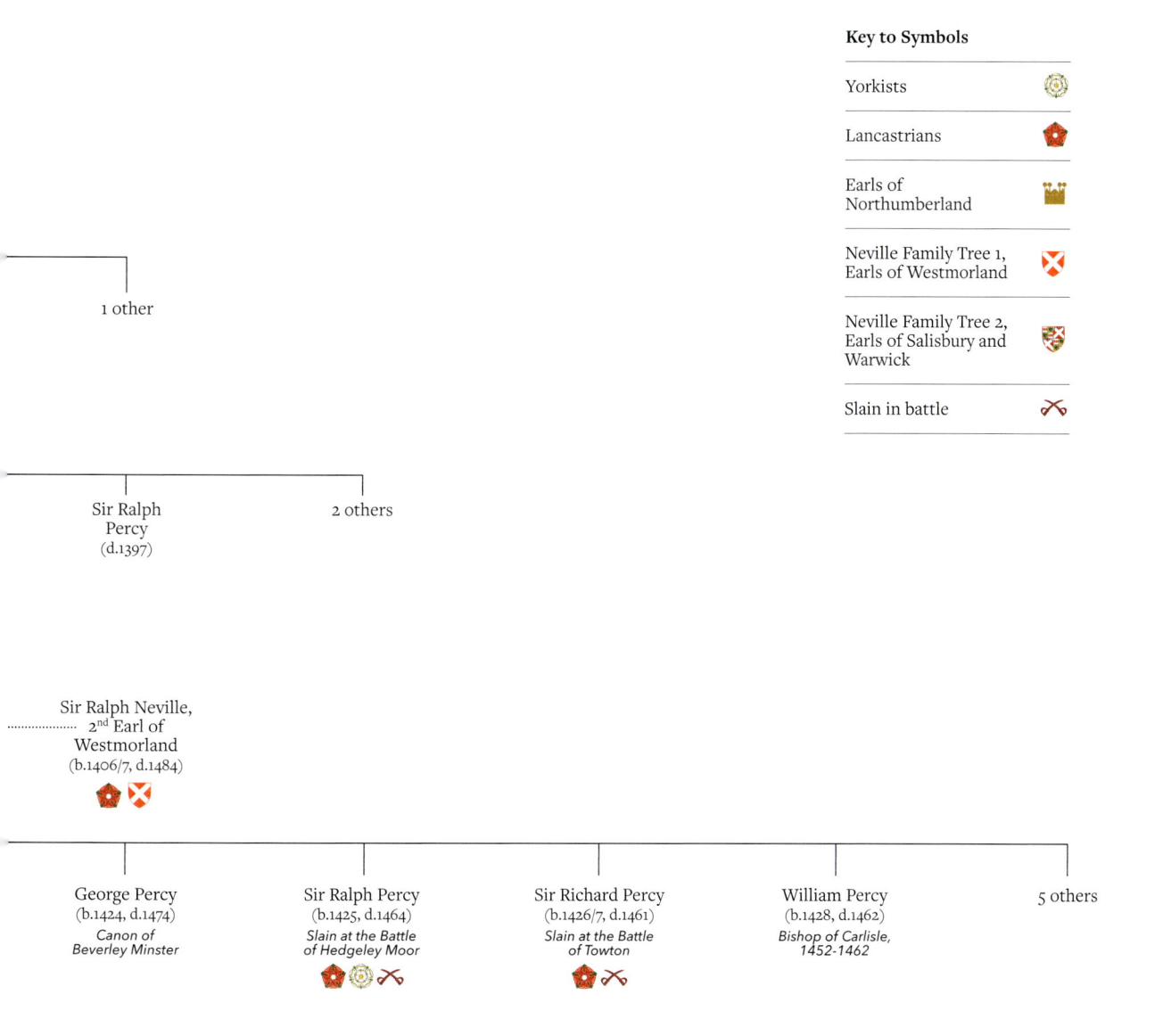

1 other

Sir Ralph Percy (d.1397)

2 others

Sir Ralph Neville, 2nd Earl of Westmorland (b.1406/7, d.1484)

George Percy (b.1424, d.1474)
Canon of Beverley Minster

Sir Ralph Percy (b.1425, d.1464)
Slain at the Battle of Hedgeley Moor

Sir Richard Percy (b.1426/7, d.1461)
Slain at the Battle of Towton

William Percy (b.1428, d.1462)
Bishop of Carlisle, 1452-1462

5 others

APPENDIX C – THE PERCY FAMILY TREE

The Neville Family Tree 1
Earls of Westmorland

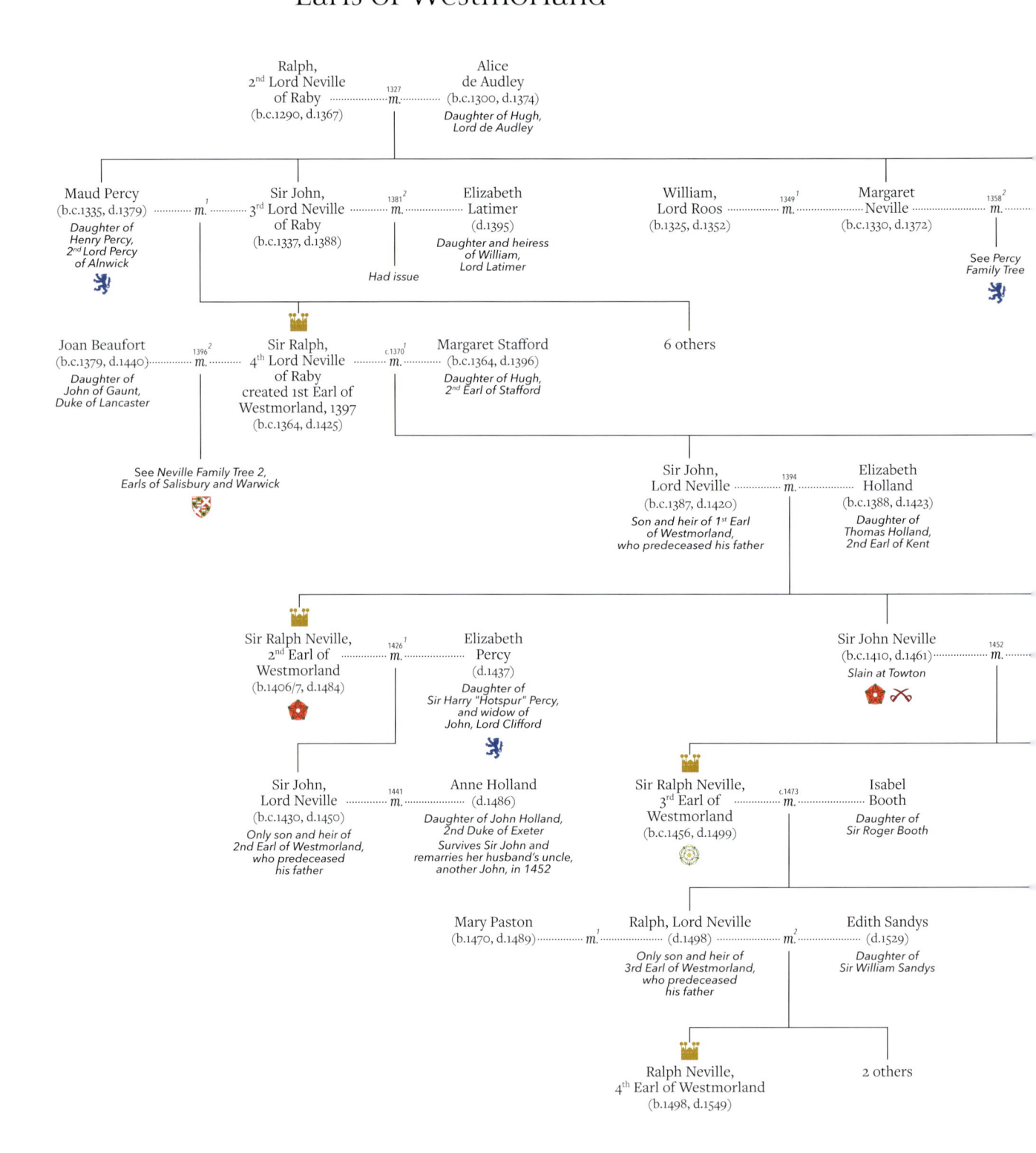

Ralph, 2nd Lord Neville of Raby (b.c.1290, d.1367) —m. 1327— **Alice de Audley** (b.c.1300, d.1374) *Daughter of Hugh, Lord de Audley*

Children:

- **Maud Percy** (b.c.1335, d.1379) *Daughter of Henry Percy, 2nd Lord Percy of Alnwick* —m.1— **Sir John, 3rd Lord Neville of Raby** (b.c.1337, d.1388) —m.2 1381— **Elizabeth Latimer** (d.1395) *Daughter and heiress of William, Lord Latimer* — *Had issue*

- **William, Lord Roos** (b.1325, d.1352) —m.1 1349— **Margaret Neville** (b.c.1330, d.1372) —m.2 1358— *See Percy Family Tree*

Children of Sir John, 3rd Lord Neville and Maud Percy:

- **Joan Beaufort** (b.c.1379, d.1440) *Daughter of John of Gaunt, Duke of Lancaster* —m.2 1396— **Sir Ralph, 4th Lord Neville of Raby, created 1st Earl of Westmorland, 1397** (b.c.1364, d.1425) —m.1 c.1370— **Margaret Stafford** (b.c.1364, d.1396) *Daughter of Hugh, 2nd Earl of Stafford*

See Neville Family Tree 2, Earls of Salisbury and Warwick

- **6 others**

- **Sir John, Lord Neville** (b.c.1387, d.1420) *Son and heir of 1st Earl of Westmorland, who predeceased his father* —m. 1394— **Elizabeth Holland** (b.c.1388, d.1423) *Daughter of Thomas Holland, 2nd Earl of Kent*

Children of Sir John, Lord Neville and Elizabeth Holland:

- **Sir Ralph Neville, 2nd Earl of Westmorland** (b.1406/7, d.1484) —m.1 1426— **Elizabeth Percy** (d.1437) *Daughter of Sir Harry "Hotspur" Percy, and widow of John, Lord Clifford*

- **Sir John Neville** (b.c.1410, d.1461) —m. 1452— *Slain at Towton*

Children of Sir Ralph Neville, 2nd Earl and Elizabeth Percy:

- **Sir John, Lord Neville** (b.c.1430, d.1450) *Only son and heir of 2nd Earl of Westmorland, who predeceased his father* —m. 1441— **Anne Holland** (d.1486) *Daughter of John Holland, 2nd Duke of Exeter. Survives Sir John and remarries her husband's uncle, another John, in 1452*

- **Sir Ralph Neville, 3rd Earl of Westmorland** (b.c.1456, d.1499) —m. c.1473— **Isabel Booth** *Daughter of Sir Roger Booth*

Children of Sir Ralph Neville, 3rd Earl and Isabel Booth:

- **Mary Paston** (b.1470, d.1489) —m.1— **Ralph, Lord Neville** (d.1498) *Only son and heir of 3rd Earl of Westmorland, who predeceased his father* —m.2— **Edith Sandys** (d.1529) *Daughter of Sir William Sandys*

Children:

- **Ralph Neville, 4th Earl of Westmorland** (b.1498, d.1549)
- **2 others**

Henry Percy,
1st Earl of
Northumberland
(b.1341, d.1408)

8 others

8 others

Anne Holland
(d.1486)
Daughter of John Holland,
2nd Duke of Exeter
Widow of her husband's
nephew, John

5 others

1 other

1 other

Key to Symbols

Yorkists	
Lancastrians	
Earls of Westmorland	
Neville Family Tree 2, Earls of Salisbury and Warwick	
Percy Family Tree, Earls of Northumberland	
Slain in battle	

APPENDIX C – THE NEVILLE FAMILY TREE 1

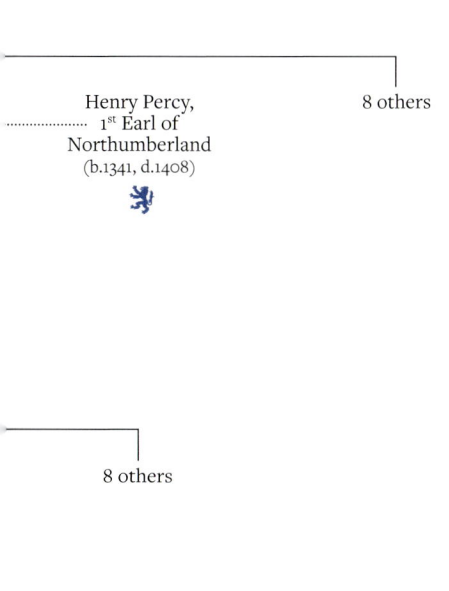

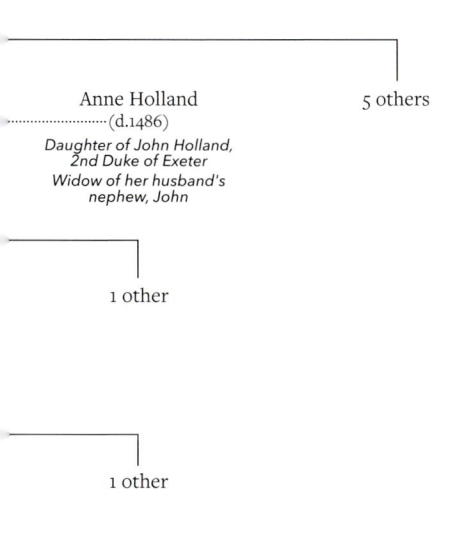

The Neville Family Tree 2
Earls of Salisbury and Warwick

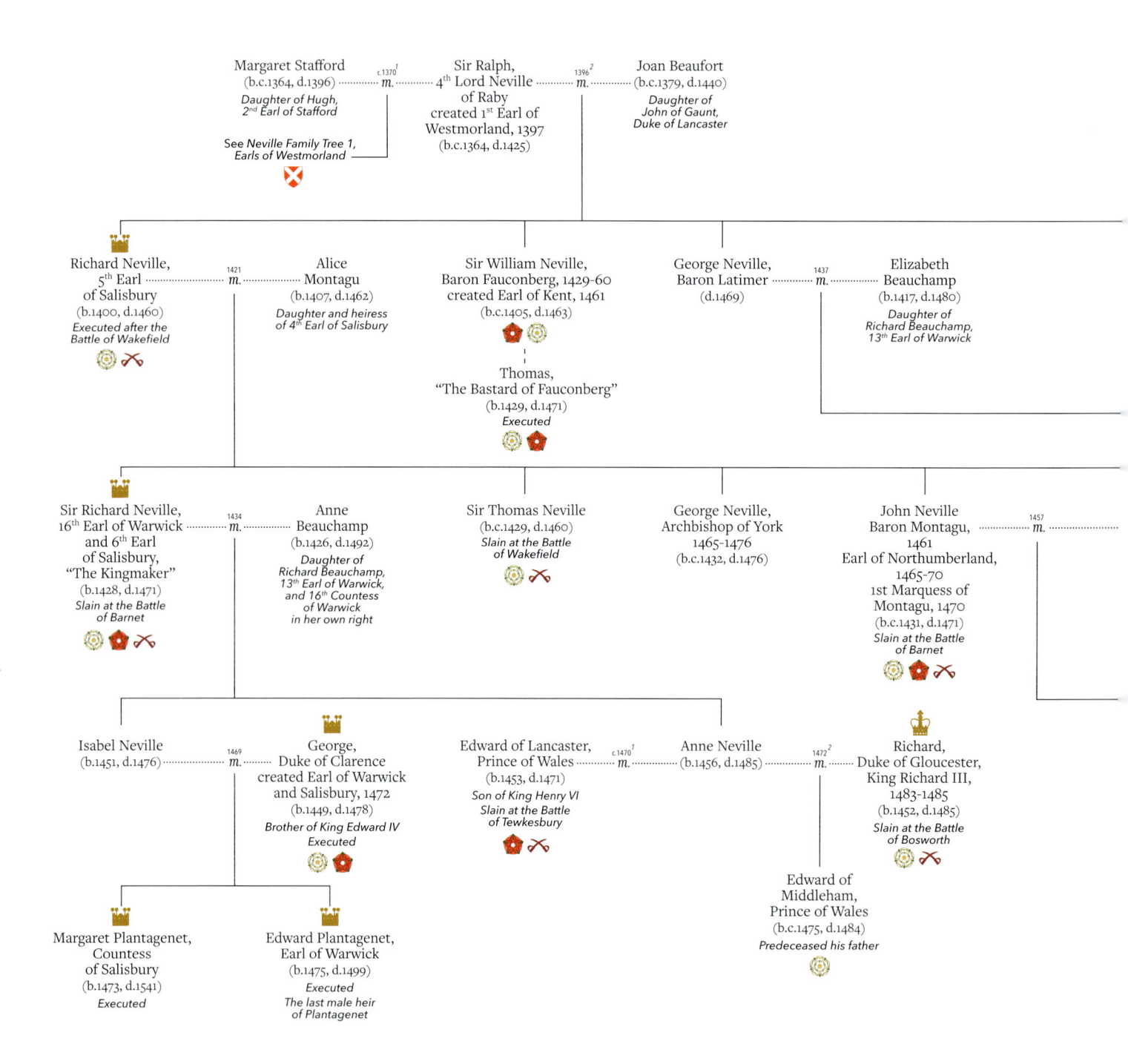

Margaret Stafford (b.c.1364, d.1396) *Daughter of Hugh, 2nd Earl of Stafford* — m. c.1370¹ — **Sir Ralph, 4th Lord Neville of Raby** created 1st Earl of Westmorland, 1397 (b.c.1364, d.1425) — m. 1396² — **Joan Beaufort** (b.c.1379, d.1440) *Daughter of John of Gaunt, Duke of Lancaster*

See Neville Family Tree 1, Earls of Westmorland

Children of Sir Ralph and Joan Beaufort:

- **Richard Neville, 5th Earl of Salisbury** (b.1400, d.1460) *Executed after the Battle of Wakefield* — m. 1421 — **Alice Montagu** (b.1407, d.1462) *Daughter and heiress of 4th Earl of Salisbury*
- **Sir William Neville, Baron Fauconberg, 1429-60** created Earl of Kent, 1461 (b.c.1405, d.1463)
  - **Thomas, "The Bastard of Fauconberg"** (b.1429, d.1471) *Executed*
- **George Neville, Baron Latimer** (d.1469) — m. 1437 — **Elizabeth Beauchamp** (b.1417, d.1480) *Daughter of Richard Beauchamp, 13th Earl of Warwick*

Children of Richard Neville and Alice Montagu:

- **Sir Richard Neville, 16th Earl of Warwick and 6th Earl of Salisbury, "The Kingmaker"** (b.1428, d.1471) *Slain at the Battle of Barnet* — m. 1434 — **Anne Beauchamp** (b.1426, d.1492) *Daughter of Richard Beauchamp, 13th Earl of Warwick, and 16th Countess of Warwick in her own right*
- **Sir Thomas Neville** (b.c.1429, d.1460) *Slain at the Battle of Wakefield*
- **George Neville, Archbishop of York** 1465-1476 (b.c.1432, d.1476)
- **John Neville, Baron Montagu,** 1461, Earl of Northumberland, 1465-70, 1st Marquess of Montagu, 1470 (b.c.1431, d.1471) *Slain at the Battle of Barnet* — m. 1457

Children of Sir Richard Neville and Anne Beauchamp:

- **Isabel Neville** (b.1451, d.1476) — m. 1469 — **George, Duke of Clarence** created Earl of Warwick and Salisbury, 1472 (b.1449, d.1478) *Brother of King Edward IV. Executed*
- **Anne Neville** (b.1456, d.1485) — m. c.1470¹ — **Edward of Lancaster, Prince of Wales** (b.1453, d.1471) *Son of King Henry VI. Slain at the Battle of Tewkesbury*
- Anne Neville — m. 1472² — **Richard, Duke of Gloucester, King Richard III, 1483-1485** (b.1452, d.1485) *Slain at the Battle of Bosworth*

Children:

- **Margaret Plantagenet, Countess of Salisbury** (b.1473, d.1541) *Executed*
- **Edward Plantagenet, Earl of Warwick** (b.1475, d.1499) *Executed. The last male heir of Plantagenet*
- **Edward of Middleham, Prince of Wales** (b.c.1475, d.1484) *Predeceased his father*

```
Richard,           Eleanor Neville      1414²   Henry Percy,              Richard of York,            Cecily Neville,         9 others
Lord Spenser ··· m.¹ ··· (b.c.1398, d.1472) ··· m. ··· 2ⁿᵈ Earl of           3ʳᵈ Duke of York ··· c.1429 ··· "The Rose
(d.1414)                                         Northumberland            and 6ᵗʰ Earl         m.         of Raby"
                                                 (b.1394, d.1455)          of March                       (b.1415, d.1495)
                                                 Slain at 1ˢᵗ Battle       (b.1411, d.1460)              Youngest of
                                    See Percy    of St Albans              Slain at the Battle           23 children
                                    Family Tree                            of Wakefield
```

Isabel Ingoldesthorpe (b.c.1441, d.1476)	Sir Henry Neville (b.1437, d.1469) *Only son* *Slain at Edgecote Field near Banbury*	Edward of York, King Edward IV, 1461-1470 and 1471-1483 (b.1442, d.1483)	Edmund, Earl of Rutland (b.1443, d.1460) *Slain at the Battle of Wakefield*	George, Duke of Clarence (b.1449, d.1478) *Executed*	Richard, Duke of Gloucester, King Richard III, 1483-1485 (b.1452, d.1485) *Slain at the Battle of Bosworth*

8 others

3 others

See Royal Houses of York and Lancaster

8 others

George Neville
created
Duke of Bedford, 1469
2ⁿᵈ Marquess
of Montagu, 1471
(b.1465, d.1483)

6 others

Key to Symbols

Yorkists	🏵
Lancastrians	⬟
Kings	👑
Earls of Warwick and Salisbury	♛
Neville Family Tree 1, Earls of Westmorland	⛊
Percy Family Tree, Earls of Northumberland	🦁
Slain in battle	⚔

APPENDIX C – THE NEVILLE FAMILY TREE 2   149

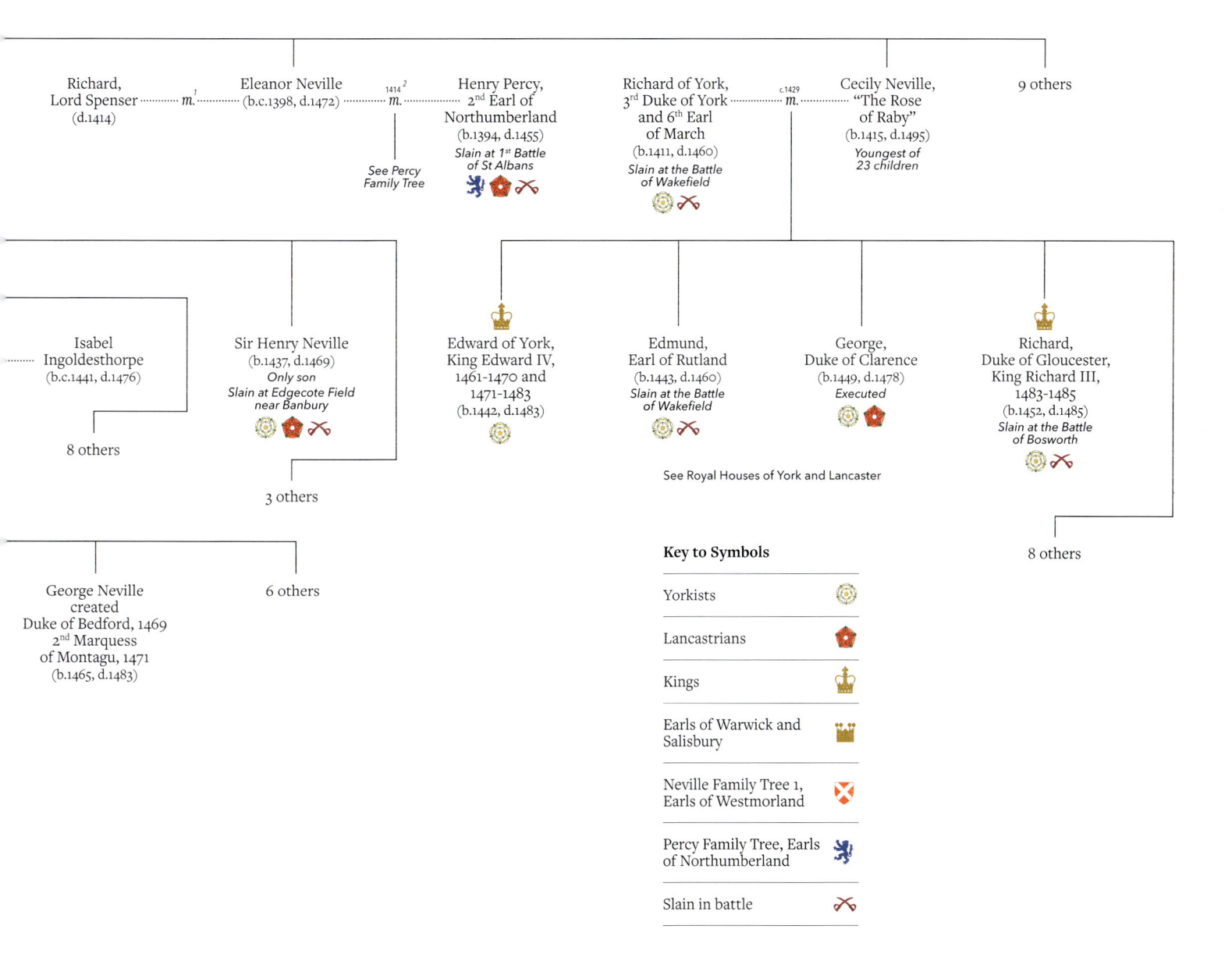

Appendix D

The Loss of English-held or Allied Territory in Continental Europe, c. 1429–1453

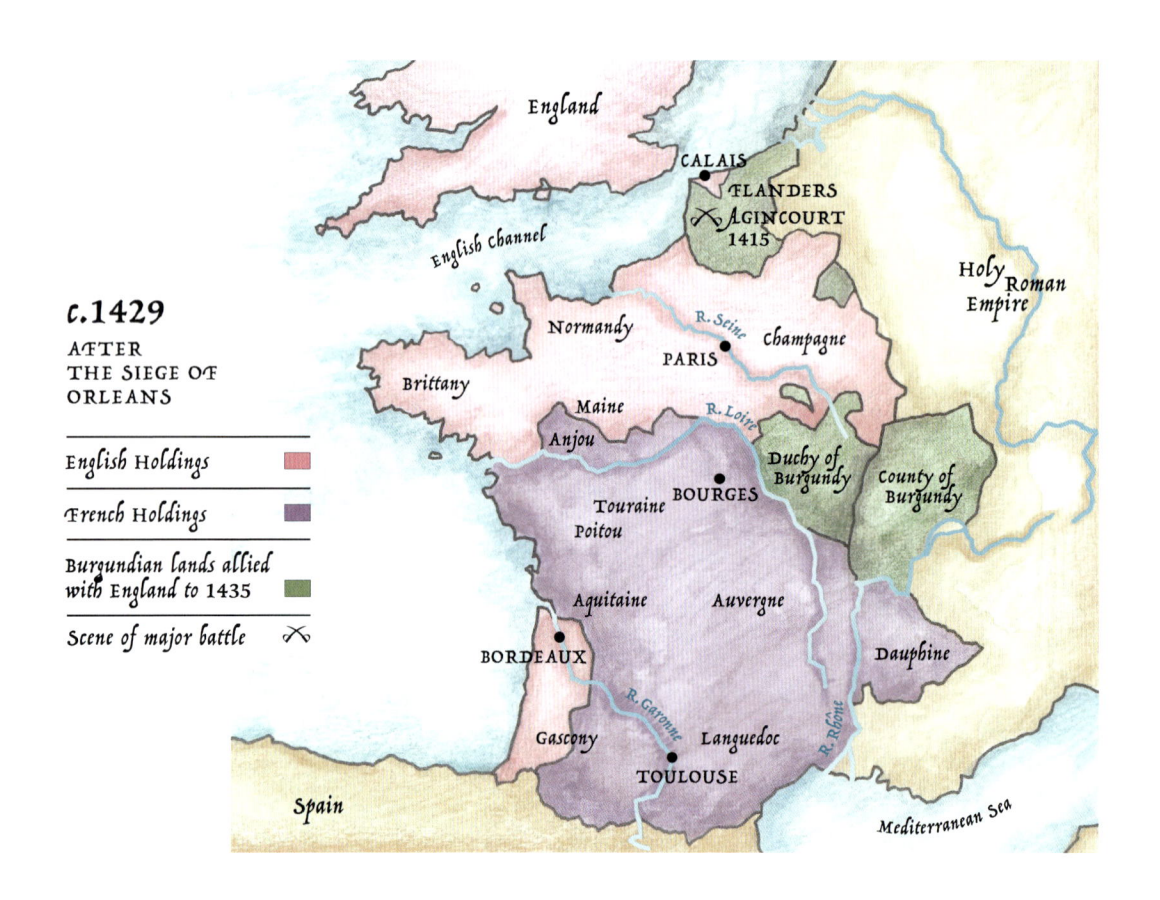

c. 1429
AFTER THE SIEGE OF ORLEANS

- English Holdings
- French Holdings
- Burgundian lands allied with England to 1435
- Scene of major battle

1453
END OF THE HUNDRED YEARS WAR

- English Holdings
- French Holdings
- Burgundian lands reconciled with France after 1435
- Scene of last battle

APPENDIX D – THE LOSS OF ENGLISH-HELD OR ALLIED TERRITORY

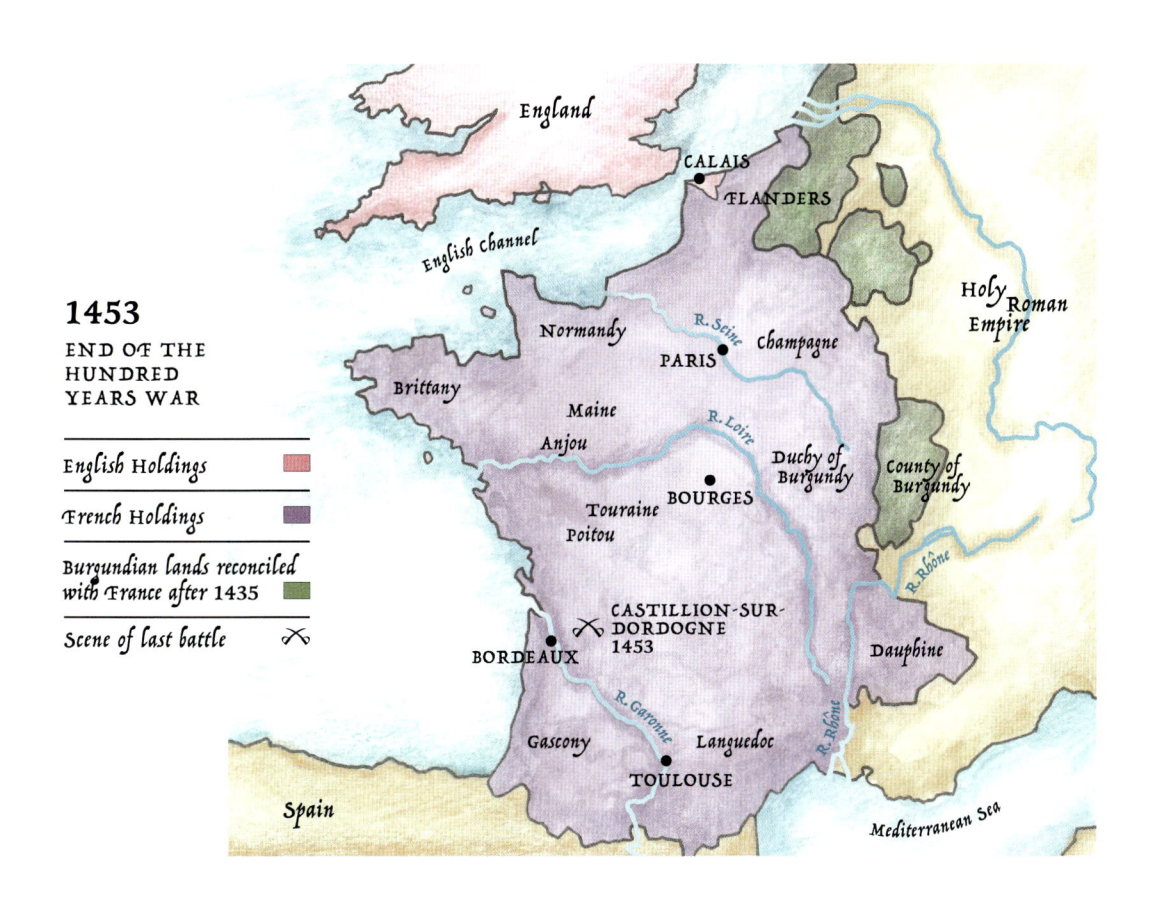

Index

Page numbers in *italics* are for illustrations.

Abingdon, black monk of 95
Accord, Act of, (1460) 61, 63
Acton Bridge 53
Agincourt, Battle of, (25 Oct 1415) 11, 15, 25, 63, 97
Aire, River 72
Albany, Dukes of *See under Stewart*
Alnwick
    Abbey 42-43
    Bondgate Tower *21*
    Castle 10, 78-85, 88, 92, 120-121 *82*
        Barbican *82*
        Chaplains of 16, 43
        Well in the Keep 85
    Town of 21-22, 28, 84, 89, 119
    Town walls 21
Ampthill, Manor of 58
Angers, France, Capital of the Province of Anjou 104
    Cathedral 114
Anglo-Burgundian Alliance 108
Anglo-French treaty, *See Picquigny*
Angus, Earls of *See under Douglas*
Anjou, Margaret of, Queen of Henry VI (b.1430, d.1482) 26-27, 34, 36, 45-47, 50-53, 56, 59, 61-64, 67-68, 70-71, 78-89, 96-97, 104-105, 107, 109-111, 114, *27*
Anjou, Rene of (former King of Naples) (b.1409, d.1480) 88
Arc, Joan of 20, *21*
Arkinholm 46
Arras, Treaty of 121
Arrowheads *74*
Artillery *See also Cannon* 11, 13, 18, 22, 60, 87, 92, 120 *58*
Arundel, Earl of, William Fitzalan (b.1417, d.1487) 53, 94, 102
Assassinations
    Henry V, 'Southampton' plot 15
    Scottish King James I, at Blackfriars Monastery in Perth, 1437 22
    Duke of York and Earl of Warwick, attempted 47
Audley, Lord, James Tuchet (b.c.1398, d.1459) 52-53
Auld Alliance, The 10, 118
Axes 41, 74, *51*
Ayton, Village of 132

Bamburgh Castle 81, 83-88, 92, 130, *87*
Banbury, Town of 100
Barnard Castle, Town of 116
Barnet, Battle of, (14 Apr 1471) 30, 84, 100, 110-112, *110*
Barnsdale, Yorkshire 130
Barville, Squire to Pierre de Breze 86

Battles *See Barnet, Blore Heath, Bosworth, Edgecote, Hedgeley Moor, Hexham, Losecoat Field, Ludford Bridge, Mortimer's Cross, Northampton, St Albans, Shrewsbury, Stoke Field, Tewkesbury, Towton, Wakefield*
Becket, Thomas, Saint 56
Beauchamp, Anne *See Neville, Anne (née Beauchamp)*
Beauchamp, Sir Richard, Governor of Gloucester (b.c.1435, d.1502/3) 111
Beaufort, Edmund, 2nd Duke of Somerset (b.1406, d.1455) 24, 27-28, 34-39, 41
Beaufort, Edmund, 4th Duke of Somerset (b.c.1438, d.1471) 45, 108, 111-113, *113*
Beaufort, Joan *See Neville, Joan (née Beaufort)*
Beaufort, Joan, *See Stewart, Joan (née Beaufort)*
Beaufort, John, 1st Earl of Somerset (b.c.1373, d.1410) 19
Beaufort, Henry, Cardinal, Bishop of Winchester (c.1375, d.1447) 19, 21-22, 24
Beaufort, Henry, Earl of Dorset and 3rd Duke of Somerset (b.1436, d.1464) 44-45, 47-48, 50-53, 55, 59, 62-65, 68, 71-74, 78, 81, 83-85, 88-91
Beaufort, Margaret, Countess of Richmond and Derby (b.1443, d.1509) 113, 124-126, *126*
Beaujeu, Anne de, Princess (b.1461, d.1522) 125
Bedford, Duke of, *See Lancaster, John of, and Neville, George*
Berwick,
    Captain of 123
    Castle 120-121
    Governor of 19, 120
    Keeper of 46
    Town of 18, 46, 61-62, 68, 78, 81, 83-85, 88, 118-121
    Wardenship of 131
Beverley Minster 23, 132-133
Bisham Abbey 110
Bishop's Lynn, *See Lynn*
'Black Jack' 86
Black Prince, Edward The, *See Plantagenet, Edward*
Blore Heath, Battle of, (23 Sep 1459) 52-53
Bona, Princess, of Savoy 92
Bondgate Tower, *See Alnwick, Bondgate Tower*
Booth, Laurence, Bishop of Durham, (b.c.1420, d.1480) 45
Bosworth, Battle of, (22 Aug 1485) 9, 11, 17, 30, 126-128, 130, 132
Bothwell, Patrick Hepburn, 1st Earl of (d.1508) 120

Bourchier, Henry, Lord Bourchier and 1st Earl of Essex, (b.c.1405, d.1483) 72
Bourchier, Thomas, Archbishop of Canterbury (b.1404, d.1486) 37, 56, 61, 94, *94*
Bower, William, Bowyer to the 4th Earl of Northumberland 119
Bowes, Ralph, Tenant of Budle and Spindlestone 103
Bramham Moor, Battle of (1408) 13
Brandon, William, Standard Bearer for Henry VII, (b.1456, d.1485) 128
Breze, Pierre de (b.c.1410, d.1465) 83, 85-88
Brittany 81, 92-93, 97-98, 113, 125
    Duke of 89, 97, 114, 125
Bruges, Flanders 81
Buchan, John Stewart, Earl of (b.c.1381 d.1424) 19
Buchan, James Stewart, Earl of (b.1442 d.1499) 118
Buckingham, Dukes of, *See under Stafford*
Burgundy 50, 56, 81, 86-87, 92-93, 96-97, 104, 108, 113, 118-119
    Duchess of, *See York, Margaret of*
    Duke Charles of (b.1433, d.1477) 92, 97-98, 104, 107-108, 113-114, 118
    Duke Philip of (b.1396, d.1467) 86, 88, 92, 97
    Mary of (b.1457, d.1482) 98, 116, 121
    Maximilian, Duke of (b.1459, d.1519) 121
    Ships of 50
Bury St Edmunds, City of 24
Butler, James, Earl of Wiltshire, (b.1420, d.1461) 45, 51, 55, 64-65, 70, 77
Butler, Eleanor, Lady, 123
Byrd, George, Possessor of the Earl's Inn, Newcastle 121
Bywell Castle 88, 90, 92, *88*

Cade, Jack, Rebellion of 27
Calais, France,
    Captain of 36, 44, 48, 55
    Port and town of 28, 48, 50-52, 54-55, 62, 81, 83, 97, 99-100, 104, 114, 118
    Staple 51
Calder, River 64-65
Caltrops 68, *69*
Cambridge,
    King's College 10, 49, 124
    Queen's College 124
    Trinity College 66
Cambridge, Richard, Earl of (b.1385, d.1415) 15, 25
Cannon 11, 40, 45, 52-54, 56, 58, 64, 83, 128
    Balls 20, *85*
    Field *60*
    Mons Meg *60*
    'The Lion' 22, 60

Canterbury, 99
    Archbishop of, *See Bourchier, Thomas*
    Cathedral 95
Carlisle, City of 29, 42, 80, 86, 119
Caernarvon, Town of 79
Castillon, France, Battle of, (17 Jul 1453) 28
Cerne Abbey 111
Chamber, John 132
Charles VI, King of France (b.1368, d.1422) 15
Charles VII, King of France (b.1403, d.1461) 20-22, 26, 28, 68
Charolais, Charles of, *See Charles Duke of Burgundy*
Chateaugiron, Treaty of 113
Clarence, Lionel, Duke of (b.1338, d.1368) 71
Clarence, George, Duke of (b.1449, d.1478) 24, 54, 78-79, 98-105, 107, 109, 114, 116, 129, *98, 101, 106, 117*
Clarence, Isabel, Duchess of (née Neville) (b.1451, d.1476) 99, 104, *99, 101*
Clifford, Elizabeth *See Neville, Elizabeth (née Percy)*
Clifford, John, 7th Lord Clifford (b.c.1389 d.1422) 15, 24
Clifford, Thomas, 8th Lord Clifford (d.1455) 34, 37-41
Clifford, John, 9th Lord Clifford, 'Butcher' or 'Blackfaced' (b.1434, d.1461) 33-34, 44-45, 47-48, 55, 63-66, 71-72, 77, *67*
Clinton, John, Lord (d.1464) 37, 53, 72
Cock, River (or Beck) 72-73, 75
Cockermouth,
    Castle 19, 32, 35-36, *36*
    Honour of, 103
Cocklodge, Percy residence 132
Conisbrough Castle 55
Conyers, John, Sir (d.1490) 98-99
Conyers, William, Sir (d.1469) 98
Coppini, Francesco, Cardinal (d.1464) 56
Coquet Island 42-43
Cork, an English spy 86-87
Coronations 105
    Charles VII in Reims Cathedral, (1428) 20
    Edward IV in Westminster, (1461) 78, *78*
    Edward V in Westminster, never took place 122
    James III in Kelso, (1460) 62
    Richard III in Westminster, (1483) 124
    Henry VI in Notre Dame, Paris, (1431) 21
    Henry VII in Westminster, (1485) 130
    Simnel, Lambert, in Dublin, (1487) 131
    Valois, Catherine, Queen, (1420) 17
    Woodville, Elizabeth, Queen, (1465) 94

Cotes, Robert, Receiver for the County of Northumberland 43
Courtenay, John, Earl of Devon (b.c.1435, d.1471) 111
Courtenay, Thomas, Earl of Devon (b.1432, d.1461) 53, 59, 62, 64, 72, 77
Coventry,
    City of 45, 56, 99, 109
    Great Council of, (1459) 52
Cromwell, Lord 33, 35, 37, 58
Crossbows 40, *40*
"Curtana", Sword of Mercy 124

Dacre, Lord, Richard Fiennes (b.1415, d.1483) 72
Dacre of Gilsland, Humphrey, Lord (b.c.1424, d.1485) 80-81, 117
Dacre of Gilsland, Randolph, Lord (d.1461) 72-73
Dacre of Gilsland, Thomas, Lord (b.1467, d.1525) 131
Daggers 66, *51*
De la Pole, William, Earl and 1st Duke of Suffolk (b.1396, d.1450) 20, 24, 26-7, *27*
De la Pole, John, 2nd Duke of Suffolk (b.1442, d.1492) 114, 124
Delapré Abbey 56-57
Denbigh Castle 59, 61
Derby, Earls of, *See Stanley, Thomas*
Devon, Earls of, *See under Courtenay and Stafford, Humphrey*
Dorset, Earls of, *See under Beaufort*
Douglas, Archibald, 4th Earl of Douglas (b.c.1369, d.1424) 18-19
Douglas, Archibald, 5th Earl of Angus (b.c.1449, d.1513) 119-120
Douglas, George, 4th Earl of Angus (b.c. 1427, d.1463) 62, 80
Douglas, Hugh, Earl of Ormonde (d.1455) 29
Douglas, James, 1st Earl of Morton (b.1426, d.1493) 88
Douglas, James, 9th Earl of Douglas (b.1426, d.1491) 118-119
Douglas, William, 2nd Earl of Angus (b.1398, d.1437) 21-22
Douglas, William, 8th Earl of Douglas (b.1425, d.1452) 28, 46
Dover,
    Port of, 27
    Straits and sands of, 26-27
Dublin, City of 131
Dudley, Lord, John Sutton (b.1400, d.1487) 52-53
Dumfries, Town of 62
Dunbar
    Castle 21
    Town 28

Dunbar, George, 10th Earl of March (b.1338, d.1422) 21
Dunbar, George, 11th Earl of March (b.c.1370, d.1457) 21
Dundas, Duncan 62
Dunstable 68-69
Dunstanburgh Castle 79-80, 83, 85, 130, *79*
Durham,
    Cathedral Priory 42-43, 84
    City of 19, 80, 85, 88, 103

Eccleshall Castle 53, 59, *52*
Edgecote, Battle of, (26 Jul 1469) 100
Edinburgh,
    Castle of, 120-121
    City of 13, 62, 67, 120-121
Edward II, King (b.1284, d.1327) 79, 84, 99
Edward III, King (b.1312, d.1377) 18-19, 24-25, 63, 71, 79, 84, 96
Edward IV, King (b.1442, d.1483) 24, 33, 55-59, 64, 69-74, 78-82, 84-86, 88-90, 92-114, 116-123, *55, 58, 70, 71, 106, 113, 123*
Edward V, King (b.1470, d.1483?) 107, 122-125, 131, *123*
Egremont, Castle and Barony 31, *34*
Egremont, John 132
Egremont, Lord *See Percy, Thomas, Lord Egremont*
Empingham, Village of, 102
English Channel 93, 109
Eton College 10, 49
Exeter,
    City of 111
    Dukes of, *See under Holland*
    Port of 104

Fauconberg, Lord *See Neville, William*
Fauconberg, Thomas the Bastard of (b.1429, d.1471) 107, 112-113, *112*
Ferrybridge, River crossing at 72
Fitzhugh, Henry, Lord (b.c.1429, d.1472) 72
Fitzhugh, Richard, Lord (b.c.1458, d.1487) 129, 131
Fitzwalter, Lord, John Radcliffe (d.1461) 72
Flanders 5, 60, 88, 125
Flodden, Battle of (1513) 11, 18
Flushing, Harbour of 108
Fortescue, John, Lord (b.c.1394, d.1479) 88
Fortune, Wheel of *106*
Foul Raid, The 18
Fotheringhay Castle 97, 120, *96*

Gargrave, Church of 32
Gascony, France 32
Gaunt, John of, Duke of Lancaster (b.1340, d.1399) 12, 19, 21, 30, 34, 79, 126

INDEX   153

Glamorgan 35
Gloucester,
   City of 111
   Dukes of *See Lancaster, Humphrey of, and Richard III*
Gray, Andrew, Lord Gray (d.1514) 120
Grey, Anne (née Holland) 94-95
Grey, Anthony, son of Lord Grey of Ruthin 94
Grey, Katherine (née Percy) (b.1423, d.c.1475) 58
Grey, Ralph, Sir (b.1406, d.1443) 22
Grey, Ralph, Sir, (b.1432, d.1464) 45, 81, 85, 89, 92
Grey, Richard, Lord of Powys and 3rd Earl of Tankerville (b.1436, d.c.1466) 37, 53
Grey, Richard, Sir (b.1457, d.1483) 122, 124
Grey, Thomas, Marquess of Dorset (b.1455, d.1501) 94
Grey de Wilton, Reginald, Lord (b.1421, d.1493) 72
Grey of Codnor, Henry, Lord (b.1435, d.1496) 72
Grey of Ruthin, Edmund, Lord (b.1416, d.1490) 56-58, 94
Greystoke, Ralph, Lord (b.1406, d.1487) 117, 131
Guelders, Mary of, Queen of James II of Scotland (b.c.1435, d.1463) 22, 60, 62, 71, 81, 83, 87

Haddington, Town of 121
Halberd 129
Halliburton, William, Sir 18
Handguns 108, *58*
Hanseatic League 51
Harbottell, John, Receiver for 4th Earl of Northumberland 119
Harlech, 97
   Castle 59, 98
Hastings, William, Lord (b.c.1430, d.1483) 81, 100, 102, 109, 114, 123
Heads on spikes 12, 27, 47, 66-67, 77
Hedgeley Moor,
   Battle of, (25 Apr 1464) 9, 89, 91
   Percy's Cross 91
   Percy's Leap 90-91
Helmsley, Town of 116
Henry IV, King (b.1366, d.1413) 12, 14, 21, 25, 30, 33, 71, 108, 125
Henry V, King (b.1387, d.1422) 11-12, 14-15, 17-19, 21, 24-26, 31, 42, 125, *17*
Henry VI, King (b.1421, d.1471) 10, 17, 21-22, 25-26, 28-29, 31, 34, 36-39, 44, 53-54, 59-61, 69, 71-72, 74, 77-79, 81, 83-84, 88-90, 95-96, 99, 101, 104-105, 108-110, 113, *10, 26, 55, 58*
Henry VII, King (b.1457, d.1509) 9, 17, 30, 70, 78, 102, 105, 113, 125-128, 130-132, *129*
   Family of *130-131*
Henry VIII, King (b.1491, d.1547) 134
Herbert, William, 1st Earl of Pembroke (b.c.1423, d.1469) 70, 79, 97-98, 102, 117, 126

Herbert, William, 2nd Earl of Pembroke (b.1455, d.1491) 117, 126
Hereford, City of 70
Heworth Moor, Ambush on, (1453) 6, 33
Hexham, 90
   Abbey and Priory 84, 90
   Battle of, (15 May 1464) 90, 92, 101, 111
   Castle 89
   Gaol Museum 90
Holderness, Robin of 99
Holland, Anne (née York), 3rd Duchess of Exeter (b.1439, d.1476) 95
Holland, Anne *See Grey, Anne (née Holland)*
Holland, John, 2nd Duke of Exeter (b.1395, d.1447) 24
Holland, Henry, 3rd Duke of Exeter (b.1430, d.1475) 34-36, 45, 47-48, 53, 58-59, 63-64, 72-74, 78-79, 83, 88, 95, 108
Holland, Principality of 98, 107
Holy Island 85
Homildon Hill, Battle of, (1402) 11, 14, 21
Honfleur, Normandy 83, 104
Horse Armour 74
Hotspur, Harry *See Percy, Henry "Harry Hotspur"*
Howard, John, Duke of Norfolk (b.c.1425, d.1485) 81, 104, 124-125, 127-128
Hull, Town of 59, 62-63
Hulne Priory 43
Hundred Years War, the 10,15, 28
Hungerford, Robert, Lord (b.c.1429, d.1464) 72, 83, 89-91

Ireland, John, Academic at the Sorbonne (b.c.1440, d.1495) 118
Ireland 27, 55-56, 60
   Lieutenant of, 55

James I, King of Scots (b.1394, d.1437) 13-14, 18-22
James II, King of Scots (b.1430, d.1460) 22, 29, 46, 60-62, *61*
James III, King of Scots (b.1451, d.1488) 62, 88, 96, 118-121, *62, 120*
James IV, King of Scots (b.1473, d.1513) 117, 119, 122
Jargeau, France 20
Jedburgh, Town of 119, 121
Jester 95, *95*
Johnson, William, a Scot 114

Kalewater 46
Kelso, Town of 22, 62
Kenilworth Castle 45, 47, 52
Kent, Earl of, *See Neville, William, Lord Fauconberg*
Kentishmen 56, 59, 72
"Kingmaker" *See Neville, Richard, Sir, 16th Earl of Warwick*

King's Lynn, *See Lynn*
Kircudbright 86-87
Koeur-la-petite Castle, France 88
Lake District, The 101
Lancaster, Anne (née Neville), Princess of Wales, *See York, Anne, Queen*
Lancaster, Blanche of (b.1342, d.1368) 34
Lancaster, Edward, Prince of Wales, son of King Henry VI (b.1453, d.1471) 34, 36, 59, 61-62, 69, 78, 80, 83, 87, 105, 111-112, *101*
Lancaster, Eleanor of, (née Cobham) Duchess of Gloucester (b.c.1400, d.1452) 24
Lancaster, Humphrey of, Prince, Duke of Gloucester (b.1390, d.1447) 17, 24, 42
Lancaster, John of, Duke of Bedford (b.1389, d.1435) 15, 19, 21, 24, 92
Landais, Pierre, Treasurer of Brittany (b.1432, d.1485) 125
Langley Castle 88
Langley, Edmund of, Duke of York (b.1341, d.1402) 18, 24, 63, 71, 96
Lauder Bridge 120
Leicester,
   City of 37, 103, 109, 129, 131
   Grey Friars Priory 129
Lincluden Abbey 62
Lisle, Robert, a Percy retainer 118
London, 27, 35, 37, 44, 47-52, 56, 61-62, 64, 70-72, 85, 95, 99, 106-110, 113, 119, 122, 124, 132
   Bishop's Palace 110
   Blackfriars 66
   Bridge 12
   Great Council of, (1458) 47-48
   Temple Bar 47-48
   Tower of 27-28, 64, 79, 96, 108, 113, 116, 122-123, 130-131, *107*
      Bowyer Tower 116
   Treaty of,
      1424 19
      1474 113
Longbows 40
Losecoat Field, Battle of, (12 Mar 1470), *See Empingham*
Louis XI, King of France (b.1423, d.1483) 81, 83, 86, 92-93, 97-98, 104-105, 108, 113-114, 118-119, 121, *81*
"Loveday", (24 Mar 1458) 49-50
Lovelace, Henry, Sir 68
Lovell, Francis, Lord (b.1456, d.1487) 130
Ludford Bridge, Battle of, (12-13 Oct 1459) 53-55, *55*
Ludlow,
   Castle *52*
   Town of 52-53, 55, 70, 122
Lumley, George, Lord (b.1445, d.1509) 131
Luton, town of 68-69
Lynn, Port town of, 107

Maces 74, 112-113, *51*
Malmsey Wine 116, *117*
Mancini, Dominic, Chronicler 122

March, Earls of,
  English *See under Mortimer, York Richard of and Edward IV*
  Scottish *See under Dunbar*
Market Drayton 52-53
"Martin of the Sea" 108
Meaux, France, Siege of 17
Melrose, town of 19
Melun, France, Siege of 15
Middleham Castle 23-24, 31, 35, 37, 52, 68, 90, 101, *24*
Middleham, Edward of, Prince of Wales, son of King Richard III (b.c.1475, d.1484) 24, 126, *101*
Milford Haven, Port of 128
Molinet, Jean (b.1435, d.1507) 129
Montagu, Thomas, 4th Earl of Salisbury (b.1388, d.1428) 20
Mortimer, Anne (b.1388, d.1411) 25
Mortimer, Edmund, 5th Earl of March (b.1391, d.1425) 25, 71
Mortimer, Elizabeth *See Percy, Elizabeth (née Mortimer)*
Mortimer's Cross, Battle of, (2 Feb 1461) 70, *70*
Morton, Earl of *See Douglas, James*
Morton, John (b.c.1420, d.1500) 83
Mountjoy, Lord, Walter Blount, (b.c.1416, d.1474) 94
Mowbray, John, Duke of Norfolk (b.1444, d.1476) 72-73, 75, 114
Mylling, Thomas, Abbot of Westminster 107

Nancy, Battle of, in the Duchy of Lorraine 118
Naworth Castle 80-81, *80*
Nene, River 57-58
Neville, Alice (née Montagu) 5th Countess of Salisbury (b.1407, d.1462) 30
Neville, Anne (née Beauchamp) 16th Countess of Warwick (b.1426, d.1492) 31, 104, *101*
Neville, Anne, Widow of Edward Prince of Wales and Wife of King Richard III (b.1456, d.1485) 24, 94, 105, 116, 124, 126, *101, 116*
Neville, Anne *See Stafford, Anne (née Neville) Duchess of Buckingham*
Neville, Cecily "The Rose of Raby" *See Plantagenet, Cecily (née Neville)*
Neville, Eleanor, 2nd Countess of Northumberland, *See Percy, Eleanor (née Neville)*
Neville, Elizabeth (née Percy) 2nd Countess of Westmorland, daughter of "Harry Hotspur" (d.1437) 15
Neville, George, Archbishop of York (b.c.1432, d.1476) 96, 99-100, 109-110
Neville, George, Baron Latimer (d.1469) 30
Neville, George, Duke of Bedford (b.1465, d.1483) 103-104
Neville, Humphrey, of Brancepeth (b.c.1439, d.1469) 89, 101-102

Neville, Isabel, *See Clarence, Isabel (née Neville)*
Neville, Joan (née Beaufort) second wife of 1st Earl of Westmorland (b.c.1379, d.1440) 15, 30-31, 53
Neville. John, Sir (b.c.1410, d.1461) 64-65, 72, 77
Neville, John, Sir, Marquess of Montagu and Earl of Northumberland (b.c.1431, d.1471) 8, 32-35, 79-81, 84-86, 89-92, 94-95, 99, 103, 106-107, 109-110, 116
Neville, Katherine, Dowager Duchess of Norfolk (b.c.1397, d.1483) 94
Neville, Margaret (née Stafford), 1st Countess of Westmorland (b.c.1364, d.1396) 30
Neville, Maud (née Stanhope), wife of Sir Thomas Neville 33
Neville, Ralph, Sir, 1st Earl of Westmorland (b.c.1364, d.1425) 12, 30-31
Neville, Ralph, Sir, 2nd Earl of Westmorland (b.1406/7, d.1484) 23-24, 53, 117
Neville, Ralph, Sir, 3rd Earl of Westmorland (b.c.1456, d.1499) 131
Neville, Richard, 5th Earl of Salisbury (b.1400, d.1460) 8, 23-25, 28-32, 34-41, 44, 46-49, 52-56, 61, 64-68, 110, *37, 55, 67*
Neville, Richard, Sir, 16th Earl of Warwick and 6th Earl of Salisbury, "The Kingmaker" (b.1428, d.1471) 8, 24, 30-31, 34-35, 37-41, 44, 47-48, 50-62, 64, 66, 68-70, 72-74, 79-81, 83-87, 89, 92-111, 113, *48, 55, 101*
Neville, Thomas, Sir (b.c.1429, d.1460) 33, 35, 66
Neville, Thomas, *See Fauconberg, Thomas the Bastard of*
Neville, William, Sir, Lord Fauconberg and Earl of Kent (b.c.1405, d.1463) 30, 57, 59, 72-74, 79
Newark, Town of 99
Newcastle,
  Castle 130
  Earl's Inn 121
  Town of 78, 86, 88-89
Newgate Prison 36, 44-45, *44, 45*
'Nicholas of the Tower', ship 26
Norfolk, Dukes of *See Howard, John and Mowbray, John de*
Norham Castle 86, 89-90, *89*
Normandy 68, 83, 97, 104, 107
Northampton,
  Battle of, (10 Jul 1460) 56-60, 132
  Town of 100
Northumberland, Earls of, *See under Percy, and Neville, John*
Nottingham, City of 64, 72, 99-100, 119-120, 128

Ogle, Robert, Sir (b.c.1370, d.1436) 18, 22
Ogle, Robert, Sir (b.1406, d.1469) 37, 40, 78
Olney, Village of 100

Orleans, France, Siege of, 1428 20
Ormond, 6th Earl of, John Butler (d.1476) 108
Ormond, Earl of, Hugh Douglas (d.1455) 25
Oxford,
  Earls of *See Vere, John de*
  University College 42, *42*

Parhelion 70, *70*
Paris, France 21, 81, 125
"Parliament of Devils" 55
Peeris, William, Chaplain to 5th Earl of Northumberland 13, 43, 77, 133
Pembroke Castle 70
Pembroke, Earls of *See Herbert, William and Tudor, Jasper*
Percy, Alianor, Daughter of 3rd Earl of Northumberland 76
Percy, Eleanor (née Neville), 2nd Countess of Northumberland (b.c.1398, d.1472) 14-15, 43
Percy, Eleanor (née Poynings), 3rd Countess of Northumberland (b.1428, d.1484) 23
Percy, Elizabeth, Daughter of 3rd Earl of Northumberland 76
Percy, Elizabeth (née Mortimer) wife of "Harry Hotspur" (b.1371, d.1417) 13, *14*
Percy, Elizabeth *See Neville, Elizabeth (née Percy)*
Percy, George, Canon of Beverley Minster (b.1424, d.1474) *23*
Percy, Henry, 1st Earl of Northumberland (b.1341, d.1408) 12-13, 33, 54, 71, 84 *12*
Percy, Henry "Harry Hotspur" (b.1364/6, d.1403) 11-15, 21, 23, 25, 30-33, 41, 54, 71, 76, 125
Percy, Henry, 2nd Earl of Northumberland (b.1394, d.1455) 9-10, 13-24, 28-30, 32-43, 45-46, 54, *29, 32, 42*
Percy, Henry, 3rd Earl of Northumberland, Lord Poynings (b.1421, d.1461) 9, 20, 23, 28-29, 35-36, 44-48, 53-56, 59-60, 62-66, 68, 71-74, 76-78, *46*
Percy, Henry, 4th Earl of Northumberland (b.c.1449, d.1489) 9, 33, 79, 82, 84, 93, 102-103, 106, 108-110, 113-114, 116-134, *108*
Percy, Henry, Sir, Cousin of 4th Earl of Northumberland 118, 121
Percy, Henry, 5th Earl of Northumberland (b.1478, d.1527) 13, 134, *134*
Percy, Henry, 9th Earl of Northumberland (b.1564, d.1632) 66
Percy, Katherine *See Grey, Katherine (née Percy)*
Percy, Margaret, Daughter of 3rd Earl of Northumberland 76
Percy, Maud (née Herbert), 4th Countess of Northumberland (b.c.1448, d.1485) 117, 126, 134

Percy, Ralph, Sir (b.1425, d.1464) 9, 45, 59, 79, 84-85, 88-89, 91, 93, *86*
Percy, Richard, Sir, Kinsman of the 2nd Earl of Northumberland 22
Percy, Richard, Sir (b.1426/7, d.1461) 9, 33, 44-45, 53, 59, 77, *44*
Percy, Thomas, 1st Earl of Worcester (b.1345, d.1403) 12, 33, 37
Percy, Thomas, Lord Egremont (b.1422, d.1460) 9, 23, 31-36, 44-45, 47-50, 53, 55-59, 66, 79, 132, *32*, *35*, *58*
Percy, Thomas, Bishop of Dromore (b.1729, d.1811) 14
Percy, William, Bishop of Carlisle (b.1428, d.1462) 23, 32, 37, 41
Percy's Cross 91, *93*
Percy's Leap 91, *90*
Petworth, Honour of 103
Picquigny, Treaty of 114, 119
Pikes 66, *51*
Piperdean, ambush at, 1436 22
Plantagenet, Edward, "The Black Prince" (b.1330, d.1376) 12
Plantagenet, Cecily (née Neville) Duchess of York, "The Rose of Raby" (b.1415, d.1495) 25, 54, 96, 99, *25*
Plantagenet, Edward, Earl of Warwick (b.1475, d.1499) 130-131, *101*
Pole *See De la Pole*
Poleaxes 128
Pontefract Castle 35-36, 66, 72, 109, 123-124
Poynings, Eleanor *See Percy, Eleanor (née Poynings)*
Poynings, Henry Lord *See Percy, Henry, 3rd Earl of Northumberland*
Propaganda 27, 47, 55-56, 68, 81, 98

Raby Castle 23
Raglan Castle 70
Rat, Cedric the *44, 135*
Ravenspur, Town of 108
Readeption, The 107-108
Rede, River 98
Redesdale, 98
    Robin of, *See Conyers, William, Sir*
Redesdalers 99, 106
Reed, Alan, Shepherd of 4th Earl of Northumberland 119
Regency,
    Council of, for Henry VI 17, 19
    Of England 19
    Of Scotland 13, 18, 21, 78
    Protectorate during Henry VI's mental incapacity 34-36, 44-45, 63
    Protectorate of Richard, Duke of Gloucester 122-124
Reims Cathedral 20
Rennes Cathedral 126
Ribaudkins 69, *69*
Ribble, River 95
Richard II, King (b.1367, d.1400) 12-13, 19, 30, 99, 108, 134

Richard III, King (b.1452, d.1485) 17, 24, 30, 55, 63, 78, 94, 96, 100, 102, 108-109, 112-113, 116-124, 126-132, 134, *101*, *106*, *129*
Richmond, Earl of *See Tudor, Edmund*
Richmond, Town of, North Yorkshire 116
Rivers, Earls *See under Woodville*
Robert III, King of Scots, (b.c.1371, d.1406) 13
Rokeby, Sir Thomas 12
Roos, Thomas, Lord (b.1427, d.1464) 64-65, 72, 83-84, 89-91
Rouen, France 15, 21
Rous Roll 48, 99, 116
Roxburgh Castle 18, 22, 60, 62, 118, 121, *22*
Rutland, Edmund, Earl of (b.1443, d.1460) 63-67, 97, *67*

St Albans 110
    Abbey 41-42, *40*
    Castle Inn 41
    Clock Tower *41*
    First Battle of, (22 May 1455) 9, 37-40, 43-44, 46, 48, 59, 71
    John Wheathampstead, Abbot of 10, 41
    Second Battle of, (17 Feb 1461) 68-69
    Town Bell, Gabriel *41*
St Andrew *120*
St Andrew's,
    Bishop of, 78, 80-81
    City of, 13
St Cuthbert 43
St Denys Church, Walmgate, York 32, 77
St Paul's Cathedral, London 44, 49, 71, 110, *49*
Salisbury,
    Bishop of, Richard Beauchamp (d.1481) 56
        See also Woodville, Lionel
    City of, 125
Salisbury, Earl of, *See Neville, Richard*
Sand Hutton 33, 35
Sandal Castle 37, 63-65, *63*
Sandwich, Kent 52, 56
Sark, River 28
Savage, John, Sir (b.1444, d.1492) 128
Savoy, Philip, Duke of, (b.1438, d.1497) 92
Scales, Anthony Woodville, Lord, *See Woodville, Anthony*
Scarborough
    Castle 55
    Lordship of 116
Scott, Sir Walter (b.1771, d.1832) 8
Scrope, John, Lord, (b.1437, d.1498) 72, 117, 131
Scrope of Masham, Thomas, Lord (b.c.1459, d.1493) 131
Seals
    1st Earl of Northumberland *12*
    2nd Earl of Northumberland *19, 23*
    4th Earl of Northumberland *103, 115*
    Lord Egremont *59*

    Lord Poynings as Warden of the Eastern March *28*
    Richard III, Great Seal *125*
Severn, River 111-112
Shakespeare, William, (b.1564, d.1616) 8, 66, 129
Shaw, Ralph, Dr 123
Sheriff Hutton, Castle and lordship of 30-31, 68, *30*
Ships 11, 13, 26, 50-51, 56, 83, 86, 89, 104-108, 113, 125, *104*
Shrewsbury, Battle of, (21 Jul 1403) 12-13, 15, 21, 25, 33
Shrewsbury, Earls of, *See under Talbot*
Signet ring *19*
Simnel, Lambert (b.c.1477, d.1534) 130-131
Skipton
    Castle, 88
    Town of, 116
Somerset, Dukes and Earls of *See Beaufort*
Somme, River 114
"Southampton Plot" 15
Southwark, Town of 113
Spencer, Christopher, squire to Lord Poynings 28
Spenser, Richard Lord (d.1414) 14
Stafford, Anne (née Neville) 1st Duchess of Buckingham (b.c.1408, d.1480) 30, 55
Stafford, Henry, 2nd Duke of Buckingham (b.1455, d.1483) 94, 122-126
Stafford, Henry, Sir (b.c.1425, d.1471) 126
Stafford, Humphrey, Earl of Stafford and 1st Duke of Buckingham (b.1402, d.1460) 30, 37-38, 40, 45, 47, 52-54, 56-58, 102
Stafford, Humphrey, Earl of Devon (b.c.1439, d.1469) 99-100
Stafford, Humphrey, Sir (b.c.1427, d.1486) 130
Stafford, John, Earl of Wiltshire (d.1473) 102
Stafford, Margaret, *See Neville, Margaret (née Stafford)*
Stafford, Thomas, brother of Sir Humphrey 130
Stamford Bridge 35-36
Stanley, Thomas, Lord Stanley and 1st Earl of Derby (b.1435, d.1504) 53, 107, 120-121, 125-129
Stanley, William, Sir (b.c.1435, d.1495) 127-129
Stirling Castle 46
Stewart, Alexander, Duke of Albany (b.c.1454, d.1485) 96, 117-118, 120-121
Stewart, Joan (née Beaufort), Queen of Scotland (b.1404, d.1445) 19, 22, 61
Stewart, Margaret, Sister of James III of Scotland 80, 87, 118
Stewart, Margaret, Dauphine of France (b.1424, d.1445) 22
Stewart, Murdoch, Duke of Albany (b.1362, d.1425) 14-15, 18-21
    Sons of, Walter and Alexander 20

Stewart, Robert, Duke of Albany (b.c.1340, d.1420) 13-15, 18, 21
Stewart, Robert, plotter 22
Stillington, Robert, Bishop of Bath and Wells (b.c.1405, d.1491) 123
Stoke Field, Battle of, (16 Jun 1487) 9, 131
Stony Stretford, Town of 122
Strange, John, Lord (b.c.1440, d.1477) 94
Strange, George Stanley, Lord (b.1460, d.1503) 128
Suffolk, Earls and Dukes of, *See De la Pole*
Swords, *See also Curtana* 17, 27, 59, 72, 74, 124, *51*
Swynford, Katherine (b.1350, d.1403) 30

Tadcaster, Town of 72-73, 75
Tailboys, William, Sir (b.c.1416, d.1464) 80-81
Talbot, Gilbert, Sir (b.1452, d.1517/18) 128
Talbot, John, 1st Earl of Shrewsbury (b.c.1387, d.1453) *26*
Talbot, John, 2nd Earl of Shrewsbury (b.1413, d.1460) 45, 53, 56-58
Talbot, John, 3rd Earl of Shrewsbury (b.1448, d.1473) 107
Tattershall Castle 33, *33*
Tempest, John 95
Tempest, Richard, Sir 95
Teviot, River 22, 46
Tewkesbury,
 Abbey 112, *112*
 Battle of, (4 May 1471) 111-113, 116, *111*
 Town of 111, 113, *113*
Thirsk, Town of 132
Tiptoft, John, 1st Earl of Worcester (b.1427, d.1470) 37
Topcliffe Castle 35, 132
Tours, Treaty of, 1444 26
Towton, Battle of, (29 Mar 1461) 9, 19, 72-78, 84, 102, *75*
Treaties, *See Accord, Arras, Chateaugiron, London, Picquigny, Tours, Troyes*
Trent, River 55, 59 62, 68, 109
Trinity, The, Ship 104
Trollope, Andrew, Sir (d.1461) 54, 64-66, 69, 72
Troyes, Treaty of, (21 May 1420) 15
Truces, 19, 21, 26, 28, 38, 46, 64, 72, 81, 88-90, 93, 97, 117
 "Truce Days" 118
Tudor, Edmund, Earl of Richmond (b.c.1430, d.1456) 125-126
Tudor, Henry *See Henry VII*
Tudor, Jasper, Earl of Pembroke (b.1431, d.1495) 45, 59, 70, 79, 81, 83-85, 88-89, 98, 106-108, 111, 113, 126, 128

Tudor, Owen (b.c.1400, d.1461) 17, 45, 70
Tunstall, Richard, Sir 83, 95
Tunstall, William 83
Tweed, River 18, 22, 62, 78, 86
Tynemouth
 Castle 83, *83*
 Priory 42-43

Umfraville, Sir Robert (b.c.1363, d.1437) 18

Valois, Catherine of, Queen (b.1401, d.1437) 17, *17*
Vaughan, Thomas, Chamberlain (b.c.1410 d.1483) 122, 124
Vere, John de, 12th Earl of Oxford, (b.1408, d.1462) 81
Vere, John de, 13th Earl of Oxford (b.1442, d.1513) 107-109, 113, 127-128
Verneuil, France, Battle of, 1424 19
Vinci, Leonardo da (b.1452, d.1519) 69, *69*

Waddington Hall 95
Wakefield, Battle of, (30 Dec 1460) 24, 63-68, 70, 97
Wales, Princes of *See Lancaster, Edward of, and Middleham, Edward of, see also Henry V*
Wallingford Castle 36
Warbeck, Perkin (b.c.1474, d.1499) 131
Wardens of the English and Scottish Marches 10, 12, 15, 19, 22-23, 28-29, 31-32, 36, 44, 46, 79, 85, 103, 114, 117-118, 121-122, 126, 130
Wark Castle 18, 78, *18*
Warkworth
 Castle 33, 43, 83-85, 114, *84*
 Hermitage 14, *14*
 Town of 28
Warwick Castle 100, 101, 109 *100*
Warwick, Earls of, *See Neville, Richard; Plantagenet, Edward*
Watling Street 68
Waynflete, William, Bishop of Winchester (b.c.1398, d.1486) 45
Wedryngton, John, servant of 4th Earl of Northumberland 118
Welles, Richard, Lord (b.c.1428, d.1470) 102
Welles, Robert, Sir (d.1470) 102
Wenlock, John, Lord (b.c.1400, d.1471) 104, 111-112
Westerdale, John, Captain 108
Westminster, 47-48
 Abbey 35, 78, 94, 105, 107, 122-123, 130, *105*
 Abbot of, *See Mylling*
 Palace of 34, 50-51, 61, 71, 97, 110
Westmorland, Earls of, *See under Neville*

Wheathampstead, *See under St Albans*
Wiltshire, Earls of, *See under Butler, James and Stafford, John*
Woodville, Anne, Viscountess Bourchier (b.c.1438, d.1489) 94
Woodville, Anthony, Lord Scales, 2nd Earl Rivers (b.c.1440, d.1483) 94, 104, 120, 122-124, *123*
Woodville, Edward, Lord Scales (d.1488) 94
Woodville, Eleanor 94
Woodville, Elizabeth, Queen (b.c.1437, d.1492) 92, 94-98, 104, 107-108, 117, 122-124, *92, 123*
Woodville, Jacquetta, Lady Strange (b.1445, d.1509) 94
Woodville, John, (b.c.1445, d.1469) 94, 101
Woodville, Katherine, Duchess of Buckingham (b.c.1458, d.1497) 94
Woodville, Lionel, Bishop of Salisbury (b.1447, d.1484) 94, 122, 124
Woodville, Margaret, Countess of Arundel 94
Woodville, Martha, (d.c.1500) 94
Woodville, Mary, Countess of Pembroke (b.c.1456, d.1481) 94, 117
Woodville, Richard, Sir, 1st Earl Rivers (b.1405, d.1469) 72, 92-94, 101
Worcester, Earl of *See Percy, Thomas, and Tiptoft, John*
Wressle Castle and manor 33, 49, 132, *33*

York,
 Archbishop of 12, 34, 96, 99, 100, 123
 Castle *102*
 City of 35, 62-63, 66-68, 71-72, 77, 89-90, 101-102, 119,
 Micklegate Bar 12, 66, *67*
 Minster 13, 42, 76, 130
York, Anne, Wife of King Richard III, *See Neville, Anne*
York, Cecily of, Duchess of York, *See Plantagenet, Cecily*
York, Cecily of, Daughter of King Edward IV (b.1469, d.1507) 117-118, 121-122
York, Edward of, 2nd Duke of York (b.1373, d.1415) 25, 63, 97
York, Elizabeth of, Queen (b.1466, d.1503) 9, 97, 104-105, 114, 119, 122, 125-126, 130, *131*
York, Margaret of, Duchess of Burgundy (b.1446, d.1503) 92, 98, *98*
York, Richard, Prince, Duke of (b.1473, d.1483?) 122-123
York, Richard, 3rd Duke of, 6th Earl of March (b.1411, d.1460) 24-28, 30, 34-41, 44-48, 52-56, 60-67, 77, 96-97, *27, 53, 55, 66, 67*

Zealand, Principality of 98

INDEX 157

Acknowledgments

Thanks to:

Thanks to Clare Baxter, Chris Hunwick and Daniel Watkins for their invaluable help; Peter Phillips for his artistic and editorial contribution; and Chris Wilson for all his help with publishing this book.

Select Bibliography

Bassett, Margery, *Newgate Prison in the Middle Ages*, (Chicago, 1943)

Brenan, Gerald, *A History of the House of Percy*, (London, 1902)

Cokayne, George Edward, *The Complete Peerage or a History of the House of Lords and all its members from the earliest times, Second Edition, Volumes 1-13* (London, 1910-1959)

De Fonblanque, E. B., *Annals of the House of Percy*, (London, 1887)

Ed. Egerton Brydges, Samuel, *Collins's Peerage of England; Genealogical, Biographical, and Historical, Vol II*, (London, 1812)

Goodwin, George, *Fatal Colours: Towton, 1461... England's Most Brutal Battle*, (London, 2012)

Griffiths, Ralph A., *Local Rivalries and National Politics: The Percies, the Nevilles, and the Duke of Exeter, 1452-55*, (Chicago, 1968)

Hall, E., *Hall's Chronicles*, (London, 1809)

Hicks, Michael, *Richard III, the Self-Made King*, (London, 2021)

Ed. Horrox, Rosemary, *Beverley Minster: An illustrated history*, (Beverley: Friends of Beverley Minster, 2000)

Ingram, Mike, *The Battle of Northampton 1460*, (Northampton Battlefields Society, 2015)

Langley, Philippa, *The Princes in the Tower*, (London, 2023)

Ed. Matthew, H. C. G. and Harrison, Brian, *Oxford Dictionary of National Biography, 60 Volumes*, (Oxford University Press, 2004)

Newcome, The Reverend Peter, *The History of the Ancient and Royal Foundation, called the Abbey of St Alban, in the County of Hertford*, (London, 1793)

Pollard, Anthony, *The Wars of the Roses*, (Basingstoke, 2013)

Rose, Alexander, *Kings in the North: The House of Percy in British History*, (London, 2003)

Royle, Trevor, *The Wars of the Roses, England's first civil war*, (London, 2010)

Skidmore, Chris, *Bosworth: The Birth of the Tudors*, (London, 2013)

Weir, Alison, *Lancaster and York: The Wars of the Roses*, (London, 2009)

Picture Credits

All images, unless listed below, are by Peter Phillips. The copyright belongs to Northumberland Estates.

All images from the Collections and Archives of the Duke of Northumberland are © Collection of the Duke of Northumberland, with thanks to Paul Hindmarsh and John McKenzie for their photography.

p2: BHSL.HS.0236, f5r. © Ghent University Library.
p8: The Archives of the Duke of Northumberland at Alnwick Castle (henceforth 'Alnwick Castle Archives'), Sy: D.I.10.a.
p9: © Phil Wilkinson, Photographer.
p10: The Collection of the Duke of Northumberland at Syon House (henceforth 'Syon House Collection'), DNC: 04266.
p12: De Fonblanque, Edward Barrington, *Annals of the House of Percy, Vol I*, (London, 1887), p480.
p13: Alnwick Castle Archives, DNP: MS 79.
p14: De Fonblanque, Vol I, p204.
p14: Percy, Thomas, *The Hermit of Warkworth*, (Catnach of Alnwick, 1807).
p16: Alnwick Castle Archives, Sy: D.III.27.
p17: BL Cotton MS Julius E IV/3, f22r. British Library, London, UK. © British Library Board. All Rights Reserved / Bridgeman Images.
p17: NPG 545. © National Portrait Gallery, London.
p19: Alnwick Castle Archives, DNP: MS 761/19.
p19: British Museum AF.771. © The Trustees of the British Museum.
p20: Alnwick Castle Archives, DNP: MS 80.
p21: Johan of Arc – Archives nationales (France) – AE-II-2490 by Vinzez Sozvr Zovzanza (taken from Wikimedia).
p23: De Fonblanque, Vol I, p480ff.
p23: Poulson, George, *History of Beverley*, (Liverpool, 1829).
p25: Horae ad usum Parisiensem, f34v. © Bibliothèque nationale de France.
p26: BL Royal MS 15 E. vi, f2v. British Library, London, UK. © British Library Board. All Rights Reserved / Bridgeman Images.
p27: BL Royal MS 15 E. vi, f3r. British Library, London, UK. © British Library Board. All Rights Reserved / Bridgeman Images.
p28: Alnwick Castle Archives, DNP: MS 761/22.
p29: Syon House Collection, DNC: 04425/8.
p32: Drake, Francis, *History of York* (London, 1736), p306.
p34: Buck, Samuel and Nathaniel, *Ruins of Abbeys and Castles*, (1733-1739).
p35: Syon House Collection, DNC: 04425/10.
p36: Buck, Samuel and Nathaniel, *Ruins of Abbeys and Castles*, (1733-1739).
p37: The Salisbury Roll of Arms, c1463. © Duke of Buccleuch.
p38: Arms of Henry VI by Sodocan (taken from Wikimedia).
p38: Arms of Duke of Buckingham by unknown (taken from Wikimedia).
p38: Arms of Duke of Somerset by Sodocan (taken from Wikimedia).
p38: Arms of Earl of Northumberland by Thom.lanaud (taken from Wikimedia).
p38: Arms of Lord Clifford by Wikimandia (taken from Wikimedia).
p38: Arms of Duke of York by Sodocan (taken from Wikimedia).
p38: Arms of Earl of Salisbury by Rs-nourse (taken from Wikimedia).
p38: Arms of Earl of Warwick by Rs-nourse (taken from Wikimedia).
p40: Buck, Samuel and Nathaniel, *Ruins of Abbeys and Castles*, (1733-1739).
p42: The Collection of the Duke of Northumberland at Alnwick Castle (henceforth 'Alnwick Castle Collection'), DNC: 43536.
p43: Alnwick Castle Archives, Sy: C.III.1.a.
p43: Alnwick Castle Archives, DNP: MS 79.
p46: Syon House Collection, DNC: 04425/9.
p48: BL MS 48976, 'Rous Roll', f7br. British Library, London, UK. © British Library Board. All Rights Reserved / Bridgeman Images.
p53: Richard Duke of York, St Laurence's Church, Ludlow, Shropshire. © Alamy.
p54: Alnwick Castle Archives, Sy: D.I.3.
p55: Harley MS 7353. British Library, London, UK. © British Library Board. All Rights Reserved / Bridgeman Images.
p56: Arms of Henry VI by Sodocan (taken from Wikimedia).
p56: Arms of Duke of Buckingham by unknown (taken from Wikimedia).
p56: Arms of Viscount Beaumont by Wikimandia (taken from Wikimedia).
p56: Arms of Earl of Shrewsbury by Rs-nourse (taken from Wikimedia).
p56: Arms of Lord Egremont by unknown (taken from Wikimedia).
p56: Arms of Lord Grey by Thom.lanaud (taken from Wikimedia).
p56: Arms of Earl of Warwick by Rs-nourse (taken from Wikimedia).
p56: Arms of Earl of March by unknown (taken from Wikimedia).
p56: Arms of Lord Fauconberg by Rs-nourse (taken from Wikimedia).
p58: Harley MS 7353. British Library, London, UK. © British Library Board. All Rights Reserved / Bridgeman Images.
p59: Alnwick Castle Archives, Sy: X.II.9/A/1/2.
p61: PG 683, Unknown artist, James II, 1430 – 1460. Reigned 1437 – 1460, National Galleries of Scotland.
p62: BM, 1854,0901.125. © The Trustees of the British Museum.
p64: Arms of Duke of Somerset by Sodocan (taken from Wikimedia).
p64: Arms of Earl of Northumberland by Sodocan (taken from Wikimedia).
p64: Arms of Earl of Wiltshire by Rs-nourse (taken from Wikimedia).
p64: Arms of Lord Neville by Thom.lanaud (taken from Wikimedia).
p64: Arms of Lord Clifford by Wikimandia (taken from Wikimedia).
p64: Arms of Lord Roos by Wikimandia (taken from Wikimedia).
p64: Arms of Sir Andrew Trollope by Grünen (taken from Wikimedia).
p64: Arms of Duke of York by Sodocan (taken from Wikimedia).
p64: Arms of Earl of Salisbury by Rs-nourse (taken from Wikimedia).
p64: Arms of Earl of Rutland by Sodocan (taken from Wikimedia).
p66: Richard Duke of York. © The Master and Fellows of Trinity College, Cambridge.
p66: Portrait of John 'Butcher' or 'Blackfaced' Clifford. © Private Collection.
p69: Berol. Ms. Germ. Qu. 132, Jagiellonian Library Kraków.

p69: Codex Atlanticus, sheet 157 recto. © Veneranda Biblioteca Ambrosiana/Metis e Mida Informatica/Mondadori Portfolio.

p70: Harley MS 7353. British Library, London, UK. © British Library Board. All Rights Reserved / Bridgeman Images.

p71: Syon House Collection, DNC: 04290.

p71: Harley MS 7353. British Library, London, UK. © British Library Board. All Rights Reserved / Bridgeman Images.

p72: Arms of Duke of Somerset by Sodocan (taken from Wikimedia).

p72: Arms of Duke of Exeter by Sodacan (taken from Wikimedia).

p72: Arms of Earl of Northumberland by Sodocan (taken from Wikimedia).

p72: Arms of Dacre Family by Jimmy44 (taken from Wikimedia).

p72: Arms of Edward IV by Sodocan (taken from Wikimedia).

p72: Arms of Duke of Norfolk by Saltspan (taken from Wikimedia).

p72: Arms of Earl of Warwick by Rs-nourse (taken from Wikimedia).

p72: Arms of Lord Fauconberg by (taken from Wikimedia).

p75: The Battle of Towton, by Richard Caton Woodville, 1922 from *Hutchinson's Story of the British Nation, Vol II*, (London, 1922-24), p538.

p76: Alnwick Castle Archives, Sy: H.I.1.

p77: Alnwick Castle Archives, DNP: MS 79.

p78: Anciennes chroniques d'Anglettere, Jean de Wavrin, Francais 85, f165r. © Bibliothèque nationale de France.

p81: Portrait Louis XI of France by Jacob de Littemont (taken from Wikimedia).

p85: Alnwick Castle Collection, DNC: ACAT 1288/1-15.

p90: Alnwick Castle Archives, DNP: MS 187A/68.

p90: Arms of Duke of Somerset by Sodocan (taken from Wikimedia).

p90: Arms of Sir Ralph Percy by Wikimandia, modified (taken from Wikimedia).

p90: Arms of Lord Hungerford by Thom.lanaud (taken from Wikimedia).

p90: Arms of Lord Roos by Wikimandia (taken from Wikimedia).

p90: Arms of Lord Montagu by Rs-nourse (taken from Wikimedia).

p90: Hexham Abbey, HEXAB2198, Dallison Collection Lantern Slide.

p92: RCIN 404744, Royal Collection Trust. © His Majesty King Charles III 2023.

p93: Alnwick Castle Archives, DNP: MS 187A/4.

p94: Thomas Bourchier, Archbishop. Sevenoaks Church, Kent. © Alamy.

p98: Portrait of George Plantagenet, Duke of Clarence, oil painting by Lucas Cornelisz de Kock, 16th century. Private Collection Photo © Philip Mould Ltd, London/Bridgeman Images.

p98: Portrait of Margaret of York, oil painting c1470. 2023. © RMN-Grand Palais /Dist. Photo SCALA, Florence.

p99: BL MS 48976, 'Rous Roll', f7br. British Library, London, UK. © British Library Board. All Rights Reserved / Bridgeman Images.

p101: BL Cotton Julius E. IV, art. 6, f28. British Library, London, UK. © British Library Board. All Rights Reserved / Bridgeman Images.

p103: *The National Archives*, ref. WARD 2/12/40/29.

p106: Harley MS 7353. British Library, London, UK. © British Library Board. All Rights Reserved / Bridgeman Images.

p108: Syon House Collection, DNC: 04425/11.

p110: BHSL.HS.0236, f2r. © Ghent University Library.

p111: BHSL.HS.0236, f5r. © Ghent University Library.

p112: BHSL.HS.0236, f9v. © Ghent University Library.

p113: BHSL.HS.0236, f7v. © Ghent University Library.

p115: Alnwick Castle Archives, DNP: MS 761/24.

p116: BL MS 48976, 'Rous Roll', f8ar. British Library, London, UK. © British Library Board. All Rights Reserved / Bridgeman Images.

p118: Alnwick Castle Archives, Sy: Y.II.28r.

p119: Alnwick Castle Archives, Sy: C.III.2.a.

p120: RCIN 922153, Royal Collection Trust. © His Majesty King Charles III 2023.

p121: Alnwick Castle Archives, DNP: MS 96/19.

p122: Syon House Collection, DNC: 04272.

p123: MS 265, Lambeth Palace Library, London, UK © Lambeth Palace Library / Bridgeman Images.

p124: Alnwick Castle Archives, DNP: MS 468, f2.

p125: Alnwick Castle Archives, Sy: D.I.7.

p126: Syon House Collection, DNC: 04280.

p126: Arms of Henry Tudor by Sodocan (taken from Wikimedia).

p126: Arms of Earl of Oxford by Thom.lanaud (taken from Wikimedia).

p126: Arms of Richard III by Sodocan (taken from Wikimedia).

p126: Arms of Duke of Norfolk by Saltspan (taken from Wikimedia).

p126: Arms of Earl of Northumberland by Sodocan (taken from Wikimedia).

p126: Arms of Lord Stanley by Geraldiker (taken from Wikimedia).

p126: Arms of Sir William Stanley by Thom.lanaud (taken from Wikimedia).

p128: British Museum: 2003,0505.1. © The Trustees of the British Museum.

p129: Photograph of Richard III taken from Richard Buckley, Mathew Morris, Jo Appleby, Turi King, Deirdre O'Sullivan, Lin Foxhall, '*The king in the car park*': new light on the death and burial of Richard III in Grey Friars church, Leicester, in 1485, (Cambridge University Press, 2015). © Antiquity Publications Ltd.

p129: Syon House Collection, DNC: 04275.

p130: Syon House Collection, DNC: 04286/2.

p131: Syon House Collection, DNC: 04286/1.

p132: Alnwick Castle Archives, DNP: MS 761/25.

p133: Alnwick Castle Collection, DNC: T1094.

p133: Alnwick Castle Archives, DNP: MS 79.

p134: V&A E.401-2013. © Victoria and Albert Museum, London.

p138: Giovanni di Bicci de' Medici by Agnolo Bronzino – Public domain (taken from Wikimedia).

p138: Bronze lion in Forbidden City, Beijing © Shutterstock.

p138: '*The Birth of Venus*', by Sandro Botticelli – Public domain (taken from Wikimedia).

p139: Johannes Gutenberg – Public domain (taken from Wikimedia).

p139: '*The Coronation of Moctezuma I*' – Public domain (taken from Wikimedia).

p139: Machu Picchu © Shutterstock.

p139: '*The Fall of Constantinople*', by Theophilos Hatzimihail – Public domain (taken from Wikimedia).

p140: William Caxton – Public domain (taken from Wikimedia).

p140: Ferdinand and Isabella – Public domain (taken from Wikimedia).

p140: Vlad 'The Impaler', anonymous – Public domain (taken from Wikimedia).

p141: '*Columbus Taking Possession*', L. Prang & Co., Boston – Public domain (taken from Wikimedia).

p141: Vasco de Gama – Public domain (taken from Wikimedia).

p141: '*Portrait of Mona Lisa del Giocondo*', by Leonardo da Vinci – Public domain (taken from Wikimedia).